MASTED STRUCTURES
IN ARCHITECTURE

BUTTERWORTH ARCHITECTURE NEW TECHNOLOGY SERIES

Series Editor
Chris Grech

Published titles
The Building Envelope: Applications of New Technology Cladding
Supersheds: The Architecture of Long-Span Large-Volume Buildings 2nd Edition
Connections: Studies in Building Assembly
Masted Structures in Architecture

Forthcoming titles
Component Design
Portable Architecture
Space Frame Structures

MASTED STRUCTURES
IN ARCHITECTURE

James B. Harris
Kevin Pui-K Li

Butterworth Architecture
An imprint of Butterworth-Heinemann
Linacre House, Jordan Hill, Oxford OX2 8DP
A division of Reed Educational and Professional Publishing Ltd

 A member of the Reed Elsevier plc group

OXFORD   BOSTON   JOHANNESBURG

NEW DELHI   SINGAPORE

First published 1996

British Library Cataloguing in Publication Data
A CIP record for this book is available from the British Library

ISBN 0 7506 12827

Library of Congress Cataloguing in Publication Data
A catalogue record for this book is available on request

Designed and typeset by The Pinpoint Group, London
Printed in Great Britain by The Bath Press, Avon

CONTENTS

FOREWORD

This book began some years ago as an original dissertation by Kevin Li and, at that time, I was asked to comment on its content and accuracy. It was, even then, a major work with wide coverage of most of the masted structures that I knew about. That dissertation has now become a comprehensive book which is definitive, the only one of its kind and will certainly become the standard reference source.

Every conceivable example and type of masted structure is represented in the book, which is divided into two parts. First is a review of principles and development, including some fascinating history of early examples. The second section consists of a Taxonomy of different types defined according to number of masts and number of "cells". This part goes on to discuss, as special cases, masted membrane and masted grandstand structures.

The book is necessarily rather dense overall and is not for reading at one session, but it is a reference work. There are two aspects of the book which are particularly good: one is that the descriptions of the structures are extremely clear and secondly the chronology of who did what first is fascinating and very revealing.

Of course, as with every other similar type of book, there will be the problem of how and whether to keep it up to date – this could be a long running task for the authors and publisher!

I think that students and practitioners of both Architecture and Structural Engineering will want a copy of this book and it will be an essential for university libraries for both those disciplines.

The authors have produced a work of immense value to the professions and I know that I and my fellow colleagues in engineering and architecture will all have a copy in their offices. I recommended it strongly and look forward to having my copy alongside the original dissertation. ■

Tony Hunt
Anthony Hunt Associates

ACKNOWLEDGEMENTS

This book could not have been written and illustrated without many contributions from architects and engineers, and from a number of other individuals and companies in related fields; it gives the authors much pleasure to thank them here.

So far as the largest UK practices are concerned, we have had substantial contributions from Ove Arup and Partners, initially through discussions with John Thornton and, more recently, with much help from Patrick Morreau. We have had invaluable contributions too from the offices of Sir Norman Foster and Partners, via Katy Harris, from Nicholas Grimshaw and Partners with the help of Sarah Hawkins, from Michael Hopkins and Partners, thanks to Antonia Wade and Clare Endicott and the Richard Rogers Partnerships through Harriet Watson.

Mr. A. E. Ozveren of the GMW Partnership, and Alan C. Jones of Anthony Hunt Associates gave our requests their personal attention, as did Lorenzo Apicella and Cedric Price from their offices, and Neil Thomas from Atelier One. We are naturally very pleased indeed that Tony Hunt has written a Foreword for the book.

Further essential information regarding masted structures of their own design came from Brookes Stacey Randall Fursden, via Nick Randall, and Aukett Associates, through Paul K. Newman, and Weston Williamson Ltd; Ian Ritchie Architects very kindly discussed the design of Eagle House at a meeting in their office. Chris Wilkinson and Paul Baker of Chris Wilkinson Architects made some extremely helpful suggestions during the course of our later research; lastly, Mr N. C. Derbyshire and Miss G. Talbot of the Architects Department of the British Railways Board (since privatised) organised an office visit and provided drawings of the Poole station structure.

Outside London, and at an earlier stage in the research, Mr K. P. Sherry, the then Chief Architect of the Borough of Thamesdown, gave an encouraging response to our enquiries. Further afield, Faulkner Browns of Killingworth, Newcastle upon Tyne, and Eric Brown of the Napper Collerton Partnership, also in Newcastle, provided extra drawings, as did Feilden Clegg Design in Bath, the Glendinning Hanson Partnership in Halifax, and Derek Walker Associates in Milton Keynes, through Derek Walker personally.

We have been able to use excellent drawings and photographs very kindly sent from outside the UK by B V Articon of Amersfoort, Cepezed B V of Delft and Antwerp, and Kaag + Schwarz Architekten BDA of Stuttgart; invaluable Japanese material was sent by Yoshiko Amaya of Arato Isozaki and Associates of Tokyo, and Shoie Yoh + Architects of Fukuoka-Shi.

Particularly good photographic material also came from Sybolt Voeten Architectuurfotographie of Breda in Holland, from Professor Philip Cox and Michael Rayner, earlier, and through Janet Roderick latterly, all of Philip Cox, Richardson, Taylor and Partners Pty Ltd, in the Sydney, Australia office, and from Noel Robinson of Noel Robinson Architects in Brisbane; Arato Isozaki's photographer, Yasuhiro Ishimoto, of Shiagawa-ku, Tokyo has allowed us to use his high quality artwork.

Very useful black and white brochures were sent to us by Hans Maurer in Germany, and Aarno Ruusvuori in Finland in relation to their respective buildings; from the USA, Don Rothe, an architect in Facilities Planning and Construction of Central Washington University, and Kaki Strause of SOM, Chicago, provided useful cross sections early in the research.

Information on 19th century structures came from Ms Susan Day, Chief Librarian at the Institut Francais d'Architecture in Paris, and Martine Pitallier at the Pavillon de l'Arsenal, also in Paris.

We have been graciously helped personally, too, by Signora Flora Savioli in Florence, by M. Maurice Bianchi in Montrouge, France, and M. Jean-Pierre Duval in Nîmes. The complex details of the Plant House in Edinburgh came to light as the result of the efforts of John Wilson and Angus Greenslade of TBV Consult, Edinburgh, and of Ian Lawrie of the Estates Office at the Royal Botanic Garden site. Mr Eddie Hasselder helped in the translation of articles in Dutch.

It has been particularly enlightening to have structural engineering advice and comments from Mr Michael Maidens of the School of Architecture in the University of Manchester, from Dr Adrian Bell of UMIST, Manchester, and from Mr J. J. Hart of the Bridges Division of Mott MacDonald Limited in Croydon. In the above School of Architecture, too, John Archer provided very welcome advice on many aspects of the project, Dr Frank E. Brown made some very helpful points regarding the charting of complete topological possibilities, and Professor Peter Dovell was not only a source of constant encouragement when the project was flagging but also helped with additional information, in collaboration with the Librarian of the School, Mrs Val Gildea.

We were glad to receive informed comments and advice on paint protection and anti-corrosion measures generally from Mr Graham S. Worrall of W. and J. Leigh and Company of Bolton, England.

Lastly, it is particularly important to mention that the basic research for this study was supported at an early stage with the aid of the Anthony Pott Memorial Fund Award made to Kevin Li by the Architectural Association in London in 1987. We are indebted to Mr Edouard le Maistre for all his help and support in this connection.

The typing and formatting of the text has been in the capable hands of Ms Elizabeth Brodie of the Office of the Academic Secretary, the University of Manchester, with later additions and amendments by Terry Curthoys in Ludlow.

The authors are more than grateful for all of the contributions made by those mentioned above; we could not have produced this book without your help. If we have inadvertently overlooked any person or organisation, we apolgise and will do our best to make amends in a later edition; responsibility for the interpretation and use of the material remains, of course, with ourselves. ■

Part One: A REVIEW OF PRINCIPLES AND DEVELOPMENT

Since the end of the Second World War, a new family of 'masted structures' has arrived on the architectural scene. In these buildings, the roof construction takes the form of a tensile structure based on tall masts from which suspension cables or rods are taken down to provide additional intermediate supports to the roof structure. This may consist of a rigid framework of primary and secondary beams supporting a decking system, a flexible membrane or a cable net system.

Mast architecture of this kind comes in all manner of shapes, sizes, materials and colours, and in a range of building types from small offices and stations to vast supermarkets and warehouses. They can be delightfully charming or impressively spectacular – and are always eye-catching. Although most of the significant examples are in Europe, mast architecture is a world-wide addition to the present day architectural language.

The elements of this language are structural, i.e. the number and arrangement of the masts, the profile and pattern of the roof elements, and the configuration of the tension members and their connectors and anchorages. By these means, a new architectural grammar and syntax has been constructed, and a new semantics of meaningful functional elements has been added to the visual scene.

In structural terms, masted structures are theoretically efficient because the masts effectively resist the direct compressive forces; the cables and rods transmit direct tension, and supporting the roof at more frequent intervals reduces the spans and consequently the bending stresses in the supporting members. But the broad scale, architectural economics of masted structures is a complex matter involving individual circumstances such as the site and the pattern of spaces required, as well as factors which are more difficult to quantify such as appropriateness in context and the publicity value of an eye-catching structure.

The post-war development of mast architecture can be seen to have its origins in two principal historical precedents. The most common of these is the vernacular tent which grew in size from the simple awnings and poles of nomadic peoples to the complex, decorative encampments of medieval courts, the 'big tops' of modern travelling circuses and the spectacular undulating tented forms of Frei Otto and his collaborators.

The second source of masted structures, the cable-stayed version of the suspension bridge, originated during the 19th century. In parallel with the arched and framed structures of the architectural 'iron revolution', suspension bridges of more substantial and permanent form than hitherto were introduced and the cable-stayed, radiating cable form made its appearance. It was whilst these engineering advances were being made that a small number of space enclosing, architectural tension structures were successfully erected, using masts and tensile cables for the first time since the rope and canvas 'velaria' which had shaded the stadia of ancient Rome.

However, the full force of technological development was brought to bear on masted structures only in the second half of the 20th century. By this time, the theoretical understanding of the dynamic behaviour of tensile structures could be simulated and tested in computer form and physically expressed in new materials and constructional techniques. Initially, the resulting buildings were sporadic and limited to only a small number of building types. But, from 1970 onwards, the design and erection of masted structures gathered momentum in terms of numbers, in differentiation in form and function and in an increasingly high level of architectural and structural engineering quality. This in turn led to a virtual explosion of interest in the 1980s and, in this way, masted structures began to coalesce from a series of individual examples into a new, comprehensive architectural genre.

This review explains how and why these structures have come about, discusses their advantages and disadvantages, and identifies the factors which have to be borne in mind in making them work satisfactorily from all points of view.

A surprising feature which emerges from a formal analysis of the examples, is that underlying the apparent confusion of the various configurations of masts, cables and roofs is an architectural 'deep structure', an ordered pattern of formal relationships in terms of which the buildings can be related to each other, compared, contrasted and understood.

These last two topics form the basis of the general content of the two parts of the book: Part One, a review of principles and development, begins by locating masted structures in the general context of architectural tensile structures. This is followed by a chapter which outlines the basic principles of structural mechanics and explains how the exploitation of these principles characterises the appropriate use of a masted structure in particular circumstances. The next chapter reviews the two principal sources of masted forms: the cable-stayed bridge and the vernacular tent, including an account of modern forms of tented constructions. This is followed by two chapters which describe, chronologically, the development of mast architecture in the 19th and 20th centuries, the second of which is divided into different time segments, reflecting the increasing number of examples over the period.

Part Two mainly consists of a series of short descriptions of individual buildings in the context of a formal taxonomy of masted structures. The basis of this taxonomy is explained in an Introduction and this is followed by a series of chapters based, initially, on the major divisions of the taxonomy,i.e. single mast, two mast, four mast and eight mast arrangements. Three further chapters deal, respectively, with structures incorporating membrane roofs, grandstand structures, and rotational structures which differ formally from those in the initial categories. The two remaining chapters consist of a structural case study and the conclusions which result from our explorations, together with analyses of the subject.

The study has made use of material drawn from a wide range of sources and these are noted in the two remaining sections of the book. The Gazetteer reveals that these sources range from complete and detailed descriptions, written sometimes from several points of view, to other accounts which are frustratingly brief, whilst the Bibliography notes other sources of more general information.

We hope that the book will prove interesting, informative and, above all, enlightening. What began as a relatively small scale field has expanded in recent years into a fascinating range of innovative, imaginative and exciting structures. The pattern of differentiation in the field should, as a result of the book, become understandable, and its account of the underlying principles and their examples will, we hope, provide a springboard for further development and design.

We shall be pleased to learn, via the publishers, of additional proposals and projects which might be included in a later edition. Meanwhile, responsibility for errors and omissions remains, as always, our own. ■

James B. Harris Ludlow, England
Kevin Pui-K Li Hong Kong

TENSION STRUCTURES IN ARCHITECTURE

The term 'tension structures' is a general one referring to several groups of different architectural forms. These sub groups have become identifiable, mainly since the 1950s, following the completion of a relatively small number of buildings in comparison with the total architectural population. Amongst these buildings, tension members play a major structural role in every case, but the basic structural concepts and the associated building forms differ widely between the groups. We summarise them here so that masted structures can be understood in relation to the overall pattern of tension structures in architecture.

1.1
SUSPENDED CABLE ROOFS

Buildings embodying this principle have a roof structure based on parallel catenary cables which form the support for the roof decking and its weatherproof layer. The smallest built example of this, and the one which was mainly responsible for generating the initial interest in the concept, was Paul Rudolph's tiny holiday house constructed in Florida in 1954 whose 6.7m span of steel flats was small enough to avoid the wind-induced problems of larger structures. This early demonstration of the architectural potential of tension structures was followed by Robin Boyd's Melbourne house of 1958, and the very much larger structures of Saarinen's Dulles Airport

terminal (Fig. 1.1) and P.L. Nervi's Burgo Paper Mill at Mantua in Italy, which is virtually a suspension bridge structure supporting an open steel trussed roof some 250m long (Fig. 1.2). In this group, the essential characteristic is that the roof curvature is one-dimensional.

1.2
ARCHED SUSPENSION ROOFS

In contrast to the previous category, these roof curvatures are two dimensional so as to generate a form which is structurally stable.

Suspension structures of this kind have taken two generic forms: the simplest, exemplified by the Yale Hockey Rink of 1960, consist of a parabolic

Fig. 1.1
Suspended cable roof structure; Eero Saarinen: Dulles Airport Terminal, Chantilly, Washington DC, USA, 1964.

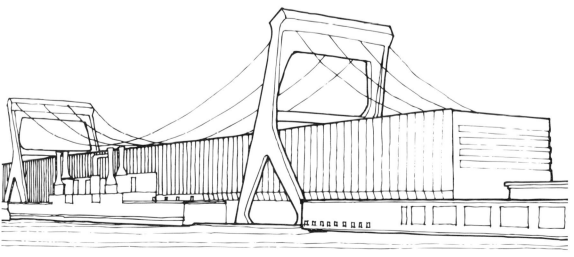

Fig. 1.2
Architectural version of a suspension bridge structure; Pier Luigi Nervi: Burgo Paper Mill, Mantua, Italy, 1961.

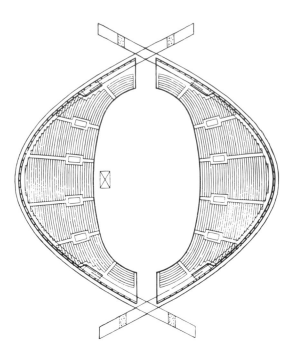

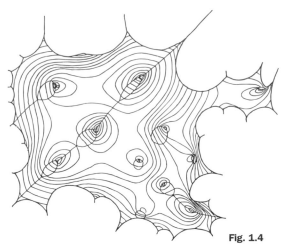

Fig. 1.4

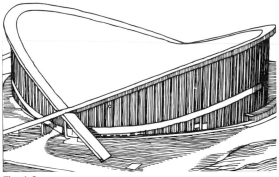

Fig. 1.3

building, completed in 1952 by Matthew Nowicki and Fred Severud (Fig. 1.3), which was the first of the modern generation of architectural suspended roofs. Another notable example, despite its subsequent collapse, is the Berlin Congress Hall, designed by Hugh Stubbins, Jnr. and completed in 1957.

A third form of catenary roof occupies any intermediate position between the arched structures of this general category and the free, complex tented forms of the next. Two examples of this are the Japanese national gymnasia at Tokyo, designed by Kenzo Tange and completed in 1964. The larger of the two structures is based on two pylon type 'horns', swept up from their respective interlocking helical seating structures. Between the two pylons, twin steel ridge cables provide the top anchorage for a steel catenary cable network to which the innumerable steel roof plates are welded. This structure makes an interesting comparison with Friedrich Schnirch's theatre roof design of 1824 described later (Fig. 4.4). The smaller gymnasium used a single pylon as the high level suspension point for a similar, anticlastic catenary roof on a circular plan.

arch from which roof cables are stretched to the sides of the building. The second earlier but equally striking form, is based on two sloping and intersecting arches from which a cross grid of cables forms an anticlastic or saddle surface. Below ground level, tie rods hold the scissored ends of the arches together so that only vertical force components are transmitted to the ground. The most notable example in this group is the Raleigh Arena

1.3

PRE-TENSIONED CABLE NETWORKS AND MEMBRANES

This group of structures originated in the explorations and experiments of one man: the architect Frei Otto. The constructions, which are rarely fully enclosed, are of two kinds: the first is characterised by an undulating mesh of steel cables, the peaks of which are either drawn up from above, using external masts, or propped up by internal masts from below. The network is again curved in opposing directions to form the pre-stressed, anticlastic surface necessary for structural stability. A separate weatherproof membrane is attached to this structural network at the intersection points.

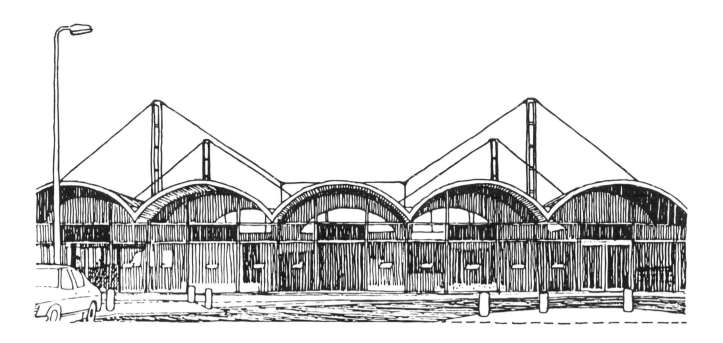

The most spectacular examples of these are the German Pavilion at Expo '67 in Montreal, and the roof over the stadia at the 1972 Munich Olympics (Fig. 1.4).

In a second group, this dual system is replaced by a single, lightweight material which fulfills both functions of structure and weatherproofing. This development occurred in the 1970s when Teflon-coated glass fibre membranes became available. These are light in weight, high in tensile strength, resistant to weather and degradation by ultra violet light, and self-cleaning by wind and rain in most climates. PVC-coated polyester has been more widely used but is only really suitable for lighter, and less permanent structures. Oustanding examples of this group are the Schlumberger Research Centre of 1985 in Teflon-coated glass fibre (Figs. 1.5, and 9.10-9.12), and the new Mound Stand at Lords Cricket Ground of 1987, in PVC-coated polyester (Figs. 10.5-10.7).

1.4

EXTERNALLY EXPRESSED MASTED STRUCTURES

The group of buildings under this heading is characterised by tall masts which provide the high level anchorages for systems of tension cables or rods. These, in turn, support the roof construction which can be expressed in a wide variety of forms and materials. The buildings can be formally differentiated according to the number of masts associated with a basic structural cell. This may be repeated along one or two dimensions to produce aggregations of cells in larger buildings. In all the examples, the presence of the masts gives the group a recognisable identity (Figs. 1.6 and 7.33).

1.5

CABLE-STAYED, CANTILEVERED BEAM STRUCTURES

This group of buildings has several features in common with the previous group, but the mast, the primary distinguishing feature, is absent. In all cases, there is a cantilever beam system, cable-stayed to a high level anchorage, but no continuous mast running from ground level to the

Fig. 1.6 (above) Externally expressed masted structure; Poole Station, Poole, Dorset, England, 1988.

Fig. 1.7 (below) Typical cable-stayed cantilevered beam structures of the post-war period.

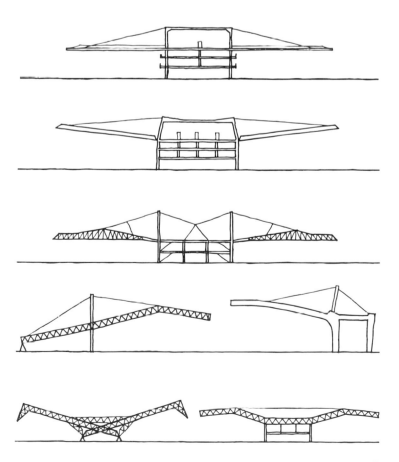

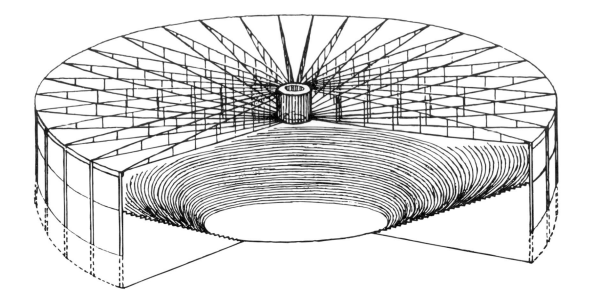

Fig. 1.8
Typical cycle
wheel structure;
Lev Zetlin:
municipal
auditorium,
Utica, New York,
1960.

apex. In its place there may be fin walls above roof level, various forms of A-frames, or even stub columns set on some form of sub-structure. This can lead to rather cumbersome structural 'hybrids' (Fig. 1.7).

Fig. 1.9
Typical
suspended
floor building;
Standard Bank
Headquarters,
Johannesburg,
1970.

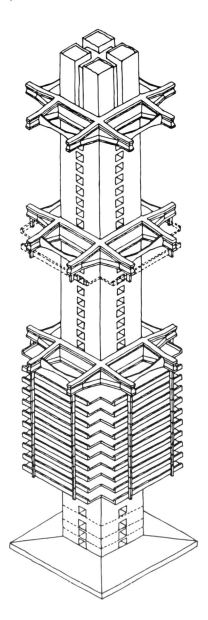

1.6
BICYCLE WHEEL STRUCTURES

The modern form of dual-spoked, tensioned cycle wheel was invented by James Starley of Coventry in 1874. In circular roof frameworks which take this form, two sets of pre-stressed cables span between an outer compression ring and an inner tension ring or 'hub'. The prestressing enables both sets of cables to share in supporting the dead and live loads and the system is economic for spans between 60m and 550m. The first architectural example of this form was developed by the engineer Lev Zetlin for the Municipal Auditorium at Utica, New York, completed in 1960 (Fig. 1.8). The two systems of unequally stressed cables span 73m and are held apart by tubular spreaders. An equally celebrated example was the US pavilion at the Brussels Expo of 1958 designed by Edward D. Stone with a span of 100m and with its central hub open to the sky.

1.7
SUSPENDED FLOOR BUILDINGS

This is a form of tower block structure in which the floors are supported centrally by a substantial core structure, and at the perimeter by steel cables hung from an anchorage framework at roof level. A concrete core can be conveniently constructed by 'slip form' methods. The slender cable supports enable column-free space, with minimal obstruction to light and view, together with an open ground floor. Typical examples are the West Coast Building in Vancouver of 1958, and the Standard Bank, Johannesburg of 1970 (Fig. 1.9).

1.8
AIR SUPPORTED STRUCTURES

These form a totally different group of tension structures: they are constructions in which a

Fig. 1.10
An air-supported structure; Foster Associates: office accommodation for Computer Technology Ltd., Hemel Hempstead, 1970.

membrane is pre-stressed, not by applying tension to its surface, but by pressurising a volume of air inside it so that it is forced into tension from the interior. Although this idea was patented by F. W. Lanchester in 1917, it was only in the 1930s, when synthetic fibres such as nylon and polyesters were developed, that suitable air-tight and durable fabrics could be produced. Inflatable structures can take the form of simple, low pressure balloons, or create a rigid enclosure by maintaining pressure in membrane ribs or between the double skins of a cellular roof. One of the earliest, and simplest examples was the temporary office accommodation designed by Norman Foster in 1963 (Fig. 1.10).

It should be noted that even these very general categories of tension structures in architecture are not exhaustive: buildings based on the 'suspenarch' principle, for example, might be considered to form a further category. Moreover, many examples represent such individualised variants as to comprise a 'class' of one structure only! However, amongst the masted structures which make up the present subject matter, several distinct sub groups can be identified, and these will be analysed in detail in Part Two. ∎

2 STRUCTURAL FUNDAMENTALS

The development of mast architecture has been encouraged by the combined effects of a number of structural concepts and factors. The fundamental concepts are those of equilibrium, force and load-bearing efficiency. The important factors are those of span, depth and load, and the load/span relationship in respect of particular building elements. An understanding of these structural fundamentals is an essential basis for the appreciation of masted structures in general and the appropriateness of an individual example.

2.1
STRUCTURE – ITS DEFINITION, FUNCTION AND CRITERIA

We need first to make a distinction between the building *envelope* and the building *structure.* This distinction can be made because the fabric of a building has to perform two physical functions: firstly, that of space enclosure, involving weather-proofing and thermal insulation and, secondly, that of structural action, involving loads, spans and supports. In traditional masonry buildings, both functions are carried out simultaneously by the wall, floor and roof elements, but in framed structures, including most of the masted structures which concern us, they are represented by two distinct constructional systems i.e. by a space-enclosing and weather-protective building envelope and by the particular type of structural framework which supports it. These two systems have to be integrated constructionally and visually, and can be mutually supportive to a greater or lesser degree.

The structural system has to resist all the dead and live loads which impinge on the building fabric, and transmit them to the ground as quickly and directly as possible. The better it does this, the more efficient the structure will be. How well it does so is assessed in terms of four criteria: whether it is safe, functionally adequate, economic and appropriate to the architectural requirements.

2.2
EQUILIBRIUM AND FORCE

In discussing structural behaviour, the two fundamental concepts of 'equilibrium' and 'force' need to be considered. The ensuring of equilibrium is basic: the initial axiom with which designers must begin and end their calculations is that the various forces in and around the structure must be put into a state of balance so that it is stable under all circumstances. Unexpected movements in structures are often accompanied by equally unplanned movements of their designers to the law courts!

The concept of force is the basis of all structural principles: it is classically defined as anything that changes or tends to change the state of rest of a body or its uniform motion in a straight line. In buildings, it is the external loads on the structure, plus its own weight, which induce internal forces in the structural members. These forces come in different orders of magnitude and act in different directions over large and small areas. It was Isaac Newton who pointed out that if equilibrium is to be maintained, all the originating force actions must be resisted by equal and opposite reactions. The internal forces in the members can take only five different forms, namely tension, compression, bending, shear and torsion.

2.3
TENSION AND COMPRESSION

Tension and compression are axial forces which either pull apart from or press towards each other in opposing directions. Where axial forces in straight members pass directly through the centroid of the member without causing any tendency towards bending they are referred to as 'direct' tension and compression. Resisting these axial forces in a member involves the strength of the material in tension and compression, which may not be of the same value, and the cross-sectional area over which they act.

In theory in these situations, all the material in the cross-section should be fully used. In practice, however, this is only true for tension-loaded members. These usually fail through excessive extension when the material reaches its yield point and can be thus highly efficient – a significant attribute for tension structures. On the other hand, members in compression usually fail by buckling, i.e. by sideways bowing, at a stress level well below the 'squash load' of the material. The tendency to bow is governed by the slenderness of the member and hence initial straightness is of the utmost importance – the greater the lack of straightness, the sooner the member will buckle. This situation does not occur with tension members where the applied load has a straightening effect, even on a slender member. It follows that the most efficient tension members are minimum volume solids, whereas the most efficient compression members are maximum volume hollow sections.

2.4
BENDING AND SHEAR

In spanning members subject to non-axial loading, such as simple rectangular beams, flanged beams and girders, the internal force action is mainly in the form of bending and shear. In resisting the flexural effects of bending, the extreme fibres at the top and bottom parts of the beam are subjected to higher compressive and tensional stresses than those around the neutral axis; moreover, accompanying longitudinal stresses are developed at critical points along the beam due to the tendency of parts of the member to slide past or shear across one another.

These higher bending and shear stresses demand additional material to resist them so that members in bending are less efficient in terms of material than those in direct tension or compression. Consequently, there is a hierarchy of load-carrying efficiency with members in direct tension being first; those in compression second, and those in bending and shear last and least efficient. For this reason, it is often a general objective in structural design to attempt to avoid or at least minimise bending and shear forces in the interests of efficiency and economy. It follows that masted structures are likely to be inherently economic in some respects because they include primary suspension members which are highly efficient by being in direct tension, and masts which are only slightly less so by being in direct compression, albeit that buckling has to be resisted. In addition, supporting the roof at more frequent intervals reduces the spans and hence the depths of the main structural members which should, therefore, need significantly less material to resist the bending and shear stresses.

However, the comparative ability of a structure to resist the forces imposed on it, and the consequent amount of material needed, are not the only or often even the most important matters to be taken into account in design. So far as masted structures are concerned, three other structural fundamentals have had a significant effect on their development, these being the factors of spans and loads, structural depth and the building elements themselves.

2.5
SPAN

Span is technically important because bending moments grow with the square of the span and deflection increases with the cube of the span, or to the fourth power of the span for distributed loads. As span increases, simple rectangular beams soon reach a point at which they can no longer support even their own weight and need to be strengthened. Over longer spans, different forms of prestressed concrete structures and var-

ious types of steel beams, plate girders and lattice trusses become increasingly necessary until they reach the limits of structural feasibility and safety. But tensile structures easily extend these limits, partly because of the efficiency of suspension rods in direct tension, and partly because the wire-drawn steel in cables can resist stresses up to three and a half times as great as the rolled steel in conventional steel beams. Partly for these reasons, long span bridges are always in suspension form, and in architecture, tension-stayed, masted structures are particularly suitable for wide span buildings.

2.6
DEPTH

Structural depth is important both in spanning members and in the system as a whole. The greater the depth of the beam, and thus the greater the distance of its mass from its centre of gravity, the better it will be at resisting bending moments, and the bending stresses in the member will be smaller. The same principle applies in lattice structures. In tensile systems such as suspension bridges and masted structures, the effective depth is represented by the spatial distance to the top of the towers or masts so that, as this is increased, the system as a whole can support heavier loads and span longer distances.

2.7
LOADS

Types and sizes of loads make up a third important factor. This is not only because, over long spans the self weight of the structure becomes critical, but also because the load/span relationships have significant effects on bending and shear. For example, heavy loads acting over long spans will obviously incur penalties in terms of excessive bending and deflection which the structure has to resist. In contrast, heavy loads over short spans induce relatively minimal bending but high levels of shear. Relatively light loads over long spans will lead to low levels of bending and shear but may introduce a danger of buckling.

These differing load/span implications apply to differing building elements. For example, in modern multi-storey buildings the intermediate floors are required to be level, even in arched construction, and also of limited depth and able to bear relatively heavy loads over comparatively short spans. For these reasons, beam and column systems are conventionally used, despite the levels of bending and shear involved.

In contrast, the requirements for roofs, particularly in single storey buildings, pose an entirely different structural problem, i.e. that of supporting relatively light loads over long spans. In these circumstances, and for the reasons outlined earlier, masted structures have many advantages. The tension stayed system reduces the lengths of the roof members to a series of shorter spans, for which either simple or lattice beams can be used, whilst the structure transfers the loads to the ground, albeit indirectly, by suspension elements which are very effective in tension, and masts which are acting in compression. Simultaneously, the masted configuration increases the effective depth of the structural system as a whole whilst reducing the depth of the main spanning members and also the height of the building envelope itself – particularly if the roof is slung below the beams. The system may be arranged as a series of tension-stayed balanced cantilevers or be maintained in equilibrium by a system of back stays and tie-downs leading to ground anchorages. These general characteristics apply, as we shall see, to a wide range of tensile structures.

In summary, the basic characteristics of masted structures originate in a number of general structural fundamentals which are a potent stimulus towards their selection and design in particular circumstances. On its own, however, this is not a sufficient reason to account for the post war development of mast architecture, which has been generated largely by social and cultural circumstances and advances in technology and engineering expertise. The historical origins of these influences need also to be taken into account. ■

HISTORICAL ORIGINS: BRIDGES AND TENTS

3

The characteristic features of masted structures can be seen in two earlier types of tensile structure: first in the cable-stayed version of the traditional suspension bridge and, secondly, in the various forms of traditional vernacular tents. These two kinds of structure, the one concerned with the bridging of space, the other with its simple enclosure, help to explain how modern masted structures originated in response to human social needs, to the available structural materials and to the development of theoretical and practical knowledge of structural behaviour.

3.1

CABLE-SUSPENDED AND CABLE-STAYED BRIDGES

In response to the problem of bridging over a ravine or a river or, as often happens, over both at once, two basic types of tensile structure have been developed. These are the catenary, cable-suspended bridge and the cable-stayed bridge. Although some hybrid, practical combinations of these two basic principles have been designed, they differ fundamentally in the ways in which the bridge deck is supported by the main cables.

In cable-suspended bridges – the familiar, 'classic' suspension bridge type – the relatively flexible main cables take up a natural, catenary curve

between the anchorages or intermediate supports. Suspended from the main cables at frequent intervals are vertical hangers which support the deck and its imposed loads. The main cables, therefore, support the deck only indirectly, that is, via the hangers (Fig. 3.1).

In cable-stayed bridges, the bridge deck is supported directly by a number of relatively taut and inflexible main cables which connect the deck and the supporting tower, or towers, at much less frequent intervals along the main span. The cables may radiate in a fan pattern from a common origin or they may run in parallel, as do the strings of a harp, from a series of points up the supporting towers (Figs. 3.2, 3.3).

The classic form of cable-suspended bridge

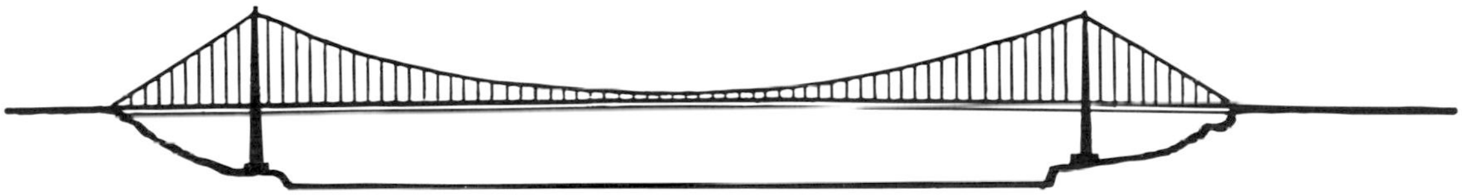

Fig. 3.1
Typical suspension bridge form.

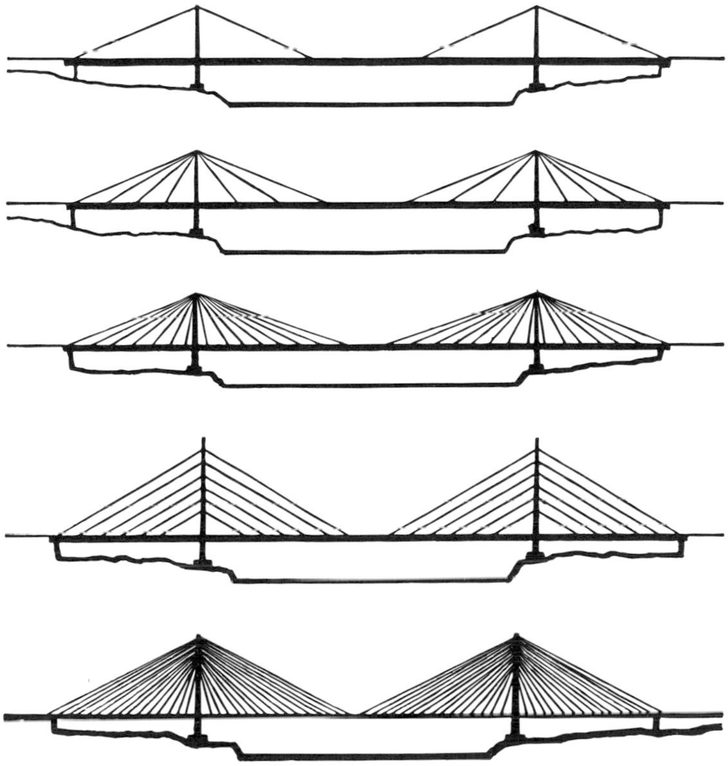

Fig. 3.2 (far left)
Typical cable arrangements of dual-masted, cable-stayed bridges.

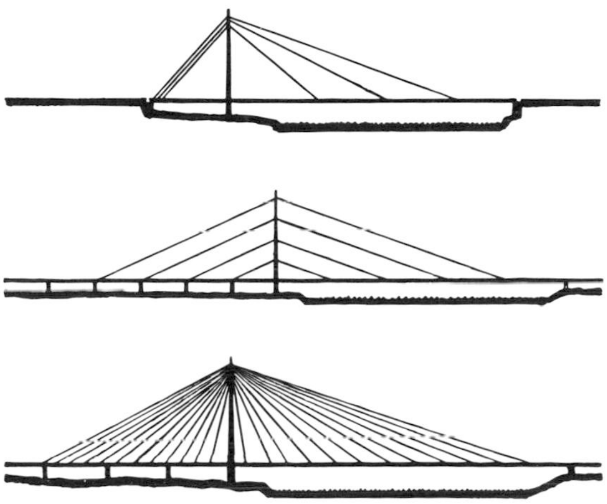

Fig. 3.3 (below)
Typical cable arrangements of single mast, cable-stayed bridges.

*Fig. 3.4
Faustus
Verantius:
proposal for a
chain link cable-
stayed bridge,
1616.*

*Fig. 3.5
C.J. Loscher:
design for a
timber-framed
cable-stayed
bridge, 1784.*

originated in areas which combined high mountains and impassable gorges with rain forest able to provide the long vines for the main cables. Bridges of this kind were needed for social life amongst the civilisations of the Eastern Himalayas and China, and in Peru. But in the south west of China, which had a developed metallurgy, an alternative tensile material was available as early as 200 BC in the form of wrought iron chains and iron bars with pinned connections. Later, between the 1st and 6th centuries AD, these components were introduced into bridge building in South East Asia generally.

Descriptions of Chinese bridges filtered through to Europe from about 1650 onwards and by the early 1800s European bridges began to overtake their Chinese forerunners. The development of the cable-suspended bridge in the 19th century is characterised by parallel progress in England,

France and the USA. In England, although a small iron chain footbridge had been thrown across the river Tees in 1741, it was Thomas Telford (1757-1834) who established the basic, cable-suspended form in his Menai Bridge, designed in 1817-18 but only opened in January, 1826. This bridge used chains of flat links and connecting pins over a main span of 176m.

In the USA, the first suspension bridge with a level deck for wheeled traffic was completed by James Finlay over Jacob's Creek, Pennsylvania in 1801. This was also a chain bridge, but in 1816, and virtually simultaneously in the USA and Scotland, wire cables were used for the first time. During the 1830s, the development of wire cable technology was continued, particularly in France, together with the formulation of a systematic body of theory. At this point, the basic elements of the cable-supported bridge had been established and, with the addition of high tensile steels and sophisticated theoretical and mathematical understanding, its future development was assured.

In contrast to the long history of cable-supported bridges, the cable-stayed bridge is a much more recent phenomenon. It was first only hinted at in the rather naive design put forward by a Venetian engineer and former Bishop, Faustus Verantius, in his work *Machinae Novae*, published in 1616 (Fig. 3.4). However, this initial idea is not a pure cable-stayed design but a structural hybrid consisting of a pair of main catenary chains supporting central hangers, and four sets of parallel stays anchored through openings in the sides of massive masonry towers built over the abutments. The stays end in

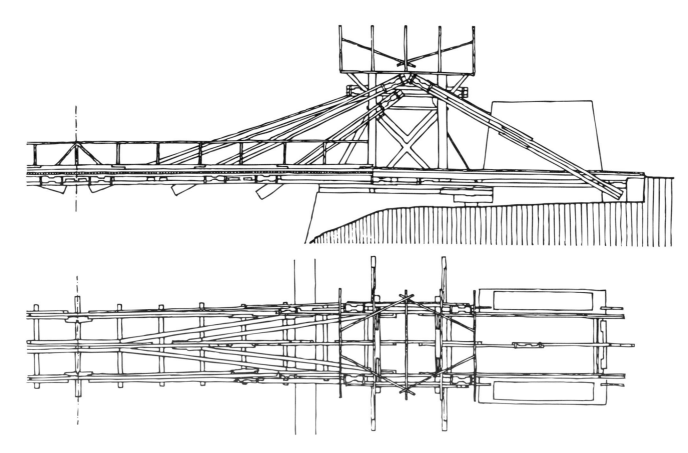

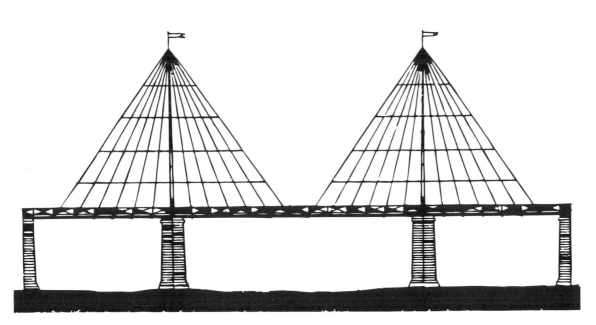

Fig. 3.6
*Bernard Poyet:
outline proposal
for a major cable-
stayed bridge,
1821.*

the links between the short deck beams, across which span the planks of the footway.

The first practical applications of the cable-stayed principle took the form of two small scale footbridges. In 1784, a timber-framed version of a stayed bridge is reputed to have been built by a Swiss engineer, C. J. Loscher, although it seems to have been nearer to 16.5m in clear span than the 32m sometimes quoted (Fig. 3.5). There is more reliable evidence of the wire-stayed Kings Meadow footbridge over the river Tweed near Peebles in Scotland, built by Redpath and Brown in 1817 to span 33.5m. These simple, experimental forms lasted for only a few years before collapsing.

The first proposal for a major, cable-stayed bridge of some length was put forward by the French architect, Bernard Poyet (1742-1824) in 1821 (Fig. 3.6). He suggested a bridge in which a series of stays radiated outwards from the tops of wooden masts to the panel points of the lattice girders which formed the parapets of the bridge deck. This design was also premature and the cable-stayed bridge as a structural solution failed to gain the confidence of engineers in a favourable set of circumstances until after the Second World War.

In the meantime, inclined cable-stays were used in several major bridges but only as a comforting, secondary back-up system to the main catenary cables and hangers. It was hoped to minimise the susceptibility of the structure to adverse wind loading in the absence of reliable theories concerning stiffness and aerodynamic stability. Typical examples of these combination bridges are the pioneering Niagara Falls Bridge of 1855 and the Brooklyn Bridge of 1869-83, both by J. A. Roebling (1806-1969) and the Albert Bridge London, designed by R. M. Ordisch and completed in 1873, which is a suspension bridge stay-assisted by wrought iron flats.

The temporary abandonment of the cable-stayed bridge in the late 19th and early 20th centuries occurred primarily because of a number of collapses at a time when knowledge of the behaviour of forces in highly indeterminate structures was unable to ensure such events would not happen again. However, as spans increased, the heavier weight of the bridge deck itself improved the stiffness of bridges for a time. Nevertheless, observations had shown that uplift movement could be analysed into longitudinal undulations and transverse sway, and it was realised that their combination could produce additional torsion. It became apparent that these forces had to be resisted by the form of the structure itself, not simply by weight alone. Consequently, James Finlay introduced stiffening girders-cum-parapets in the form of open trusses with diagonal stays in the Jacob's Falls Bridge of 1801. Later, James Matthews Rendel (1799-1856) combined designed stiffness in the bridge girders, in the deck itself and in the interconnection between girders and deck to give adequate strength in torsion, an essential requirement for all future designs.

So far as the cables of the cable-stayed bridge were concerned, the need for the stays to remain in tension at all times without being pre-stressed meant that substantial deformations had to be introduced into the structure itself, and this endangered the strength of the whole bridge. In addition, the structural steel available at the time had insufficient strength to resist the high stresses in the cable stays of the primary support system. For these reasons it was not until after the Second World War that the true potential of the cable-stayed bridge could be realised.

In the meantime, probably the most alarming bridge collapse of all time – that of the Tacoma Narrows bridge of 1940 – shook the confidence of engineers, revealed the wholly inadequate theoretical understanding of aerodynamic forces in relation to suspension bridge stability and gave an enormous impetus to basic research. As a result, knowledge of the behaviour of cable-suspension and cable-stayed bridges under conditions of wind loading was vastly improved and the confidence of engineers was restored. At the same time, although steel was in short supply, higher stresses had become permissible through the development of new materials and minimum weight design was encouraged. For these reasons, cable stayed bridges up to 40% lighter than pre-war examples, and with faster erection times, could be considered as possible solutions to long span bridge problems.

In the context of the need for about 15,000 replacement bridges in Germany following the enormous destruction of the Second World War, it is perhaps not surprising that the prime initiative for the revival of the cable-stayed bridge in its modern form came from German engineering. It was a German company, Demag, in collaboration with a German engineer, F. Dischinger, which built the Stromsund bridge in Sweden in 1955-56. This bridge had a span of 183m with steel portal frames supporting cables radiating from both sides.

A more elegant group of three cable-stayed bridges over the Rhine at Dusseldorf was proposed in 1952, although the first member of the 'family', the Theodor Heuss or North Bridge of 260m clear span, was not completed until 1958.

Cable-stayed bridges gained rapidly in popular-

ity during the 1960s and, by 1975, over 50 examples had been constructed. The general principle has been interpreted in practice in several ways: for example there have been variations in the arrangement and number of cables and in the design of the pylons. Two patterns of cable arrangements can be seen: firstly, of cables radiating in a fan pattern from the tops of the supporting pylons and, secondly, of cables inclined in parallel, as in the strings of a harp, from different points up the height of the pylons. The number of cables has also varied, although the earlier bridges used only a small number of cables on each side of the pylons. In these cases, because the bridge deck receives support at only a limited number of points, large bending moments have to be resisted by the supporting beams which therefore have to be of substantial depth. Increasing the number of cables not only reduces the bending moments in the bridge deck, enabling its depth to be reduced and its appearance to be more elegant, but also simplifies and thereby speeds up the erection procedures (Fig. 3.7).

The lightness, elegance and inherent economy of this form of bridge construction was an important factor in the development of masted structures in architecture. The two cable arrangements have recognisable counterparts in particular examples, and many of the theoretical and practical problems are common to both fields.

Fig. 3.7
A modern cable-stayed bridge.

3.2

VERNACULAR TENTS AND THEIR MODERN COUNTERPARTS

To appreciate the historical antecedents of masted structures, which are space enclosing as opposed to merely space spanning, we need to explore the earliest forms of rural and urban tents – structures which are amongst the simplest and most effective ways of providing protection against environmental extremes; we also need to understand the more recent series of modern tented constructions which have formed part of the mast architecture of our own time.

Rural tents

The traditional vernacular tent has been an accompaniment to nomadic life since before recorded history and such tents occur along three geographical bands which sweep across areas of northern Europe and Asia, Central Asia and North Africa, and the Middle East. These great swathes of cultural development, in the context of different climates, topographies, vegetation and wild and domestic animals, have brought with them distinct varieties of tented forms. In terms of structure, shape, covering material and areal distribution, these vernacular tents fall into three broad groups, within which are several sub-regional variations.

The first group comprises the cone-shaped and predominantly skin-covered tents of the most northerly inhabited regions of Europe, Asia and North America. The conical tent is, in effect, a circumpolar form extending across northern and central Siberia, Lapland and the lands of the Eskimo and American Indian. In their simplest forms, the tents of these cultures are based on an internal skeleton of three or four main poles, plus intermediate poles connected at the peak, with occasional horizontal hoops. In northern Siberia, such tents tended to be larger, with a central pole and regular side framing to vertical walls, whilst a variation in Lapland used arched ribs as additional internal supports. Eskimo tents included ridged and domed forms using whalebone in addition to the conical type. The Indian tepee is another archetypal form of the conical tent (Fig. 3.8).

The second group of tented structures is characterised by the various forms of the Kibitka (tent) of Central Asia, a region stretching from the River Volga and the plateau of Anatolia in the West to the Khingan mountains of Afghanistan in the East. In contrast to the conical form of the more northerly areas, the Kibitka tent is basically cylindrical and has two variants in the shape of domical or conical roofs. Its cylindrical walls are made up of a series of collapsible, diagonally-slatted trellises up to 1.7m high, from the tops of which inclined straight or curved rafters converge upon and support a roof

Fig. 3.8
The Indian tepee form of conical tent.

ring, or roof 'wheel'. This neatly solves the constructional problem of connecting the ends of a large number of rafters at one point, although internal posts may also be used to support the central ring on occasions. To resist the outward thrust of the rafters, an encircling rope or woven strap runs around the top of the trellis wall framework. The covering of this skeleton is not by animal skins but by various kinds and sizes of felt mats, used in untailored form and secured by ropes running diagonally over the walls and across the roof (Fig. 3.9).

The conical and the cylindrical tents just described share the common feature of an internal framework to which either skins or mats are applied. The third form of tent, the 'Black Tent' of North Africa and the Middle East, is radically different in form, structure and material.

The Black Tent type occurs in a zone between the latitudes of 25° and 40° North, most commonly between 30° and 35° North, from North Africa in the West, through the Arabic cultures of the Middle East, to Iran, Afghanistan and the borders of Tibet in the East. Its name comes from the black goats

Fig. 3.9
The Central Asian Kibitka form of cylindrical tent.

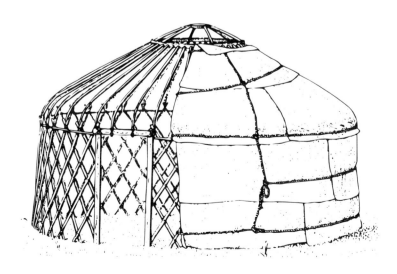

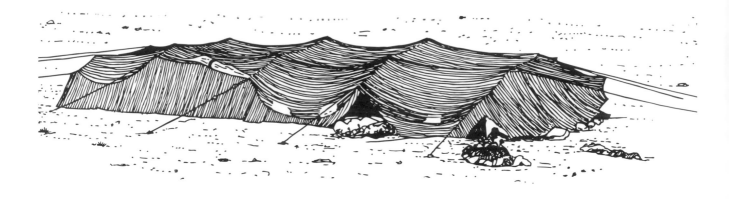

Fig. 3.10
The African and
Middle Eastern
form of variable
geometry 'Black
Tent'; general
view.

hair which is woven to form long lengths of covering material. The distribution of this form of tent therefore closely follows that of the domestic goat, the dromedary and the Tibetan Yak, which is a goat substitute.

The main functions of the Black Tent are sun protection, low night temperature resistance and wind protection. Structurally, it is quite different from the two types described so far, being a non-skeletal tent with a pre-stressed membrane of woven fabric or of skins sewn together. It is also more advanced aerodynamically: its adjustable side stakes and long guy ropes make it a variable geometry tent which can be modified in shape in high winds and sandstorms (Figs. 3.10, 3.11).

The precursors of the Black Tent were the tents of the Tuaregs, originally a Mediterranean people who drifted to the Central Sahara. Their tents were of two kinds, corresponding on the one hand to a relatively settled existence and on the other to a more mobile lifestyle. The first, a 'mat' variant, used an internal, rectangular frame resting on forked uprights, and had mats fixed to this structure. The second, a 'skin' tent, was a portable type in which the skin covering was not anchored to the structure but stretched over it to pegs, stones or poles outside it. A combination of these prototypes forms the basis of the Black Tent.

The Arabian version, a Bedouin archetype, is more regular in form than the North African exam-

Fig. 3.11
As 3.10, plan
from above.

ples, with an almost standard pattern, based on three longitudinal rows of internal poles, the central row in either direction being higher than the rest. This produces a longitudinal or lateral ridge, although the slopes on either side are very shallow. In most cases, the awning rests on goat hair straps between the posts, and is tensioned by long guy ropes. There are often outside wall stakes which can be removed to lower the profile of the tent, and wall curtains which can be rolled up or down. In Baluchistan, a barrel vaulted form is produced by the use of one or more internal hoops, set at right angles to the lengths of cloth and the main guys. In all these forms of tented structures, the internal masts, pre-tensioned membranes and guys are fundamental components.

Urban tents

The urban tents of the ancient world were more uniform in shape and their configurations were largely independent of geography. They originated in the leading countries of the Middle East: Egypt, Palestine, Assyria and Persia, and most of the evidence for their existence comes from Assyrian Palace reliefs and Persian miniatures. They show numerous instances of their use. In Egypt, for example, the transitory nature of the Royal tents contrasts with the permanence of the religious monuments; elsewhere Cubiform, 'sentry-box' tents were used as shelters for precious copies of the Koran and as sanctuaries during pilgrimages to Mecca, whilst Assyrian Royalty used tents combining semi-conical shapes connected by a ridged roof.

These early urban tents fall into two groups: the parasol tent and the pavilion tent. The parasol version had a central pole, a conical roof awning, a cylindrical wall and radiating guy ropes. The pavilion version consisted of two half cones connected by a ridge roof – or there may have been a simple, rectangular, hipped roof form. Both types of structure had enclosing envelopes raised on poles and restrained by ground stays, and both were similar to Black Tents in being pre-stressed membrane

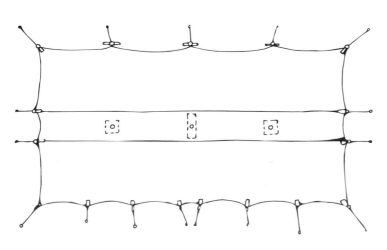

constructions rather than covered frameworks.

Inscriptions on the column of Trajan in Rome show three types of Roman military tent, related to rank: a butterfly form for the rank and file; a central ridge and gable end version for officers and a marquee for commanders. The Romans also used retractable fabric over amphitheatres from 70 BC. These fabric 'vellaria' – the word 'velum' means 'sail' – were suspended on ropes radiating from vertical wooden masts fitted through holes in locating stones and on to stone brackets built into the topmost parts of the walls. There is evidence of this in the surviving stonework of the Coliseum in Rome and the theatres at Orange and Aspendus, but the capability of wooden masts alone to support an extensive retractable fabric awning without some form of backstay is difficult to believe.

Military tents, magnificently lined with gold and more architectural in form, functioned as the real homes of the Ottoman rulers until as late as the 15th century. Indeed, throughout the Middle Ages the use of tents reflects the interests of royalty and its retinues. Fetes, masques, jousts and revels were accompanied by an increasingly ambitious range of tents. In England, the Office of Keeper of Tents ran from the time of Henry I (1100-1135) and lasted for 550 years. Similar officials were responsible for Royal tents in other countries of Europe.

The culmination of combinations of parasol and pavilion tents in England, France and Italy occurred in June 1520 at the meeting of Henry VIII and Francis I of France at the 'Field of the Cloth of Gold'. In fact, the name itself was derived from the magnificence of the tents deployed – as many as 300-400 of various kinds on each side. The meeting was in part a political conference, an athletics event, a music and drama festival and an occasion for state banquets. All these functions were accommodated in groups of basic tented forms, combined into inter-connected tented clusters for the main participants. The French encampment was designed as part of a giant, high yet compact composition, the centre-piece being Francis I's own pavilion and three ancillary tents. The British encampment was more uniform, modular and additive, low and dispersed, but equally well appointed and decorated.

After the decline of this kind of medieval magnificence it was not until the expansion of the real 'travelling circus' that large urban tents were seen again. The modern form of circus, traced out by circling horses, dates from 1768 in England, but it was in American that the real 'Big Top' developed as circus companies began to travel by rail and needed structures which could be easily erected and dismantled. The one ring travelling circus of J. Purdy Brown began to tour in 1825, but other circuses introduced two rings in 1827 and three rings in 1881. By this time the enclosing structure of the American Tent was based on a central row of poles almost 20m high; the largest examples, of the

Ringling Brothers and Barnum and Bailey, housed more than 10,000 people and covered a hectare of land.

In England, the circus was always a one ring affair with the tents correspondingly smaller – though still large in themselves. Around the ring, four King poles defined the main volume of the classic 'Chapiteau' form of tent; next came a ring of Queen poles, inclined outwards at 60 degrees, and lastly an outer ring of perimeter poles supporting the edge of the tent, which was as much as 50m in diameter.

The descendants of these structures still survive to this day, albeit in less ambitious form, in the shape of 'marquees' at innumerable summer shows, sporting events and wedding receptions. But in the mid 20th century an entirely new series of modern tents came into existence.

Modern tents

The design of tents took off at a tangent in the 1950s as the result of original research and experimental modelling techniques developed by the German architect Frei Otto. His interests, and the explorations of his collaborators, extended over every type of tension structure and led to some spectacular constructions. The initial impetus for this original work came from seeing the working drawings for the saddle roof of the Raleigh Arena during a study tour of the USA in 1951. On his return to Germany in 1952, Otto began a systematic and comprehensive study of the then unknown field of suspended roofs; his successful doctoral thesis was published as Das Hangende Dach in 1954.

In that year, Frei Otto began to collaborate with Peter Stromeyer, a partner in Europe's largest tent-making firm, in the development of new types of pre-stressed tents and pre-stressed cable networks. Stable structures of this kind are based on doubly curved saddle surfaces in which pre-stressing is achieved by tensioning one set of cables against another. The more curved the surface, the greater is its surface stiffness, but the curvature must be relatively uniform so that excessive differences in stiffness (strengths and weaknesses) do not occur. For this reason, soap bubble models, which are uniform surface tension membranes, are the essential first visualisations which Frei Otto uses in the development of tented forms. They are followed by more detailed fabric models to check measurements and cut, and lastly by very accurate, structural testing models to confirm the stress levels in the net and to determine the lengths of the cables. A good account of this process is given in Otto, et al., 1970.

There is no real difference between membrane and cable net structures of uniform mesh. The

Fig. 3.12
*Some simple
configurations
of masted
membrane and
cable net
structures.*

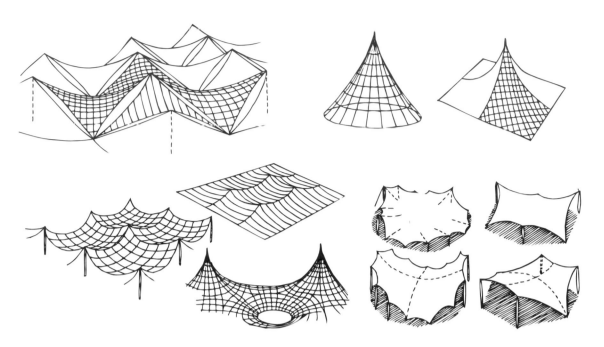

same design principles can be applied to both, and when stretched between identical support frameworks their shapes will be closely related.

Frei Otto and his researchers have shown that here is a huge range of possible configurations of pre-stressed and non pre-stressed cable net and membrane structures based on numerous methods of internal or external supports, different edge conditions and countless permutations and combinations.

The main interest in relation to mast architecture is that Frei Otto's early tents were the precursors of the masted membrane structures of the 1980s which are discussed in chapter nine. They embody three types of surfaces: 'saddle', 'undulating' and 'humped' forms, each capable of so many combinations and permutations that only the simplest shapes can be outlined here (Fig. 3.12).

Saddle surfaces are of two kinds: that closest to a 'real' equine saddle is a warped plane, developed from a square plane which has its diagonally opposite pairs of corner points either raised or lowered in relation to a basic datum. In the generation of this surface in a cable network, cables running parallel to the diagonals produce a minimal surface with a sharp and therefore stiff curvature. Cables parallel to the sides of the saddle are straight line generators and produce a hyperbolic paraboloid. Saddle, or 'anticlastic' surfaces of this kind can have numerous detailed edge treatments and matching units can be added together to form extended compositions covering larger areas.

The second type of saddle or anticlastic surface takes the form of the peaked tent. As the name indicates, a single tall pole supports the peak of a complex, but broadly conical membrane which sweeps down from and partially around the pole to short radiating guys along the bottom edge of the tent.

When saddle surfaces are added together they merge into the undulating forms of the second group of surfaces. In this group, 'gentle' undulations result from sets of cables and continuous membranes in structures which are larger, but have stronger curvatures and correspondingly smaller stresses. In contrast, 'accented' undulations are saddle surfaces stretched between two kinds of cables: sagging, carrying cables which connect the tops of perimeter poles and continue outwards as backstays, and arching, tensioning cables which run in the valleys between the ridge cables and are taken to ground anchorages. Tents of this kind are broadly rectangular, and can be added incrementally, but they can also have tapered sides and be combined into star-shaped arrangements. The perimeter poles of this kind of structure perform a similar function to those of some masted structures we shall come across later.

Lastly, 'humped' surfaces in this context are formed by replacing the highly stressed, internal support points of a tented surface by broader, gently rounded shapes at the tops of the poles. Here again, there are countless structural and formal possibilities. Moreover, in addition to normal humped surfaces, certain points on the surface can be drawn up by cables from very high masts or drawn down by tension stays from below. These high and low points can occur side by side or above and below one another. They can also be formed in vertical membranes by the application of lateral force via struts and cables, an example of this being Renzo Piano's Italian Industry pavilion at the Osaka Expo of 1970 (Fig. 9.12).

Doubly-curved tents to Frei Otto's designs were sewn together for several Federal Garden Exhibitions and other national exhibitions and trade shows between 1955 and 1965. They form a developing series of experiments in shape, stress resistance and erection technique, using different types of fabric and jointing. Two strategic ways of arranging the poles or masts can be distinguished: the membrane can be forced upwards by internal struts from below, or it can be supported from above by carrying cables from external masts. The latter are of more interest in our own context.

Three examples need to be noted: first, the ice rink designed for Villars in 1959 in which a 'high point' membrane is suspended from three carrying cables, each of 62.5m span, stretched between three high timber masts; secondly, the open air theatre at Wunsiedel where the asymmetrical ridge of a circular tent is supported by a cable system from two external lattice masts to produce a series of high points which reflect the characteristics of the particular site and the need to generate adequate saddle-shaped curvature. This structure was designed between 1962 and 1968 but has not yet been constructed. Lastly, the project for covering a ship unloading dock at Bremen involved an enormous masted membrane structure with an average length of 1500m, a width of 380m and a quayside height of 44m to clear the jib crane booms. Outwardly raking masts, 85m high at 170m intervals were intended to pierce the dual-network roof membrane. This project, too, remains to be constructed.

However, several major non externally-masted schemes did proceed to completion: the German pavilion at the Montreal Expo of 1967 covered an area of 10,000m² by a system of peaked surfaces constructed with an underslung polyester membrane, and in 1972 Frei Otto collaborated with Fritz Leonhardt to advise Gunther Benisch and Partners on their exuberantly spectacular covered areas for the Munich Olympic Games, a combination of peaked, tented surfaces with masts which pierce the membrane and support it from the outside (Figs. 3.13, 3.14).

In summary, Frei Otto's contribution to tented structures has been unequalled: his significance lies not only in the range of his imaginative structural concepts and realisations but also in the modes of conception and detailed methods which have led to them. These were employed in pursuit of a most ambitious objective: nothing less than the formulation of a complete, minimal theory of structures, couched in comprehensive terms and applicable to all types of structure. However, it must be remembered that his work is not a direct development from conventional tent construction, but it has been inspired by fundamental, research-based concepts and structural principles, and only marginally by traditional suspension bridges and historical tents.

The initial 'Frei Otto series' which we have just outlined, comprises a first phase in the progression of modern, tented constructions which form an important part of mast architecture. A second phase of more varied, and more ambitious fabric

roofed structures began in 1982 and is still in progress. The organising concepts and the characteristic buildings of this second phase will be described in detail in Chapter 9. Meanwhile, so far as the main stream of mast architecture is concerned, this has its sources in the previous century, to which we can now turn. ■

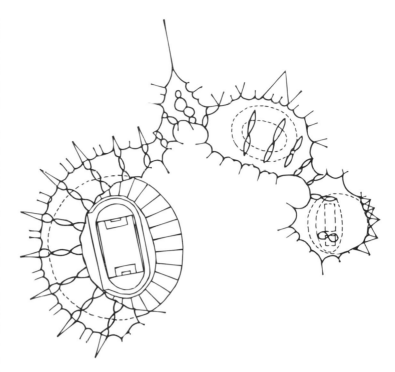

Fig. 3.13
Frei Otto and Fritz Leonhardt with Gunther Benisch and Partners: covered areas of the Olympic Games Stadia, Munich, Germany, 1972; plan.

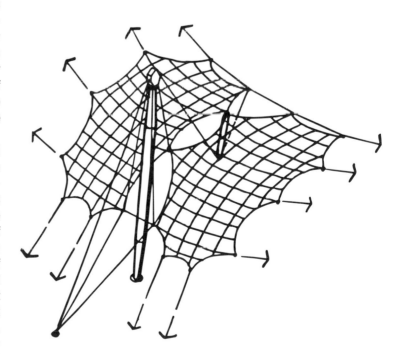

Fig. 3.14
As above, typical module of mast and its associated cable nets.

4

19th CENTURY SUSPENSION STRUCTURES IN ARCHITECTURE

The principles of suspension and support adopted in the two main types of vernacular tensile structures, i.e. bridges and tents, came to be used in more permanent architectural form in the 19th century – but only rarely, and in widely-spaced locations.

As the industrial revolution intensified, the increasing population and consequent growing scale of human industrial and cultural activity brought with it the need for large, unobstructed spaces in a wide range of building types. Railway stations, exhibition halls, markets, auditoria and other institutional and civic buildings were needed and erected. It was the adoption of cast and wrought iron for building purposes which enabled the unprecedented spans of these buildings to be realised, and their structures to be made more fire-resistant for public safety.

The overwhelming majority of these early iron and later steel structures took the form of conventional post and beam, arched or trussed frameworks, the development of which has been thoroughly studied and become well known. Tensile structures are extremely rare, although some of the ideas do provide hints of the kinds of developments to come. Broadly speaking, four characteristic types of structures can be distinguished, but three of these are really forms of suspension structures in general rather than being masted structures in particular. The examples can be categorised as:

i)   Buildings which incorporate suspension bridge elements;

ii)   Suspended chain and cable roofs;

iii)   Two-way cable networks in floor structures;

iv)   Buildings which incorporate masts, either internally or externally.

4.1

BUILDINGS INCORPORATING SUSPENSION BRIDGE ELEMENTS

Fig. 4.1
Suspended roof structure: ship's mast factory, Lorient, France, 1835.

The catenary form of suspension bridge was the source of a key structural element in two 19th century buildings. The first of these, the ships' mast factory built in 1835 in the French port of Lorient to a design by M. Laurent, consisted of two rectangular buildings aligned end to end with a 44m gap between them (Fig. 4.1). This gap was spanned along the line of the external walls by two catenary cables running from corner towers and tied back to the main flanking walls of the buildings. As in a

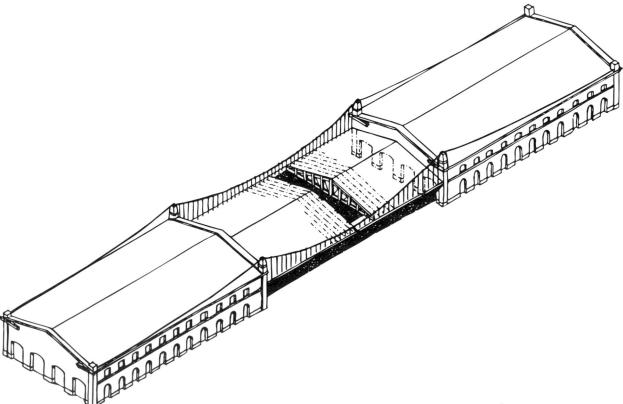

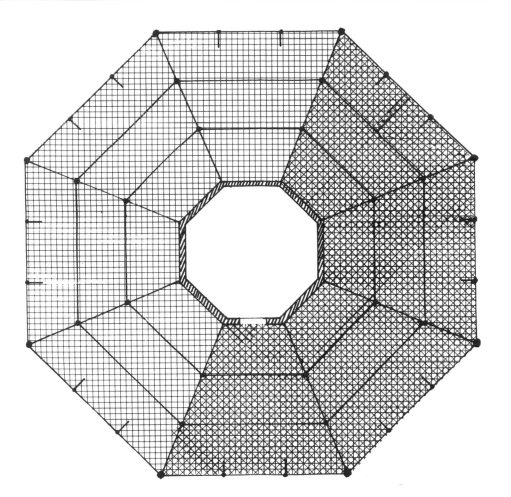

Fig. 4.2
*Friedrich Rabe:
aviary on the
Pfaueninsel,
Berlin, 1834;
tower and
roof plan.*

typical suspension bridge, hangers ran down from the catenary cables; they supported a line of inverted 'saddles' into which rested the ends of 37 trussed rafters spanning 24m across the open yard between the buildings. This ingenious construction enabled masts to be brought through arches in the gable walls and rolled out diagonally for transport to the ships (Locointe, 1843).

A second suspension structure of this kind partly supported the sloping glass roof to the loading bay of the Marshall Field wholesale store in Chicago, designed by H.H. Richardson and completed in 1885. The outer edge of this roof was carried by hangers from a catenary cable spanning 44m and anchored to the flanking walls. By this means unobstructed lorry access was provided to the loading platform. This structurally straightforward construction was demolished in 1930 (O'Gorman, 1978).

4.2

SUSPENDED CHAIN AND CABLE ROOFS

The earliest of these roofs can be credited to Friedrich Schnirch (1791-1868), who built the first Austrian chain suspension bridge in 1824. Schnirch's architectural projects were based on a method of iron roofing patented in Vienna in 1826.

In that year, he began a series of small houses in Czechoslovakia in which the normal rafters are replaced by iron chains to form a fire-proof roof. The chains run from an anchorage of multiple flat bars at the ridge (itself supported on a central spine wall), to the eaves, and from there to anchorages near the plinth of the building. The resulting inward horizontal forces in the copings of the outer walls are absorbed by stone arches resting on the floor of the attic area. At least one of these small houses is said to have been still in existence in 1954 (Ferencik, 1975).

Two later, but very much larger projects were intended to have iron chain roofs. These are the circular exhibition hall for New York, designed by James Bogardus in 1852 (Siliman and Goodrich, 1854) and an enormous steel and masonry tent for the World Exhibition of 1893 in Chicago, designed by Leroy S. Buffington (Hatton, 1979). Neither of these ambitious projects seems to have progressed beyond the design stage, but their basic principle of using a central masonry tower as the high level anchorage for a circular, suspended roof system had, in fact, been put into practice earlier in Europe.

In 1834, Friedrich Rabe's small 'vollere' was constructed on the Pfaueninsel in Berlin. In the centre of this aviary was an octagonal, two storey pavilion from which wrought iron hip rafters spanned on to three rings of cast iron struts (Fig. 4.2). This basic framework was covered by a wire netting mesh to

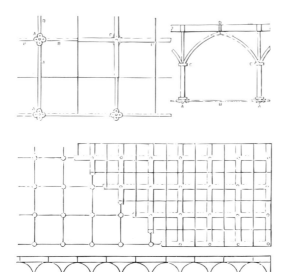

Fig. 4.3
Bridges-Adams:
proposal for a
compartmented,
cable-network
floor system,
1852.

4.3

TWO-WAY CABLE NETWORKS IN FLOOR STRUCTURES

Cable networks were shown to be built up in the roof planes of several 19th century projects, but the following examples envisage a horizontal application. Two early designs of 1852, by Bridges-Adams and E.L. Garbett, illustrated flat, pre-tensioned cable networks based on grids of steel rods. At the intersection of the square or triangular grids, cast iron struts formed a compartmented floor system, but no allowance seems to have been made for any deflection in the structure and the anchorage provisions are not explained (Fig. 4.3). Altogether, this proposal seems little more than a fanciful and structurally naive idea (Bridges-Adams, 1852; Garbett, 1852).

4.4

MASTED STRUCTURES IN THE 19TH CENTURY

Interspersed chronologically amongst the examples described above is another group of structures which are the true precursors of the masted structures of our own time. These comprise some design proposals of doubtful structural validity which were destined, perhaps fortunately, never to be realised in practice, and several more impressive structures which seem fresh and structurally innovative even today.

Fig. 4.4
Friedrich
Schnirch: design
for a suspended
theatre roof,
1824.

form the flight space for the birds. It must have been a charming and delicate structure and was probably the first attempt to derive an architectural form from the suspended profile of a tensile roof structure (Graefe, 1985).

The earliest proposal seems to have been, in morphological terms, a suspension bridge/ridge tent hybrid. It was designed by Friedrich Schnirch, the Austrian engineer mentioned earlier, and published in 1824 (Hruban, 1975). His long-span, iron roof system was intended to be of light weight, low cost and fireproof construction. The example chosen for illustration was that of a theatre roof where the need for unobstructed space and the danger of fire were amongst the prime design factors to be considered.

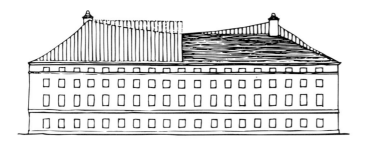

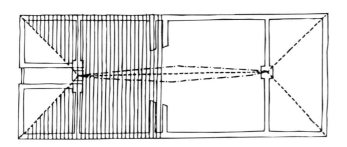

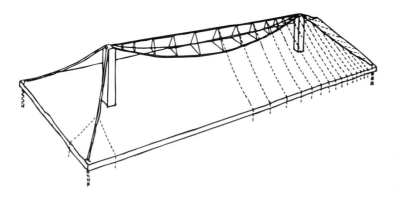

Schnirch's design was based on two internal 'masts' in the form of stone columns. From the tops of the columns it was proposed to run a ridge chain or chains, the ends of which were to be tied back to the corners of the building. The single ridge chain design functioned as a suspension bridge structure, the hangers of which supported the roof ridge and four hip ridges. The chains were thus visible above the roof and "should the concave form of the roof not suit you" the designer proposed an alternative. In this design, two chains are used, kept apart by cast iron saddles which provide support for a horizontal ridge which runs above, and thereby conceals, the structural system. Lighter chains, of 'paper clip' type links, run from ridge to eaves and are linked by lateral wires to form a metal network on which a roof covering of metal sheets or cast iron shingles can be built (Fig. 4.4).

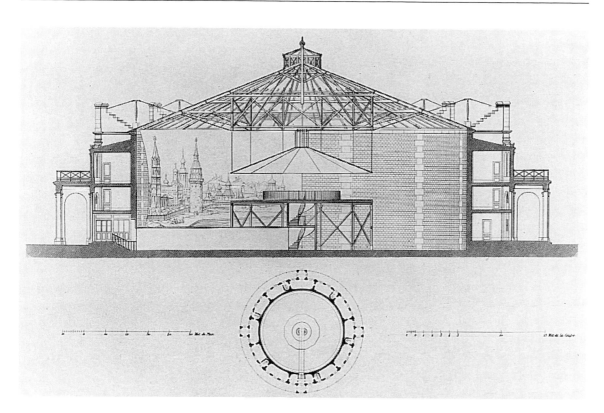

Fig. 4.5
*J.A. Hittorf:
Panorama des
Champs Elysses,
Paris, 1839;
section and plan.*

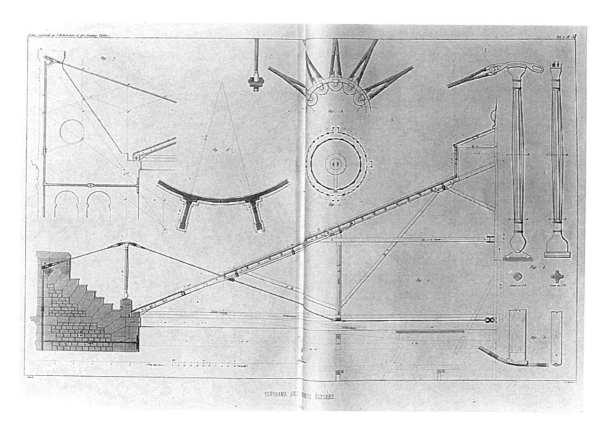

Fig. 4.6
*As above;
details of roof
construction.*

This adventurous principle seems not to have been realised in practice at this time, although it makes an interesting comparison with Kenzo Tange's gymnasium of 1964. However, in 1839, an even more ambitious and equally innovative masted suspension structure was successfully completed and opened to the public. This was the building for the Panorama des Champs Elysées, designed by J. A. Hittorf (1792-1867). The panorama itself was painted around the enclosing wall of a circular space, 14.5m high and 39m in diameter (Fig. 4.5). The scene was viewed from a central raised stage and needed a shadowless and unobstructed environment. Hittorf developed an architectural solution which satisfied the functional requirements whilst using the most advanced construction techniques of the time. He was the Peter Rice of his day – at least in respect of this example.

Fig. 4.7
Charles
MacIntosh:
design for a
cable-stayed
greenhouse roof,
1853.

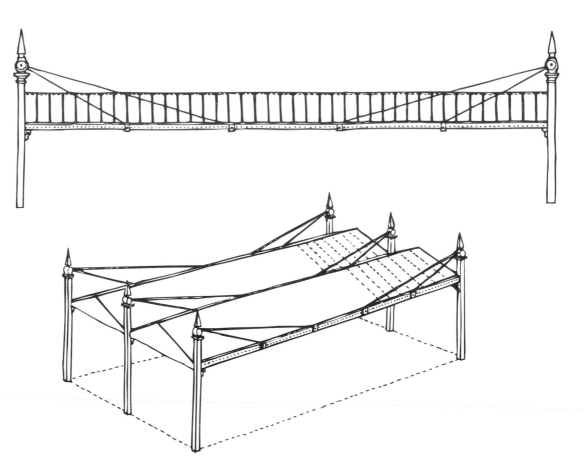

Fig. 4.8
Eduard Müller
and Ernst Giese:
auditorium for
the first German
Song Festival,
Dresden, 1865,
cross section.

The timber framed circular roof was carried by twelve cables which originated, initially horizontally, from a tension ring below the central lantern, rose at an angle to the tops of cast iron compression masts on the perimeter walls and were anchored to wrought iron tie rods extending down the walls to the foundations (Fig. 4.6). Light was admitted through a continuous strip around the roof. It was said that Hittorf could hardly conceal his joy when the scaffolding was dismantled and the immense roof appeared to float in the air. The principle of this brilliant construction could be seen from the outside, though sadly not from the interior.

Two years later, an elegant, albeit structurally unsound design for a greenhouse using a cable-stayed beam system was suggested by Charles MacIntosh in his *Book of the Garden* of 1853. The elevation shows a 'ridge and furrow' roof structure in which the valley gutters function as beams supported by four equally spaced cable stays. In elevation, these run from vertical masts which lack any backstay anchorage cables and are, therefore, certainly impracticable structurally (Fig. 4.7). Perhaps for this reason, the curious and incompatible plan shows more substantial blocks, possibly of masonry, in their place.

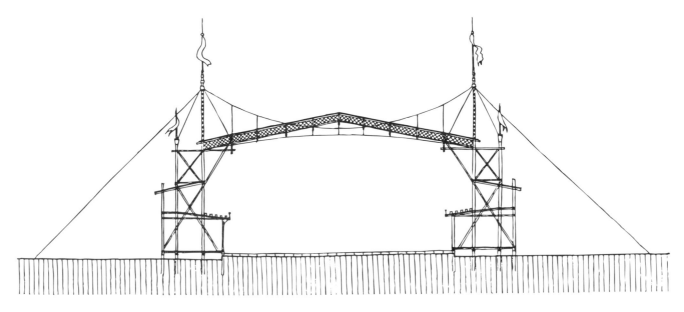

The second major masted structure to be constructed in the 19th century, following the Panorama des Champs Elysées of 1839, was a temporary and, perhaps for this reason, less well-documented structure of 1865. This was a building needed for the first German Song Festival, held over four days in Dresden. The event was attended by 12,000 singers who performed before an equally large audience. The architects, Eduard Müller and Ernst Giese, found themselves having to provide an unobstructed auditorium of 120m x 40m in floor area, which had to be quickly erected and of light weight. In answer to these requirements they designed a modular, masted structure which used suspension cables to provide support to a shallow, double-pitched roof (Fig. 4.8). The roof planes consisted of two-way frameworks of timber lattice girders hung from the main catenary cables. These cables were attached to two rows of masts located along the walls of the auditorium and tied back to ground anchorages of some kind. This is an extraordinarily innovative design for its date and it is tantalising that so few details seem to have survived.

Masts and catenary cables continued to be popular in the more fanciful schemes of the time. In the following year, 1866, the French architects LeMaistre and Mondesir published ideas for iron suspension structures over enormous spans, although their constructional details are unknown. Simplistic, and structurally naive combinations of suspension cables, and stepped roofs with clerestories are accompanied by sketch proposals for rectangular and circular masted structures. One of the latter shows an unobstructed circus building in which cables run from a central collar supporting a lantern to the tops of masts positioned on the inner wall of the enclosing masonry structure. Not surprisingly, considering their structural naivety,

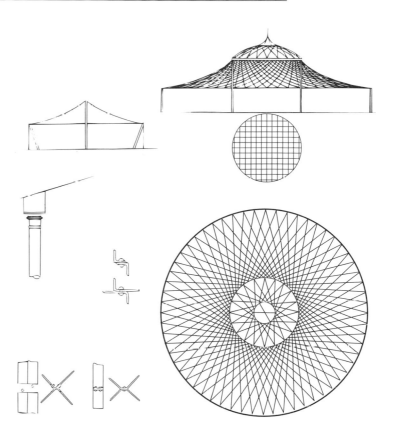

nothing was heard of these ideas again (Graefe, 1985 op.cit.).

As the end of the century approached, Schnirch's idea of using internal stone pillars to provide the peaks of an essentially tented major volume was revived in metallic form. The principle of internal 'masts' (for that is the function which the stone pillars actually performed) was re-applied using iron lattice elements as the principal supports of a series of four temporary exhibition halls for the Russian Art and Industry Exhibition at Niznij-Novgorod in 1896 (Scerbo, G. M., 1074) (Graefe, 1985, op.cil.).

Fig. 4.9 (above) V.G. Suchov: outline designs for iron geodesic roof structures, 1894.

Fig. 4.10 (below) V.G. Suchov: Russian Art and Industry Exhibition, Niznij-Novgorod, 1896; elevation and section of the circular pavilion.

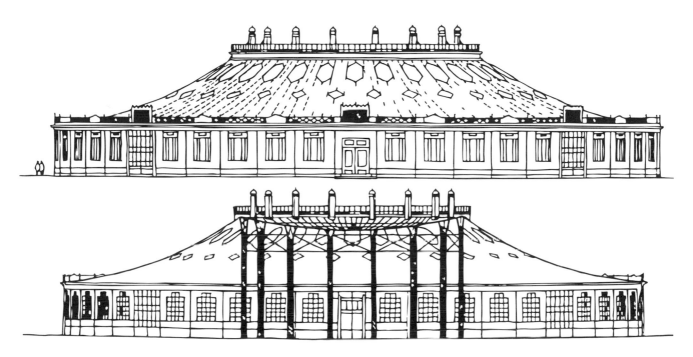

The previous year, the Russian engineer responsible, V. G. Suchov, had obtained a patent for a method of constructing geodesic networks out of lengths of hoop iron, riveted together at their intersections. His objectives were the saving of weight and the use of members subject only to tension or compression. The iron network is shown applied to the suspended roof of a circular tented structure in which a ring of internal masts props up a central shallow dome constructed in a similar way. No indication is given of any eaves anchorages or compression ring to resist the horizontal forces at that point, although one single-line outline section seems to show the provision of internal, inclined struts for this purpose (Fig. 4.9).

The four pavilions at the Niznij-Novgorod exhibition put these principles to use in a 'family' of tent-like structures, one circular, one oval and two rectangular in form, all roofed by centrally supported iron nets. The circular pavilion, 68m in diameter, is identical in its concept to the patent application drawing; the inner circle, of 16 lattice columns, supports a high level ring, 25m in diameter, from which rolled hoop iron strips span across to the outer walls, 21.5m away. The central ring was covered by a saucer-shaped, suspended bowl of soldered sheet metal (Fig. 4.10).

The oval building, 98m long, had two substantial internal lattice masts, connected by an internal lattice ridge girder in the form of an inverted arch. The rectangular pavilions, each of 70m x 30m, had a row of ten internal lattice masts, supporting a horizontal ridge from which similar hoop iron nets spanned across to the eaves and over slanting struts to the ground. These inclined struts resisted the horizontal forces at the eaves, directing them to the base of the wall construction. In these seminal iron tent constructions, the masted structures of the nineteenth century were brought to an impressive conclusion. ∎

20th CENTURY MASTED STRUCTURES

5

We conclude Part One of this study by reviewing the development of masted structures over the present century. We have divided this time span into periods of differing lengths, i.e. the years leading up to the outbreak of the Second World War in 1939; a further period of twenty years; two of ten years; two of five years, ending with a summary of the years from 1990 to mid-1995. These shortening time spans correspond to the increasing number of structures to be mentioned as the century progresses.

Our intention has been to describe how mast architecture developed in response to the social and cultural demands of the time; to review the associated building types in which it found expression, and to note the leading architects whose own intentions and objectives played a large part in the process.

In formulating this basically chronological review we have also provided sufficient constructional and formal detail to enable the general nature and scale of the buildings to be appreciated in company with their function and occurrence in the sequence. A full comparative analysis of the differing formal and structural configurations which have been developed by designers comprises the subject matter of Part Two; how those patterns of structural differentiation relate back to the general chronological development will be considered in the conclusions in Chapter 13.

5.1

BUILDINGS AND PROJECTS BETWEEN 1900 AND 1939

It will be clear from the previous chapter that 'true' masted structures were few and far between, even amongst the limited number of tensile constructions of the 19th century. In fact, twenty-six years separated the masts of the Paris Panorama from those of the Dresden Song Festival building, and it was to be a further thirty-eight years before the first masts of the 20th century were sketched out in a work of architecture.

These masts formed part of the competition version of the design for the Vienna Post Office Savings Bank building prepared by Otto Wagner in 1903 (Fig. 5.1). The cross section of the Banking Hall shows an elliptically curved glass roof, flanked by similar but lower and smaller vaults on each side. The glazing framework of these vaults is supported at intervals by cables running from a series of masts on each side of the main vault, with other cables attached to the flanking walls which enclose the hall. In the context of the more decorative Secessionist atmosphere of the Austrian Art Nouveau, the masts themselves are an aesthetic and constructional continuation of the plain steelwork, industrial lighting columns and aluminium heating outlets of the interior – technological features with which Otto Wagner would have become familiar through his polytechnic education.

It was to be another twenty years before the next group of 20th century masted designs was put forward by several Russian Constructivist architects. In 1923, Alexander and Viktor Vesnin designed a masted building for the Palace of Labour in Moscow, and the following year the two brothers outlined a design for a light field aircraft hangar

using masts and cables to support a fabric roof sloped to follow the parked profile of the biplanes of the time (Figs. 5.2, 5.3). The hangar design is direct, spare and rather like a scaled-up version of a bivouac shelter out of 'Scouting for Boys'. In its own terms it brings the transportable military tent into the era of air warfare. In 1929, Anatole Lyudvig roofed, apparently successfully, the rectangular audience area in front of the summer stage at the Moscow Central Park (Fig. 5.4). In this case, a light membrane roof, probably of fabric, was stretched between cables suspended between two lines of perimeter masts anchored to the ground by inclined back stays. The last design in this group is Nikolsky's first-round entry for the Palace of Soviets competition of 1931.

Fig. 5.1
Otto Wagner: entry for the Vienna Post Office Savings Bank Competition, 1903; cross section of the banking hall.

Fig. 5.2
Alexander and
Viktor Vesnin:
design for a light
field aircraft
hangar, 1923.

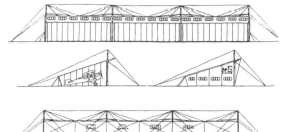

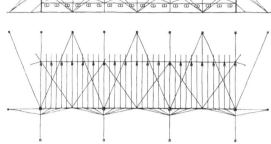

Fig. 5.2
Alexander and
Viktor Vesnin:
design for a light
field aircraft
hangar, 1923.

Fig. 5.3 (below)
Anatole Ludwig:
masted roof to
the audience
area of the
summer stage,
Central Park,
Moscow, 1929;
view of corner.

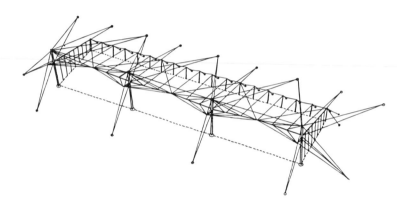

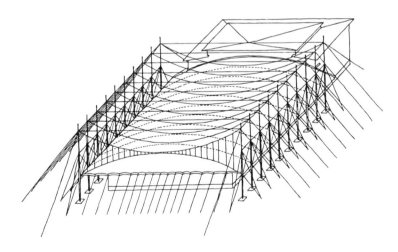

Fig. 5.4
As above;
axonometric
drawing.

This is a striking and adventurous design, despite the lack of attention paid to the structural provisions necessary to make it stand up! In the absence of any back stays to the cigar-shaped masts, the absolute necessity of some kind of substantial compression ring at the mastheads seems not to have been appreciated, nor is there any indication of the tension ring needed to support the internal tented roof and its conical peak (Fig. 5.5).

These designs have an attractive directness about them, helped partly by the fact that, in most cases, they have been recorded in outline only, lacking much structural or architectural detail. The remaining projects of the years up to 1939 are more tangible, and occurred in the USA.

The most important of these explorations was the 'Dymaxion' house design, patented by Richard Buckminster Fuller in 1927 (see Fig. 6.3). This archetypal, single-masted design, although realised only in model form, represented a significant stage in Fuller's own blend of homespun plausible rationalism and introduced, in effect, the concept of 'building performance' for the first time. Its structure and taxonomic significance are discussed in more detail in Chapter 6.

On a larger scale, the Railroad Hall of the Travel and Transportation Pavilion at the Chicago Exposition of 1933 (Figs. 5.6, 5.7) makes an interesting comparison with Nikolsky's rotunda, which was probably designed at more or less the same time. Both projects consist of a circular building, defined by a ring of external lattice masts. In the Russian example, the tensile forces from the internal roof act at the tops of the masts where they must be resisted by a compression ring, whereas in Chicago they were counteracted by a number of inclined and diverging back stays. Looking back at this design we can now see its hitherto unappreciated significance in three ways: first, it shows a mature integration of engineering expertise and architectural quality for its date – in terms of massing, the contrast between the lines and planes of the high rotunda and the lower and more straightforward rectangular block is very well judged. Secondly, it represents the first of many instances of a prominent masted structure being used for conspicuous visual effect at a major international exhibition. Finally, in visual terms, it was a stunning Art Deco concoction: the steel towers were painted black, the cables were white or silver and the main ribs were grey with silver trim. This sophisticated combination of neutral tones reflected the structural characteristics of the building and the unconcealed expression of the structure was a major innovation in 1933.

In the closing years of the 1930s, Bertrand Goldberg also used a masted form for two small structures of rather lesser significance: a rather over designed ice-cream kiosk (Fig. 6.6) and a neat petrol station canopy (see Gazetteer).

5.2

MASTED STRUCTURES FROM 1940 TO 1959

This period, which includes most of the Second World War, is characterised in terms of masted structures by sporadic experiments from individual American architects; by a number of interesting European exhibition buildings, and by the development of various kinds of hybrid hangar structures reflecting the expanding world of post war air travel. As the 1950s drew to a close, the use of masted structures began to gather momentum over a wider range of building types.

So far as individual architects are concerned, Eero Saarinen outlined an interesting two storey community centre structured around a single mast as early as 1941 (see Fig. 6.5). His later design for a four masted tent for the Goethe Music Festival at Aspen, Colorado, was erected there in 1949 (Drew, 1979, p. 198).

Bruce Goff began with a tentative use of steel tube frames and cables to support saucer-shaped external canopies in his Ledbetter House of 1947 and in 1950 he completed the delightfully idiosyncratic Bavinger House with its warped copper roof and attached activity 'pods' spiralling around a central oil well pipe mast with the help of re-cycled biplane rigging! (See Fig. 6.4). Outside this period, his 'Aparture' project of 1956 and the Minneola community centre design also included groups of masted elements in more ambitious forms.

It is noteworthy too that in 1957 a refreshingly simple and archetypal single mast design by Whitney-Smith was adopted by the Mobil Oil Company as its standard service station canopy, a square, 'parasol' design usable either singly or in groups (Fig. 5.8).

On the resumption of major exhibitions after the Second World War, masted structures soon put in an appearance. At the Milan Fair of 1948, a single monopitched roof plane was floated from raking masts over a railway rolling stock exhibit (see Figs. 7.7 and 7.8), to be followed by an improved version of the same idea at the repeated event in 1950. This was the first appearance of a masted structure in post-war Europe. It showed too that Italian design flair was fast reviving.

A more significant exhibition, to demonstrate the extent of Britain's recovery after the Second World War and to commemorate the centenary of The Great Exhibition of 1851, was held on the South Bank of the River Thames in London in 1951. The competition-winning design for its 'vertical feature' pierced the sky above the displays like a huge exclamation mark, a cigar-shaped symbol suspended from a three mast tensile system of struts and cables (Fig. 5.9). Elsewhere on the site, visitors

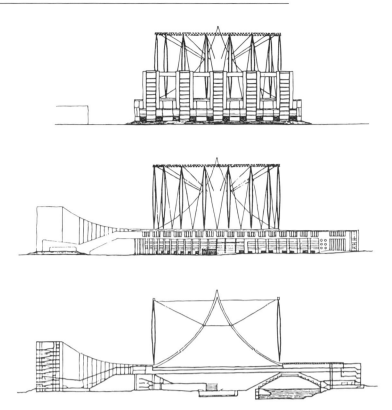

Fig. 5.5
S. Nikolsky: entry for the Palace of the Soviets Competition, Moscow, 1931.

Fig. 5.6
E. Bennett and Associates: Railroad Hall of the Travel and Transportation Pavilion, Chicago Exhibition, 1933; exterior view.

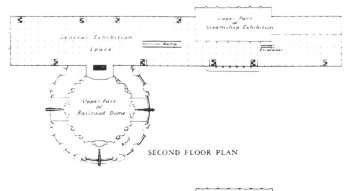

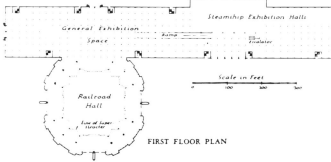

SECOND FLOOR PLAN

FIRST FLOOR PLAN

tively – the latter being a 'nave and aisles' arrangement of two lines of masted lattice 'umbrellas' supporting a central lattice-framed roof element (Fig. 5.10). There seems to be something particularly Russian about this innovative idea, expressed in conventional and somehow ungainly engineering terms.

The sequence of masted exhibition structures of this period was concluded by the circular drum and inclined external masts of the UK Pavilion at the Rand Easter Show in Johannesburg in 1959 (Fig. 11.5). This building bears little relation to the structurally rudimentary idea of Nikolsky's circular auditorium of 1931, nor does it have the ponderous monumentality of Burnham and Holabird's Chicago pavilion, also of 1931. Instead, the Johannesburg drum is classically simple and

Fig. 5.7
As Fig. 5.6: first and second floor plans.

Fig. 5.8 (below) Whitney Smith and W. Williams: masted parasol service station canopy for the Mobil Oil Company, 1957.

Fig. 5.9 (right) P. Powell and H. Moya: The Skylon, South Bank Exhibition, London, 1951.

entered the two main areas of the displays under matching conical planes, wrapped around cables radiating from two central masts. Along the river frontage, other masts and cables supported cantilever lookouts, to complete a trio of exciting masted structures appropriate to a riverside setting for a major exhibition.

The first post-war 'Expo', held in Brussels in 1958, had two masted pavilions representing the European Coal and Steel Community and the USSR respec-

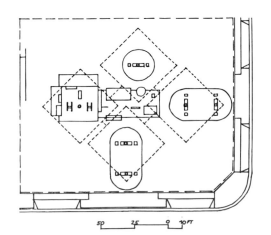

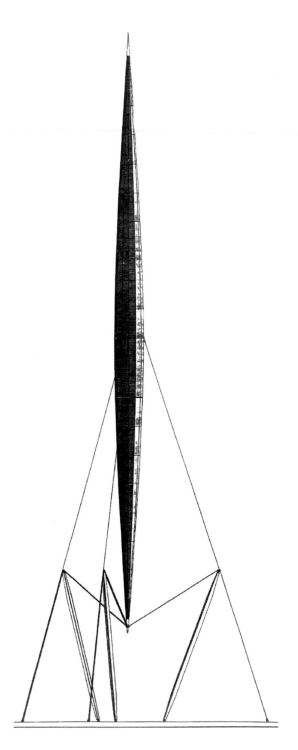

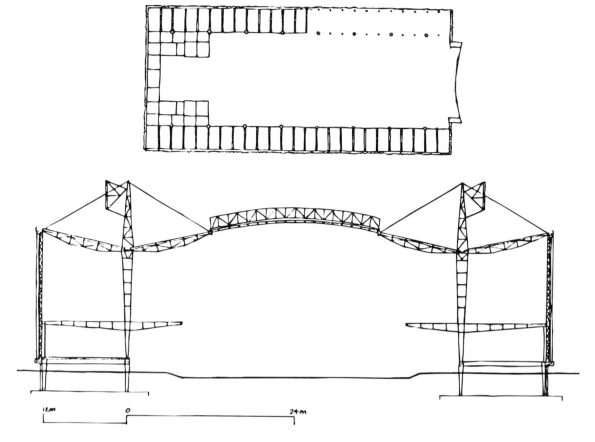

Fig. 5.10
*Boretski,
Ambramov,
Donbor and
Polanski: USSR
pavilion,
Brussels Expo,
1958.*

Fig. 5.11 *(below)
Ketchum, Gina
and Sharp:
Parkers Square
Shopping Centre
project, Witchita
Falls, Texas,
1952.*

sophisticated, but the visual ambiguity, seemingly intrinsic to all masted rotundas – that their inherent mass seems capable of supporting itself without the help of the masts – is still there (see Fig. 11.5).

In the USA, the large shopping centre project for Parker Square, Wichita Falls, Texas in 1952, envisaged a masted 'mat' building of over 18,000m² – the largest structure of its kind at that time – and in 1953 the classically simple, double-cantilevered Transcon Lines Vehicle Terminal was completed. It is interesting that these two examples of differing size are, in fact, variants of the same mast and cable-stayed beam principle (Figs. 5.11, 5.12): in the latter the structural unit is repeated along one dimension, whilst in the former it is extended over two dimensions.

The most extensive series of wide-span structures of this period was related to the demands of air travel. Differing configurations of cantilevered hangars were designed, embodying several tensile structural forms and some rather ungainly hybrids (see Fig. 1.7). However, there were very few 'true' masted structures in this building type.

5.3
MASTED STRUCTURES FROM 1960 TO 1969

Whilst the total number of masted structures in this decade seems to have differed only slightly from that of the previous period, the range of building types continued to expand. For example, the

increasing concern for physical fitness in parallel with the post-war resumption of the Olympic Games, and the consequent participation in sporting and leisure pursuits, brought with it the need for

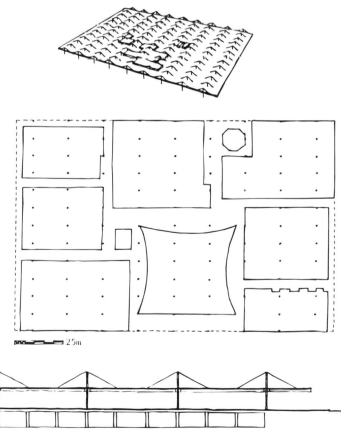

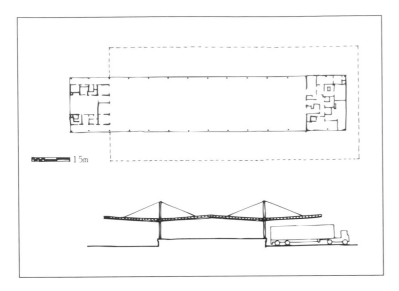

Fig. 5.12
Allison Rible, with Popp and Ropp: design for a Transcon Lines vehicle terminal, 1953.

at Laval a rearwards sloping canopy is cable-stayed from inclined masts which continue the line of the rear slope of the triangular section terracing; and at the Crystal Palace Sports Centre in London one of the most elegant embodiments of dynamic tension set a new standard in cable-stayed structures in reinforced concrete (Fig. 5.14).

In 1961, cable-stayed roof structures entered the industrial sector and were introduced to Japan for the first time. In that year, Kenzo Tange's factory for the Tosho Printing Company (see Fig. 8.28) initiated the concept of a 'spine' of dual masts on a concrete substructure supporting very wide cable-stayed roofs on either side, an idea which Richard Rogers was to take further in his fully-masted Inmos design of 1979-82 (see Figs. 8.29 – 8.31).

Exhibition buildings continued to be favourite opportunities for structural and formal innovation at a number of venues including the Hannover Industrial Fair of 1962, the Swiss Expo and the New York Worlds Fair of 1964, and the Zagreb Fair of 1968. At each of these events the range of masted structures was further extended in terms of form and material. For example, the relatively simple concept of floor and roof planes hung from a central mast, devised by Buckminster Fuller in 1927, was eventually realised constructionally but in triangular form and in the material of the Aluminium Pavilion of the Hannover Fair (see Fig. 6.2b); at the New York Fair, the twenty-one tent-roofed pavilions of the New Jersey exhibit, one for each county in the state, were hung from three clusters of three masts each; at the Zagreb Fair, the German pavilion comprised a huge rectangular volume with internal columns supporting cable-stayed concrete 'mushroom' caps (see Figs. 6.26, 6.27).

At the Swizz Expo a spectacular gull-wing

large sports halls and open air grandstands. As part of this process, towards the end of the previous decade the gymnasium of the Central Washington College incorporated the first use of a cable-stayed roof in a sports hall. Moreover, in 1960, the Squaw Valley Winter Olympic Stadium approached a not dissimilar problem from a quite different architectural stand point. The former is, conceptually, a simple box on the ground, the latter essentially a double-pitched roof floated over a moulded ground surface with its masts spanning twice the distance of its predecessor (Fig. 5.13). Also during this decade, three entirely different open air structures began what was to be a continuing series of masted grandstand canopies: for the stadium at Marl, Westphalia, (see Fig. 6.23) two towering, tapered pylons pierced a cantilevered cable-stayed roof plane over simple stepped terracing; at the stadium

Fig. 5.13
Comparative cross sections:

a. *R. Buckhard: Nicholson Gymnasium, Central Washington College, Ellensburg, 1958.*

b. *Corlett and Spackman: Winter Olympics Stadium, Squaw Valley, California, 1960.*

Fig. 5.13a

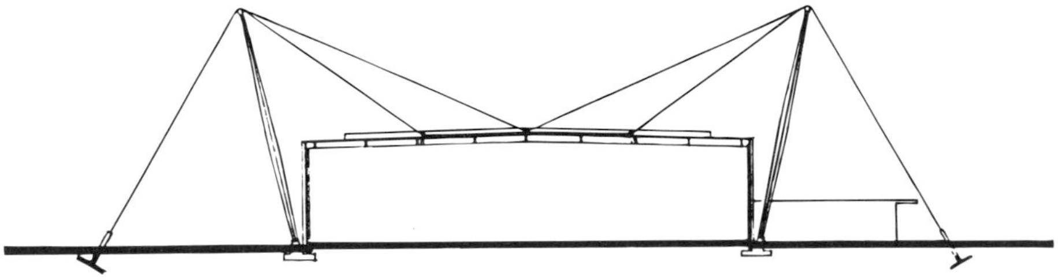

Fig. 5.13b

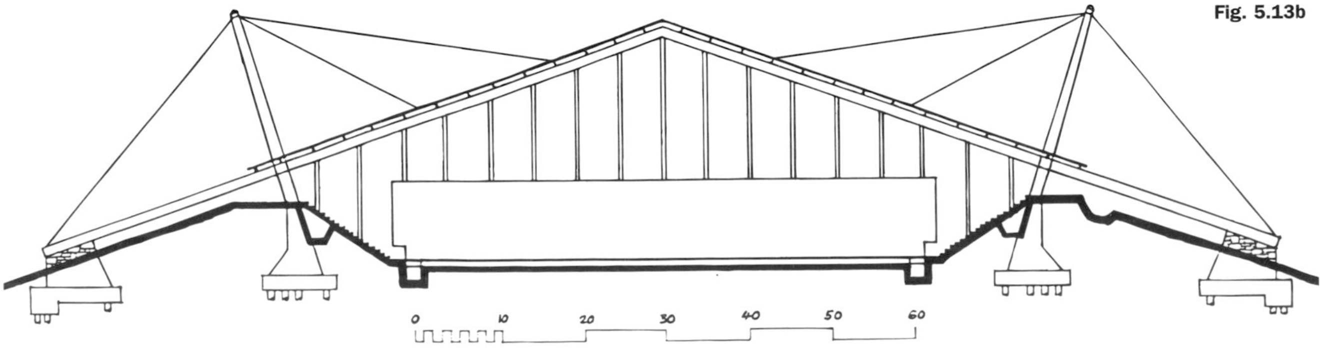

Fig. 5.14
London County
Council,
Architects
Department:
masted
grandstand
canopy, Crystal
Palace Sports
Centre, 1964.

canopy was floated over the Station platforms, hung from three soaring masts, but this basic structure made use of the suspension bridge principle of vertical hangers from catenary cables rather than radiating cable stays from a mast anchorage (see Fig. 6.21). In contrast, the station canopy at Tilburg in Holland used the currently fashionable combination of hyperbolic paraboloid roof modules partially supported by masts along the sides of the cells – a new, but rather heavy and structurally hybrid arrangement (see Fig. 8.42).

In the UK, the exhibiting of birds and plants generated the first two architectural tensile structures since the Skylon and other features at the South Bank Exhibition some thirteen years previously. The earlier of the two, the walk-through Snowden Aviary of 1965 at the London Zoo, consists of two double tetrahedra framed in tubular steel holding a cat's cradle of tension cables which give form to the black anodised aluminium mesh envelope. However, the primary supports for this netted envelope are not conventional masts as such but a pair of inverted shear-legs, or "V" frames, inclined outwards along the axis of the building (Fig. 5.15). The second UK cable-stayed structure appeared in the Royal Botanical Gardens in Edinburgh in 1967 (see Fig. 8.5). This Tropical House structure was not based on single-member masts either, but on a system of outward-sloping intersecting 'A' frames. The earliest 'true' masted structure in the UK was the Craigavon Shopping Centre of 1975 and it was not until 1980 that a mainstream masted structure was erected in the England, i.e. Hall 7

at the NEC in Birmingham. In contrast to these signs of structural and formal progress, one seemingly promising line of development seemed to have come to an end: in the field of aircraft hangars for the new generation of 'big jets' masted structures were passed over in favour of more conventional steel framed or concrete structures. Moreover, the great 60m square masted pyramids proposed for the new East Terminal at La Guardia

Fig. 5.15
Lord Snowdon,
with Cedric Price
and Frank
Newby: the
Snowdon Aviary,
London Zoo,
1965.

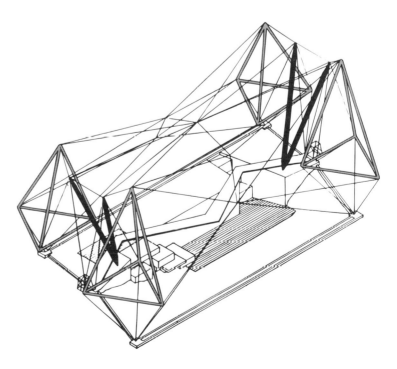

Airport, New York, never reached construction as the longer runway development of the J F Kennedy Airport took precedence over it (see Fig. 6.16).

However, despite these minor set-backs, by the end of the decade the functional and formal differentiation of masted structures was developing rapidly and we can see, in retrospect, that a number of generic structural types were becoming identifiable.

5.4
MASTED STRUCTURES FROM 1970 TO 1979

During this period, the number of new masted structures noted in journals seems to have increased by roughly 50% over the previous decade. The buildings range in size from the small, and uniquely in timber, Pabst stage canopy in Milwaukee (see Fig. 6.18), to the huge Flower Market in Pescia (see Figs. 8.7, 8.8). They fall roughly into six functional categories of which exhibition structures are the most common. The primary stimulus for this was the Osaka Expo of 1970 which reflected the increasingly confident and mature Japanese version of 'modern architecture' as it was still then known. At Osaka, the British, Italian and Kubota pavilions represented entirely different approaches to mast architecture; they comprised, respectively, an upturned 'box' hung free of the ground from four pairs of vierendeels, a square box framed by an external network of masts, cables and pvc membranes, and a twelve-sided, centrally-masted 'parasol type' structure! Seven years later, the large scale and highly competent West Japan Exhibition Centre, by Isozaki, provided further evidence, if any were needed, of Japanese design momentum (Figs. 7.23, 7.24). In March 1979, as the decade drew to a close, the architects of the new Hall 7 of the National Exhibition Centre in England were being briefed for its completion in 1980. It was to be the first true example of an enclosed masted structure in the UK (see Fig. 8.46). The comparison of these last two major-volume structures is an enlightening one: the former is a long rectangular hangar-type block with tall circular masts down the sides and a heavy concentration of tension rods, parallel and diverging; the latter is a centralised, almost square structure with two masts and minimal tension supports on each of the four faces. The two buildings represent linear and centralised cable-stayed arrangements respectively.

Other building types represented in this period include market and warehouse buildings, for example the small covered cattle market at St. Etienne (see Fig. 6.23), and the extensive set of dockside warehouses at Le Havre, both of which have the same form of square structural cells, each with a central mast and radiating cable-stayed lattice girders. The enormous but well scaled Flower Market at Peschia is also of this period (see Figs. 8.7, 8.8).

Three stadium canopies continued the sporting applications: in the raking canopy to the National Athletics Stadium at Bruce, Australia (see Fig. 10.3), Philip Cox used a masted structure for the first time on that continent, beginning a sensational series of architectural and engineering structures. In the middle range of size, the ice rinks at Braunlage and Arosa, of 1972 and 1973 respectively, make interesting parallels in end-mast and spine-beam configurations and can be studied further in relation to the similarly structured Oxford Ice Rink of 1984 (see Figs. 7.19, 7.20).

The overwhelming impression over this period is of two characteristics: first, of the developing structural differentiation noted earlier, represented in masted structures of many functional types and, secondly, of the increasingly high level of structural and architectural quality. This is, of course, the achievement of the architects and engineers concerned, amongst whom at this time the work of Philip Cox, Richard Rogers, Ove Arup and Anthony Hunt provided hints of the advances to come.

The Rogers' design of the Fleetguard Factory (see Fig. 8.9) was begun in 1978, and that of Inmos (see Figs. 8.29, 8.30) in 1979. Together they brought a freshness, sparkle and colour to industrial buildings which not only drew world-wide attention to the possibilities of masted structures but also inspired their British architectural colleagues and other designers overseas.

5.5
MASTED STRUCTURES FROM 1980 TO 1989

Compared with the previous decade, and perhaps for the reasons just mentioned, the number of masted structures we can cite in the period from 1980 to 1989 rose from twenty-eight to sixty-seven. More specifically, in the previous five years we noted thirteen buildings and projects whereas in the first five years of the new decade the number rises to twenty, and in the second to forty-seven – almost an explosion of interest in mast architecture over a range of building types. To provide a full account of the nature and scope of the field in this period, we shall therefore treat it in two sections.

From 1980 to 1984

There are three principal interlocking themes amongst the masted structures of this period: first, the popularity of sport and leisure activities is reflected in the number of related recreational buildings; secondly, there is a clutch of high quality buildings from UK architects and engineers and, lastly, a continuing increase in the size of projects up to the gigantic and so far unequalled Haj terminal of over 500,000m^2 (see Figs. 9.2, 9.3).

Amongst recreational buildings, the Oxford Ice Rink stands out technically and aesthetically for its structural logic and its visual contrasts of diamond spreaders combined with a slick metallic skin, a superb design of 1984 by Nicholas Grimshaw, Ove Arup and their respective partners (see Figs. 7.19, 7.20). However, the appropriateness of the Thamesdown Leisure Centre in unifying a complex set of activities under Anthony Hunt's strong and expressive centralised structure runs it a close second (see Figs. 8.47, 8.48). Also noteworthy in this category are the Zagreb swimming centre and Peter Cook's Frankfurt sports hall competition entry.

Indeed, competition entries incorporating masted structures are an interesting minor theme; the competitions for the Sainsbury supermarket at Canterbury and the main, permanent building at the Liverpool Garden Festival each produced innovative designs for masted structures which are more fully analysed and compared in chapter eight.

British architects and engineers led the field in this period across a spectrum of technically innovative and architecturally striking designs. To the examples already mentioned must be added Foster Associates' well-documented Renault warehouse of 1983 (see Figs. 8.11, 8.12). Here, Foster's own blend of technology transfer, or 'lateral rationalism', incorporates structural innovation, advanced materials and components, the co-ordinating use of the yellow Renault house-colour and a reduction in visual bulk – factors which influenced the local planning officers to increase the allowable site coverage from 50% to 67%, a potential financial benefit which outweighed any extra constructional costs at a stroke.

Also in the industrial sector, Richard Rogers' NAPP Laboratories Limited competition design (see Fig. 8.6), although beautifully rational in plan and section, was perhaps almost too rational in three dimensions, and did not proceed to construction. The same architect's Patscentre Laboratory at Princeton, USA (see Fig. 8.33) continues the Inmos model in its strategic concept but replaced the spinal masts by a series of 'A' frames, so we will do no more than note it here. Moreover, in any comparison between the two buildings the differences in their functional requirements must be taken into account.

Lastly, two examples of mast architecture involve very large structures indeed. In the 'Wonderworld' project of 1982, the six principal themes of the exciting and ambitious enterprise were expressed in six parallel bands of space and structure, set across a gentle slope and covering almost 40,000m^2 (see Fig. 8.16). But this extensive entertainment and educational venue represents less than one tenth of the enormous Haj air terminal in Jeddah, Saudi Arabia. This complex of 210

semi-conical fabric roof units shelters the vast number of pilgrims needing rest and shade at a necessary transfer point on their journey to Mecca. The two main units cover a total area of over 500,000m^2 (see Figs. 9.2, 9.3, 9.4).

To keep a sense of proportion, and to illustrate the vast difference in scale between the largest and the smallest masted structures by this time, we can contrast this impressive and somewhat Arabic masted megastructure of 1982 with the equally successful and exquisitely detailed miniature factory gate lodge completed by the Cepezed Studio in Holland in 1984 (see Figs. 7.3, 7.4, 7.5). This scalar differentiation was accompanied by an equally wide functional variety in the second half of the decade.

From 1985 to 1989

In this five year period we have noted forty-seven buildings and projects, an astonishing figure which continues the rising curve of examples and shows the increasing significance of mast architecture. In coming to terms with this number of buildings we can again usefully discuss them in terms of functional categories, leaving their more detailed formal classification to the next chapter.

Mast architecture for recreation, the most common category, comprises buildings at three levels: major stadia, middle-range sports centres and smaller scale facilities and canopies. However, several potentially interesting projects regrettably failed to proceed to construction: Renzo Piano's initial proposals for the Ravenna stadium – spectacular twin masts with cables to a rib cage of radiating, boomerang roof members – was superseded by a later design, and lack of local authority finance led to the postponement of Nicholas Grimshaw's centrally-masted, single volume leisure centre at Knowsley (see Fig. 6.10) until 1991. Meanwhile, the powerful raking mast design of Apicella's events venue at South Shields (see Fig. 6.12) was to remain only on paper.

Amongst the built examples, Philip Cox's marvellous, swooping 'Mexican wave in built form' at the Sydney Football Stadium (Figs.10.11 and 10.12) is a tension-stayed cantilever encircling a major arena for the first time since the Coliseum in Rome in the first century AD. This is not strictly a 'true' masted structure but rather a series of open parasols supporting a cantilevered roof. The Homebush Sports Centre is large, but not particularly inspiring – it seems to represent too much of the NSW Government architects and not enough of the Philip Cox office – but has some important, albeit cautionary design lessons (Fig. 7.22).

The modernisation and extension of transport systems brought with it two masted and vaulted structures of great charm: the delightful small station at Poole (Figs. 1.6 and 7.33) and the elegant small airport terminal at Bundaberg (Fig. 8.19); the striking, but unrealised proposal for another part-vaulted, air/rail interchange at Frankfurt (1986, see Gazetteer), and the Nice Airport terminal complete this functional group, the latter on a much grander scale and with an unusual lenticular roof (Fig. 8.25).

In this quinquennium, and amongst the buildings of the highest architectural and engineering quality, the designs of the Cepezed Studio in Holland are hard to beat; the factory at Haarlem and the two groups of industrial units elsewhere in Holland set new standards of elegance in the conception and detailing of masted structures (Figs. 7.15, 7.16, 7.17). In other parts of this industrial sector, the sizeable SNECMA factory at Le Creusot (Figs. 7.11 – 7.14) and the Rotaprint Factory in Berlin by Richard Rogers' Office (Figs. 6.30 – 6.34) represent different strategic approaches to related, although not identical functional problems and the formal effects of minimal and multiple mast strategies can be interestingly compared in these two structures.

Lastly in relation to this period, we can see tangible evidence of masted membrane structures developing apace. Six examples can be cited, including two of pace-setting standard: the Schlumberger research centre in Cambridge, England (Figs. 9.9 – 9.11), and the Mound Stand at Lord's Cricket Ground in London (Figs. 10.5 – 10.7). Both buildings are by Michael Hopkins Ltd. and will be discussed in more detail in Chapter 9. Also at this level of architectural quality in its own terms, the Yulara Visitor's Centre in the Northern Territory of Australia – a fluttering, almost box-kite compostion of masts, sails and cables (Fig. 9.1) – maintains the impeccable standards which have been reached through inspired collaboration between Philip Cox and Partners and Ove Arup and Partners.

5.6

MASTED STRUCTURES FROM 1990 TO MID 1995

At the time of writing, as this quinquennium reaches the mid-point of its final year, it is clear that functional and formal variations amongst masted structures continue to be developed, despite the recession in architectural activity in many countries. Moreover, the number of recent examples and their widespread occurrence makes it more difficult than previously to review this latest period. Indeed, it is no longer possible to take a synoptic view of what has now become a global genre without a formal and sponsored architectural literature search programme. Consequently, the authors realise that the buildings mentioned in this section may constitute a smaller proportion of significant examples than those of earlier periods, and there may be important and innovative structures of which we are unaware. However, we have found it possible to review a useful number of noteworthy examples, and to identify some interesting characteristics and themes.

In terms of function, masted structures can be found in virtually every building type, from shopping and leisure centres, social and refreshment facilities, industrial buildings and buildings for transport, to the occasional museum and library. Even a small house in France has had a cable-stayed aerofoil roof floated above it in a design proposal.

The range of sizes is similarly extensive, from the enormous Benneton factory at Treviso in Italy to the small but exquisite escape stair enclosures at Biberach in Germany (see Fig 6.13). These represent the novel use of a cluster of masts to form the armature of delicate access and service towers and this underlying principle of a four-mast cluster supporting a cable-stayed projecting element on four sides also applies to the upper level office extension at Bunnik in Holland (Fig. 6.14a and b).

In terms of spatial and structural configurations over the period, we have come across examples of most of the taxonomic categories which we shall explain in detail in Part Two. Designers have incorporated single cell, dual cell and multi-cellular forms with single, double and quadruple mast arrangements, and with a variety of suspension systems. There is no correspondence between any one structural category and any particular functional type.

At the level of the single cell, the Knowsley Leisure Centre, for example, consists of a major rectangular space with a central mast conveniently located in the space between the two principal activity areas. Groups of single mast cells, with masts at either their centres or their sides, form the bases of several schemes: the Ingus factory at Cologne, Germany, positions the central masts of its two notional cells at the centres of internal courts, thus bringing views out and light into 6,000m^2 of otherwise unobstructed space; at Almere in Holland, a 'mat' of twenty single and centrally masted spaces formed the basis of the new market building in 1990.

The main elements of several buildings over the period are based on linear repeats of a basic cellular space which has one or two masts associated with it. The central library at Pret du Gard, Nimes, has a run of eleven, single-masted modules; the TV studio canteen at San Angel, Mexico City has a run of seven under a cable-stayed vaulted roof, and the Berlin Sports Centre of 1991 has a run of nine bays, the radiating mast 'fingers' of which trace the 180° path of the loads as they are taken down to the ground anchorages (see Fig.7.32). The Dyson assembly factory at Chippenham, England, has an echelon arrangement of groups of three, end-masted cells with a 'go-fast' inclination to its masts and cables in response to the line of its monopitch roofs and as an echo of the vacuum cleaner handle and body form of the product assembled in the interior (see Gazetteer).

The largest example of this group, the huge Benneton factory at Treviso in Italy, has two ranges of seven, end-masted modules reflected about a vast central spine which is wide enough for the movement of articulated vehicles. Each module has a single, twin-tube mast, 24m high, from which four pairs of twin cables, in the very rare 'harp' pattern, support the central lattice girders which span the 84m length of the module. The back-stays of the suspension ties criss-cross over the central area.

Lastly, so far as four mast cells are concerned, the new East Croydon station-portico-cum-vestibule space represents a classic single volume type with the masts at the four corners (Figs. 8.3, 8.4). Other versions of the same four mast pattern repeated are the Massy TGV station in France and the Mitsubishi pencil factory project for Gumna in Japan.

Masted membrane structures over the last five years have so proliferated in number as to be almost commonplace. Consequently, noteworthy examples have to be particularly well designed or structurally or formally innovative, to attract appreciative comment. However, two examples by Sir Michael Hopkins' office meet these criteria: first, the amenity building at the Nottingham headquarters of the Inland Revenue, described later, and secondly, the temporary ticket office for entry to the Royal Collection at Buckingham Palace. This delightful structure, which can be taken down for the winter close season, has meticulous yacht detailing and an overall nautical aesthetic of varnished timber spars, ribs and cladding to complement the white billows of the fabric canopy – an exemplary and poetic piece of work (see Gazetteer).

Two notable grandstand structures completed during the period are the Sussex Stand at Goodwood racecourse – which has close parallels with the elegance of the Mound Stand at Lords, completed in 1987 and noted earlier – and the Don Valley Stadium in Sheffield, the first purpose-built athletics stadium to be built in England. This has its own north country solidity in terms of yellow painted pairs of vertical and horizontal cable-stayed ladder elements.

The other major masted stadia projects may or may not proceed to construction but are interesting nonetheless. Arup Associates, with the HOK Sports Facilities Group, designed a stunning 'roller-coaster' stadium as part of the Manchester 2000 Olympic bid. The undulating roof, similar to the Sydney Football stadium design, is based on eighteen perimeter masts supporting prismatic lattice trusses tied back via twin 'V' outriggers to vertical tiedowns; the escape stairs from the stadium spiral around the drum features which themselves encircle the lower parts of each of the masts (see Gazetteer). In 1995, four towering silver spikes defined the four corners of the Richard Rogers Partnership's entry for the Saitama Arena complex competition for a site north of Tokyo. This exciting composition of tensile cables, flying arched lattice ribs and huge double-tapered masts regrettably only gained a second prize.

Three formal characteristics have become apparent over the period: the first is the design of numbers of shallow vaulted roofs, cable-stayed to masts at either their centre or along one or both sides. Vaulted forms have probably become popular due to the development of the technology for forming steel beams and profiled steel sheets into shallow curves, the availability of more reliable roofing membranes, and the influence of architectural fashion. Cable-stayed vaults occur in simple form at the Zushi Marina Club, in the Mexico City TV studio canteen and in the restaurant and cafe bar at the Picketts Lock Sports Centre in England. The largest examples are the Al Gallerias at Hatfield, also in England, which has masts along both sides, and Napper Collerton's entry for the Hartlepool Imperial War Museum building competition of 1994. The latter has masts along one side, cable-stayed to each pair of curved lattice girders, exposed as an exoskeleton over the roof vault. Also vaulted is the large scale Aylesbury shopping centre roof, which is cable-stayed from pairs of masts brought down into the centre of the interior. This shows an excellent way of enabling the masted structure to be appreciated from inside the building – an aesthetic opportunity which is often mishandled or simply ignored.

Not all these examples fulfilled their early design promises. The arched roof of the Picketts Lock structure was found to have sufficient inherent strength as to make a tensile structure redundant; consequently, its constructional logic became flawed and somewhat ambiguous. Sadly, the Hartlepool War Museum entry failed to win the competition and the building will be completed in another form.

The second interesting formal development is the use of a striking masted membrane structure as a foil to more orthogonal or regular building elements. At the new Inland Revenue Centre in Nottingham by Sir Michael Hopkins, the tented sports and amenity building acts as a contrasting focus amongst the more orthogonal courts and boulevards of the rest of the layout. Four outwardly inclined masts define a cat's cradle of tensile supports to a white, teflon coated glass fibre fabric roof, spanning 24m over the sports and spectators' facilities.

The form of the International School at Lyons by Jourda and Perraudin is more unusual and unexpected. It consists of a reversed question mark range of cellular spaces for living, teaching and administration, partly enclosing other functions roughly in two blocks covered by an arched roofed tent. This tent is hung from tapered steel masts, some vertical and other inclined, and it is turfed to form an irregular grassy mound at the core of the composition. The form of this tent is not defined precisely by a regular geometry in plan or mast inclination and the effect of these fairly random and very marginal departures from the still discernible underlying order is to import a reminder of nature into the man-made world of the rest of the composition.

A third thought concerning new formal characteristics is prompted by Renzo Piano's 'Il Grande Bigo' structure erected for the 1992 Genoa Expo (see Gazetteer). This structure consisted of a cluster of eight major and minor mast 'fingers', springing upwards and outwards from a common origin on an island base. Their back-stays were taken down into the water of the Grand Harbour. The major mast hoists a panoramic lift, giving views over the Expo site, whilst the smaller ones support the curved ribs of a fabric tensile structure.

This concept of a mast used simply as a crane jib was used at the South Bank Exhibition of 1961 in support of umbrella shades to cafe tables, and in the New Jersey Pavilion of the 1964 New York World Fair where two groups of six masts supported tented parasol canopies. Masted examples of this kind are thus quite rare, but they seem to comprise a distinct, identifiable group of non-enclosing structures.

In summary therefore, there seem to be few signs of any moderation in the stream of innovative masted structures: indeed, the dynamism, freshness and imagination which characterises the field is being maintained and the aesthetic and functional criteria which successful examples must meet are becoming increasingly obvious. Moreover, although not always the cheapest methods of structuring architectural space, masted constructions would not continue to be developed without significant functional and visual advantages.

5.7

ARCHITECT/ENGINEER COLLABORATION IN THE UK

The masted structures of the 20th century could not have been realised without the joint efforts of architects and engineers. This essential requirement has been particularly fruitful in the UK where a virtual genealogy of engineers has made an invaluable contribution to both professions through collaborative projects with the architectural avant-garde. The genealogy, which has now extended over four generations, had its origins in two brilliant and architecturally committed engineers, namely Ove Arup and Felix Samuely. It was maintained by their respective initial partners and has been continued by their associates and assistants. This history of mutual interests and personal contacts between architects and engineers has been a significant factor in the extensive series of masted structures in the country.

Ove Arup came to London in 1924 and advocated the creative collaboration between architects and engineers from his earliest writings in 1926. In the early 1930s he came to know the leading architects of the Modern Movement, including Berthold Lubetkin and the partners of Tecton, with whom he worked on the celebrated intertwining helical ramps of the Penguin Pool at the London Zoo in 1934 and the pioneering reinforced concrete wall and floor slab construction of the Highpoint I flats in 1935.

Felix Samuely came to London in 1934. He worked for a few months with Arup and Keir, making the calculations for the ramps of the Penguin Pool personally. He too had known Lubetkin from his time in Berlin, and also Eric Mendelsohn with whom he almost immediately began to collaborate on the structural provisions of the Bexhill Pavilion, forming his own consultancy in the process. Through the efforts of these two visionary and inspirational engineers two distinct streams of architect/engineer collaboration became established in England in the 1930s.

In the immediate post-war period, the founders of the two, initially mainly engineering consultancies were joined by members of a second generation of engineers who shared their enthusiasm for architectural projects. In particular, Peter Dunnican, who had worked with Ove Arup since 1943, became an associate partner in 1949, and Frank Newby, who had first hand American experience of Konrad Wachsmann's attitude to engineering and Charles Eames' approach to architecture and design, joined the Felix Samuely office in 1948. Samuely himself taught structures at the Architectural Association School of Architecture, and his office prepared a first design for the Pavilion of Transport at the 1951 South Bank Exhibition in collaboration with the architects 'Arcon'. The design was based on two internal lattice masts from which tension stays supported a space deck roof (Samuely, 1952). The impressive expertise of the Arup consultancy developed into an increasingly widespread network of offices whilst the Samuely team maintained an equally high level of accomplishment, albeit on a smaller scale.

As a result, the two organisations were able to nurture a third generation of gifted engineers who shared their devotion to architectural and engineering quality, and who had the commitment and intellectual capacity to achieve it. Peter Rice and John Thornton joined the Arup team, and Anthony Hunt began work in the Samuely office as an assistant to Frank Newby. It was Frank Newby's expertise in collaboration with Lord Snowdon and Cedric Price that brought the tensile structure of the Snowdon Aviary to successful completion in 1965. At that time, Tony Hunt was working as a member of 'Team 4' with Norman and Wendy Foster and Richard Rogers, initiating a three-way interplay of architectural and engineering ideas that was to lead to more intensive discussions and collaborations in the future.

During the 1980s, Ove Arup and Partners and Anthony Hunt Associates became established as the two firms of engineers most experienced in masted structures following the completion of a rapid succession of outstanding projects in association with a number of architects. Arups collaborated with Ahrendes, Burton and Koralek in producing a partially tension-assisted roof at the Cummins Engine Plant at Shotts in Scotland in 1977; the Fleetguard/Cummins Factory at Quimper was designed with Richard Rogers in 1978, and Hall 7 at the NEC, Birmingham, with Edward D. Mills in 1979-80. The Patscenter building at Princeton, USA, also with Rogers, followed soon afterwards and this series was concluded in 1983 by Arups collaboration with Foster Associates on the masted structure of the Renault Parts Distribution Centre.

Anthony Hunt's masted structures began slightly later with the Inmos Factory, in collaboration with Richard Rogers and Partners in 1982, followed by the West Swindon Leisure Centre, in association with the Thamesdown Borough Architects Department, in 1985. Also completed in that year, the Schlumberger Research Laboratory involved Anthony Hunt Associates as engineers for the structure and Ove Arup and Partners as consultants for the membrane, in collaboration with Michael Hopkins Architects.

This continuity of commissions, coupled with the genealogy of first-rate engineers and their formal and informal patterns of personal contacts, has been of immense value both to architecture and engineering. The firms concerned have made an invaluable contribution to both professions, not only in showing the tangible and demonstrable benefits of creative architect/engineer collaboration but also in the inspiration of their colleagues and in the unselfish publication of their philosophies, methodologies and working details. In particular, Peter Rice, John Thornton and their associates have provided detailed accounts of their masted structures in conference papers and articles, whilst the Arup Journal has become an invaluable source of information on architectural and engineering structures generally.

The heroic view of engineers by architects can, of course, be traced back to Le Corbusier, and to W.R. Lethaby in the 19th century, but the reciprocal interest in architecture by enthusiastic engineers is a relatively new phenomenon. Moreover, in addition to the progressive collaborations outlined above, the opening of overseas offices by UK engineers is currently spreading their beliefs, knowledge and expertise amongst an even wider set of colleagues. Meanwhile, the UK

genealogy is being continued at the present time by a fourth generation of innovative young engineers who are making contributions in an architectural context: Chris McCarthy and Guy Battle at Arups, Neil Thomas at Atelier One and the Bob Barton/Matthew Wells and Laurence Dewhurst/Tim McFarlane partnerships.

5.8
THE MAINSPRINGS OF POST-WAR MASTED STRUCTURES

We have shown in Chapter 2 that there are underlying structural characteristics which point towards the use of some form of masted structure in certain circumstances. But structural characteristics alone are not sufficient to account for the development of mast architecture over the post-war period. This has come about for five main reasons:

● The need for large, unobstructed spaces in, for example, sports halls, exhibition centres, factories, warehouses and supermarkets.

● The development of the theory and practical understanding of how tension structures behave under varying conditions of loading, coupled with the availability of computers and computer programs to make the necessary calculations.

● The availability of new, high-performance materials, components and constructional techniques.

● The need for strikingly new visual effects, for innovation, and for an immediately recognisable building identity or 'image'.

● The presence in the UK of a number of visionary and inspirational engineers who, in company with like-minded architects, were interested in architect/engineer collaboration and were together capable of the intellectual effort required in the achievement of excellence.

In preceding chapters we have shown that masted structures represent a great variety of functional and formal types of buildings. In total they comprise an apparently diverse collection of almost individualised examples. Nevertheless, the structural combination of masts, tension elements and roof frameworks does exert its own discipline which, in turn, has the effect of imposing a degree of order on the field. There is, in fact, an abstract 'deep structure' to which individual buildings can be related and this morphological taxonomy is the subject of Part Two. ■

Part Two:
A TAXONOMY OF MASTED STRUCTURES

A real understanding of the nature and use of masted structures must be based on an analysis of how they vary. They come in many shapes and sizes comprising, at first sight, a random collection of differing configurations of masts, cables and roof beams with few apparent similarities. However, if we want to compare one structure with another, explore their development, and discuss their appropriateness in differing circumstances, the examples must be brought into some kind of orderly relationship with each other. In the following chapters we present a way of doing this in terms of an organising framework of basic concepts, physical attributes and developmental principles, in relation to which individual buildings may be compared and discussed.

A formal taxonomy of this kind, that is, a classification based on physical attributes, is as necessary and valuable in analysing and understanding a group of buildings as it is in analysing the far greater diversity of the natural world. Indeed, it is possible to unravel the complex variety of masted structures in architecture by adopting principles similar to those used in constructing taxonomies of animals and plants – without which the progress of biological understanding would have been seriously retarded. In architecture, meanwhile, our morphological understanding of the primary subject matter is still impoverished by the lack of an equally developed 'architectural systematics'.

However, some formal taxonomies of built forms do exist – and are by no means new. The first classification of architectural forms according to physical attributes was the analysis of Greek temple forms by Vitruvius around 30BC (Morgan, 1960). More recently, Sir John Summerson described the evolution of the 18th century classical English Country House (Summerson, 1959) and latterly several related studies have explored patterns of variation in the villa plans of Andrea Palladio (Stiny & Mitchell,1978), and in the 'Prairie Houses' of Frank Lloyd Wright (Koning and Eizenberg, 1981). These two later studies showed that the formal diversity of the buildings was built up from a limited number of elements such as the wall, column, arch and vaulting compartment in the first instance, and from the hearth, window and door modules in the second. In both cases the basic elements were shown to have been organised by the architect according to certain self-imposed compositional rules, usually based on the operations of symmetry such as translation, reflection, and rotation. These operations can be used as a production system to build up a 'genre' of similar but not identical buildings in a particular architectural 'language'.

'Generative shape grammars' of this kind have, so far, been specific to individual architects or building types, although the formal, syntactical principles could be used by anyone who wished to design in a Palladian or neo-Wrightian manner; the earlier analyses by Vitruvius and Summerson are less rigorous mathematically but show similar patterns of evolutionary variation through differing combinations of a few basic elements. Similar characteristics of a structural nature can be shown to apply to the buildings we are presently considering, although we are concerned with an analytical system rather than a productive one.

In constructing the taxonomy of masted structures presented here, our approach has been to analyse the number, position and relationships of the three basic structural elements, namely, the masts, cables and roof members in relation to the pattern of spaces which, structurally and conceptually, they define. This approach combines the spatial and structural interests of architects and engineers, and reflects that logical integration of space, form and structure which has long been a defining characteristic of a work of architecture.

The fundamental concept of the taxonomy is that of a 'cellular' unit of space with which one or more sets of masts, cables and roof beams may be associated. This basic cellular unit may be of any size and, at the initial levels of the taxonomy, of any shape. Its boundaries may be defined by physical elements, such as masts or walls and their organising and controlling geometry, or implied conceptually by the limits of the roof and floor planes in more open structures.

The topological relationships of one or more masts with the basic spatial cell produce a number of primary categories of examples. These categories are then further sub-divided according to two criteria: first in terms of geometry, to distinguish between rectangular forms which may have masts at their 'sides' or at their 'ends', and secondly in terms of successive repetitions of the basic cell to the various regular patterns in multi-cellular forms of masted structures. These variations can be analysed in terms of the following operations:

(i) Translation: that is repeating the basic spatial/structural 'cell' along either its long or cross axis to produce two-way patterns of cells in the form of a variety of rectangular blocks. We shall call these one-way and two-way repetitions of the basic cellular unit.

(ii) Articulation: that is, introducing a minor planning module between the basic spatial/ structural cells for functional or visual reasons.

(iii) Rotation: that is repeating an initial spatial/structural arrangement about a nodal point to produce forms which are partially or completely circular or elliptical.

In summary, the possible topological locations of one, two, four or eight masts in relation to square or rectangular cells, plus their one and two dimensional assemblages, cover the majority of orthogonal masted structures in architecture. Abstract diagrams of the single-cell arrangements, together with typical examples of one-way, two-way and articulated translations are shown in Fig. A. To avoid visual indigestion and to save space only selective examples of the latter are shown here; more extensive coverage of the possible configurations is provided in the following chapters.

It should be noted in these diagrams that the masts are shown in topological distinct locations on the boundary of the spatial/structural cell. In practice, for constructional and visual reasons, at each location the mast is more likely to be positioned inside or outside the building envelope rather than in alignment with it. The topological implications of this are shown in Fig. B: again for reasons of space and clarity we shall not show all these possibilities here, but it should be noted that they can and do occur in the actual structures.

We have mentioned that these principles and their practical realisations cover most orthogonal masted structures. They are analysed in detail in the following three chapters which deal with buildings based on one, two, and four and eight mast arrangements and their repetitions. However, this does not deal adequately with all the types of mast architecture which occur in real life. We have chosen to add two further chapters to cover two additional and distinct morphological types. The first of these comprises structures which incorporate flexible membrane roofs. Buildings of this kind have been identified and analysed in some detail because their characteristics can not be meaningfully described within the framework and the terms used for the original structural types. The second category comprises open, grandstand structures. In the terms of our general taxonomy these are almost always single-mast or two-mast cantilever structures. However, they are not fully space-enclosing in an architectural sense and their usual association with terraced spectator seating seems to put them into a distinct formal and functional category demanding a separate analysis which will also be a useful functional reference section for designers.

The taxonomic structure which has resulted from our initial approach and its subsequent extensions is shown in Fig. C. There are several ways of constructing formal taxonomies of this kind, according to the purpose which one has in mind. Our purpose in carrying out the present study has been to investigate and explore the formal differentiation between types of masted structures so as to understand the structural and spatial characteristics of the genre. Our objective has not been to formulate an academically rigorous hierarchy, with key defining characteristics at each of several levels. It is possible to construct such a framework but it would be complex, embodying many structurally impracticable permutations, and tedious to follow and understand. In contrast, the taxonomy presented here is a simple, three-level hierarchy comprising four basic categories, each of which has a varied number of differently defined sub-groups. Each of the sub-categories is not only meaningful in its own terms but will be recognisably distinct to architects and engineers. There are occasional overlaps between the categories: for example, some grandstands have notable membrane roofs, but they are very few and

Fig. A
Standardised topological relationships of structural systems based on up to eight masts, with typical one-way and two-way translations.

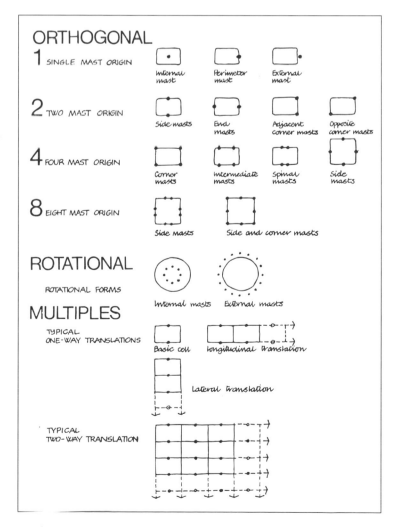

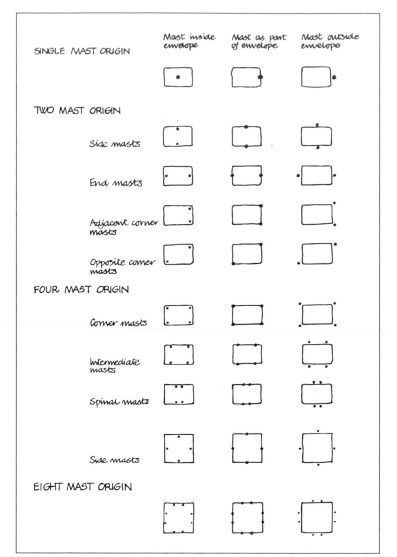

easily referred to. In summary, we believe our taxonomy to be the most appropriate and effective method of modelling the patterns of structural and spatial differentiation which occur in the real world, and that it will be able to accommodate the masted structures of tomorrow. Of course, it is not unlikely that new and surprising masted constructions will appear in the future – the pressures for structural and architectural innovation being as they are. However, we believe that the present framework will enable them to be effectively identified, compared and assessed. ■

Fig. B (above)
Standardised topological positions of masts in relation to the building envelope.

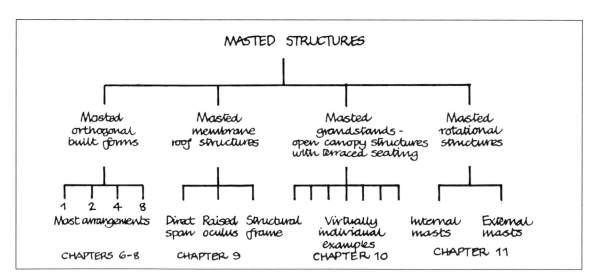

Fig. C
A formal taxonomy of masted structures.

SINGLE MAST STRUCTURES AND ASSEMBLAGES OF SINGLE MAST CELLS

6

The individual categories of the taxonomy will now be described in more detail in relation to typical and representative buildings which they include. The simplest form of masted structure is that which uses a single mast to support a straightforward roof plane. According to the size and shape of the area to be covered, and the characteristics of the site, the mast may be positioned centrally or off-centre, and the roof plane may be polygonal or circular. Moreover, although simple in form, structures of this kind can be surprisingly large, not only in buildings comprising an assemblage of masted cells but also in single volume structures.

The topological variants of single mast structures are shown in Fig. 6.1; typical roof plans of structures based on these principles are shown in Fig. 6.2. We will discuss some single mast examples first, followed by structures which consist of assemblages of cells.

6.1
SINGLE MASTED CELLS

We can reach a simple, initial understanding of the kinds of structure in this category in terms of four groups of buildings:

i) Early enclosed structures and their medium-sized successors.

ii) Open canopy structures with internal masts.

iii) Larger, single-volume structures with internal or external masts.

iv) Structures with quadruple mast elements.

Early enclosed structures and their successors

The earliest modern example of a simple, single-masted enclosed structure is Richard Buckminster Fuller's Dymaxion House project of 1927-29 (Fig. 6.3). Against the background of a boyhood spent amongst the masts and rigging of the sailing craft of Cape Cod, Fuller's approach was to use 'high performance' as a generative concept expressed in terms of structural efficiency, low heat loss, efficient environmental services, and simplicity in manufacture and erection.

To achieve a structurally effective combination of compression struts and tension ties, Fuller proposed the use of a single, hollow steel mast to provide a compression member of maximum height and minimum material. From the top of the mast, a triangulated system of tension cables supports the roof and floor planes (which act as compression rings), stabilising the walls and floor surfaces down to ground anchorages. In this way, all the structural and aerodynamic forces are resolved – although Fuller fails to provide any structural or constructional details! Moreover, when the Dymaxion House concept was finally realised in the form of the Wichita House of 1944, its structure and form were completely altered.

Fuller's use of masts and cables reflects the analytic, performance-based logic of a hard-nosed engineer. In contrast, Bruce Goff, in his Bavinger House of 1950 (Fig. 6.4) uses the mast and its

cables as the central sculptural feature of a complex composition of solid, linear and warped planar elements worthy of the Russian Constructivists. The spiralling plane of the copper roof is supported by a 16.9m mast, fabricated out of two deep-well oil drilling pipes and sixty stainless steel cables.

In between these seminal projects comes Eero Saarinen's community centre project of 1941 (Fig. 6.5). Saarinen outlined a square building,

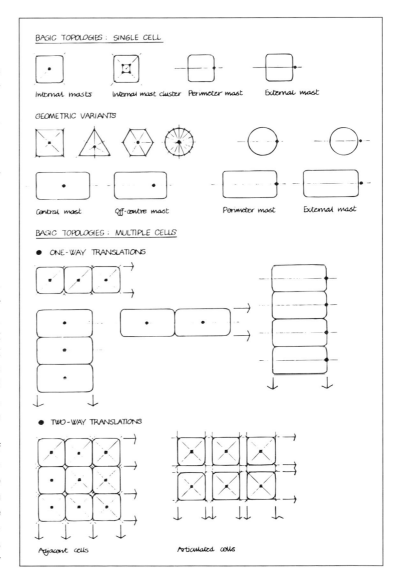

Fig. 6.1
Topological variants of single mast structures and assemblages of single mast cells.

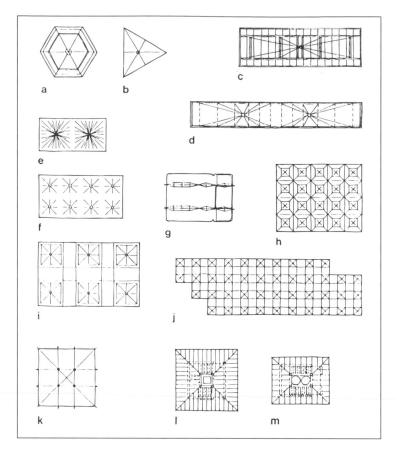

mast, medium-scale structures – passing over Bertrand Goldberg's over-designed ice cream pavilion (Fig. 6.6) – are exhibition buildings which differ in form and structure. The Aluminium Pavilion of the Hannover Industrial Fair of 1962 (Fig. 6.7) reflects the triangulated space deck roof in its over-all form and structure. From the double-tapered and hinge-jointed aluminium mast, three main cables run through the corners of the building to ground anchorages, with six additional cables to intermediate points on the roof. Six internal struts stabilise the main cables, the modest size of the building requiring no further resistance to wind up-lift forces.

Lastly, the 12-sided Kubota Pavilion, Osaka, of 1970 had a complex supporting cable network rather than several individual cables, but is similar in structural principle.

Open canopy structures

The standard Mobil Service Station canopy, designed by Whitney Smith in 1957, is an archetypal example of this simple form of masted, 'parasol' structure. The basic roof unit is 12.2m square, supported by a central mast and eight cables to provide a vehicle clearance height of 4.9m. This relatively small building relies on sufficient stiffness in the structure to resist wind uplift without external ties (See Fig. 5.8).

The single mast of the Marburg service area (Fig. 6.8) is also centrally positioned but in support of a rectangular roof related to its island location in the

Fig. 6.2 (above) Comparative roof plans of typical single mast based structures (not to scale).

a. Dymaxion House project, 1927.

b. Aluminium Pavilion, Hannover, Germany, 1967.

c. Service Station canopy, Marburg, Germany, 1971.

d. Stadium canopy, Marl, Germany, 1967.

e. Baxter Travenol facilities building, Deerfield, Illinois, 1977.

f. Printing works, Tapiola, Finland, 1965.

g. Ladkarn Haulage offices and workshop, London, 1983.

h. Market hall, Almere, Holland, 1990.

i. German pavilion, Zagreb Trade Fair, 1968.

j. Rotaprint factory competition entry, 1989.

k. Office building extension, Bunnik, Holland, 1990.

l. & m. Underground car park access staircases, Biberach, Germany, 1990.

seemingly of 12 bays x 12 bays of wall panels, with a central mast from which eight cables extend out to the ground surface, meeting the roof edges at one-third and two-third points along their length.

Two remaining noteworthy examples of single

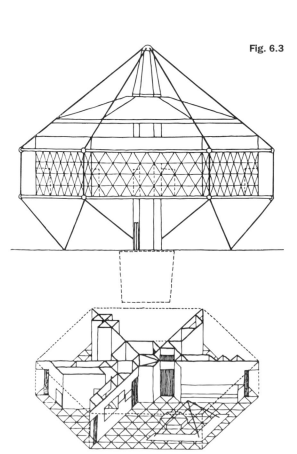

Fig. 6.3

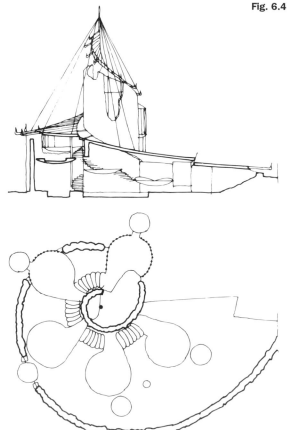

Fig. 6.4

Fig. 6.5

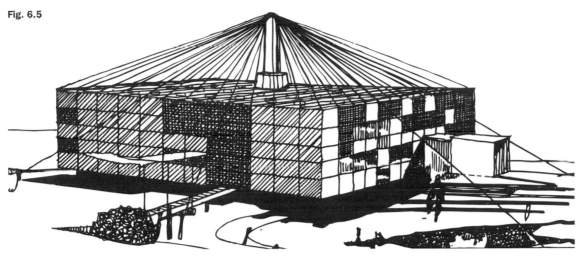

Fig. 6.6

each of which used a single mast to support a cable-stayed primary lattice beam running longitudinally above the roof of a single, large space. In the Knowsley MBC Leisure Centre project (Fig. 6.10), the central position of the mast corresponds to the location of the administrative and social facilities

Fig. 6.7

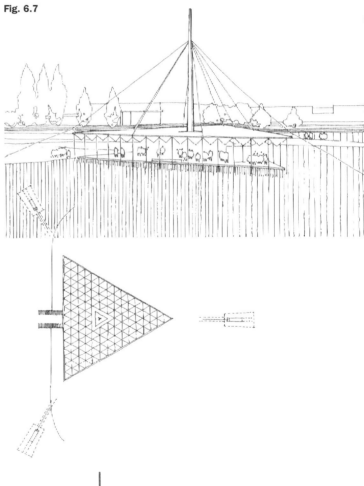

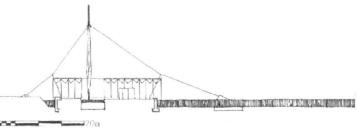

layout. Its larger size, 31m x 13m, again without any external ties against wind forces, demands a massive, hollow steel mast, 1016mm in diameter and 25mm in wall thickness. From its high level anchorage, eight cables support two massive longitudinal CHS roof beams, 508mm in diameter, which carry a relatively slender roof plane. The emphatic strength of the main tubular members in contrast to the delicacy of the cables and the roof plane is very effective in visual terms.

The even longer French canopy, covering the Ile-de-Re toll point (Fig. 6.9), also uses a single mast, but one located eccentrically in relation to the toll booths and their roof canopy. The sheer size of this roof demands a space deck structure, carried by six sets of cables. Moreover, the off-centre mast location requires a tie-down system to a ground anchorage at one end, and inclined tension members against wind up-lift under the major cantilever at the other.

Larger, single-celled structures

During the period 1986-88, the architects Nicholas Grimshaw and Partners proposed two schemes,

Fig. 6.8
Staatliches
Universitats-
bauamt: service
station canopy,
Marburg, 1971.

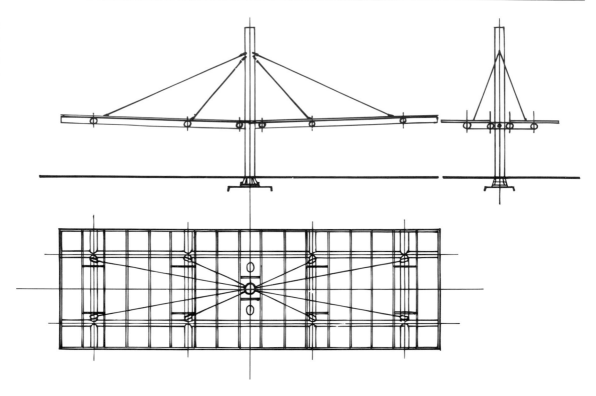

Fig. 6.9
J. Sepra,
J. Fourquier,
J. Filhol:
motorway toll-
booth canopy
L'Ile-de-Re,
France, 1988.

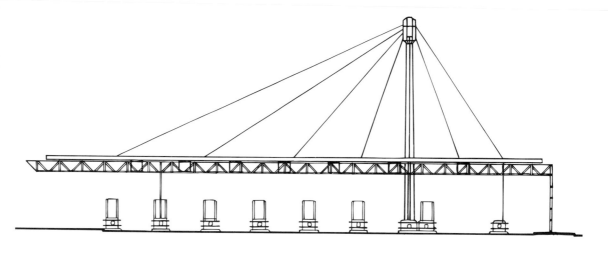

Fig. 6.10 (below)
N. Grimshaw and
Partners:
Knowsley MBC
Leisure Centre,
completed 1991.

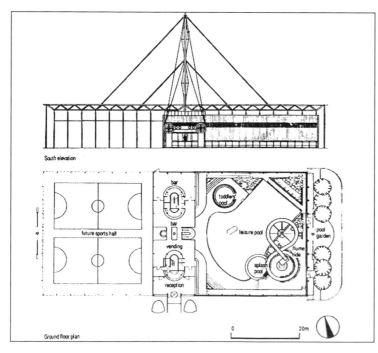

South elevation

future sports hall

Ground floor plan

which separate the two major spaces comprising the dry sports hall and the pool area. The mast itself, which has two sets of intermediate stays, is also stayed laterally, and supports longitudinally the triangular lattice roof beam from which ribs are hung to span out to the edge columns. The second half of this building was only completed in 1991.

The 'Homebase' warehouse at Brentford, London (Fig. 6.11), has a similar central lattice girder anatomy but provides a totally unobstructed space by positioning a single mast at the end of the building rather than in the centre. The mast is in the form of a rectangular vierendeel lattice made up of four CHS tubes 33m high. It supports the 100m long rectangular lattice ridge beam by four tension rods running to its mid-point. At the mast end of the beam, its structure projects to form an out-rigger from which eight restraining ties run to the ground anchorage of the whole system.

A single, massive, external mast was also

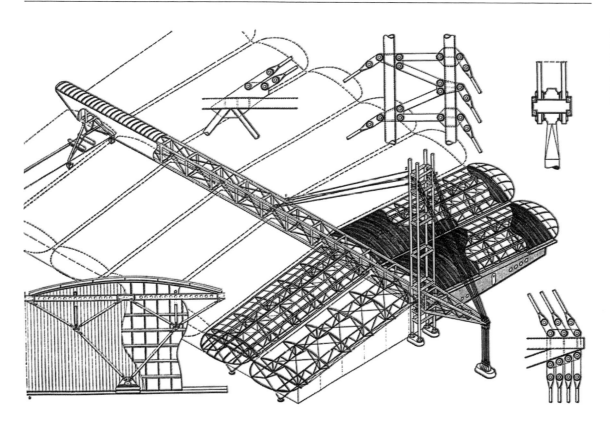

Fig. 6.11
N. Grimshaw and Partners: 'Homebase' warehouse, Brentford, London, 1988.

proposed for the Events Venue at Brents Park, South Shields, by Apicella Architecture and Design (Fig. 6.12). The design is based on a circular, dished ground slab, sunk into the ground as a permanent amphitheatre. Above it, a removable pvc roof and cladding membrane is stretched from two arched ribs to the eaves supports, these ribs being further supported by cables radiating from points on the raked lattice masts. Although membrane roofs are dealt with in Chapter 9, this particular

structure is included here because its form is not generated primarily by the characteristics of the membrane, but to a greater extent by the structural framework.

Structures with quadruple mast elements

The replacement of the single mast element by a cluster of four structural components opens up a range of structural and architectural possibilities

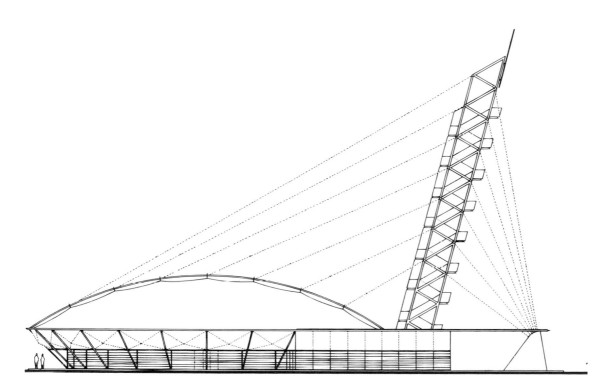

Fig. 6.12
Apicella Architecture and Design: Events Venue, Brents Park, South Shields, 1989.

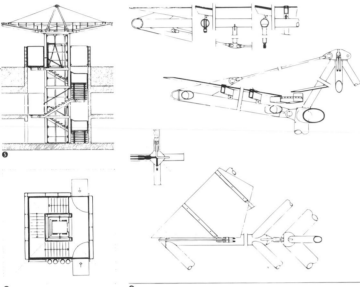

and the most delightful are the two car park access stair enclosures at Biberach, Germany, designed by Kaag + Schwarz of Stuttgart (Fig. 6.13). In each case, a set of four CHS supports defines a core area for either a glass lift or a shining aluminium extract duct, around which run steel stairs with cast glass treads set inside glass enclosures. Cable stays stiffen the tops of the four masts and support the inclined glass and tube canopies. This brilliant solution transforms a normally dingy and unwelcoming hole in the ground into a light, top-lit place of movement and interest.

On a larger scale, a group of four columns also forms the structural core of a light, self-supporting roof-top extension to an office building at Bunnik in Holland, designed by Articon of Amersfoort (Fig. 6.14). The square block, of up to 400m² of office accommodation is characterised visually by being suspended by cables from four masts, each 15.40m high and 40cm in diameter. These have orthogonal and diagonal outriggers from the suspension cables of which the roof and floor slabs are hung. This masted solution was chosen because the existing structure could not support an additional floor, because of the minimal spatial interference of the four columns, and because the separation of the upper floor from the existing building produced a visually light and attractive appearance which was a good advertisement for the company when seen from the main road between Utrecht and Arnhem. The design was also sound economically and was completed in three months.

The Ontario Place development in Toronto,

Fig. 6.13 (above) Kaag + Schwarz: four mast cluster framing underground car park staircase enclosure, Biberach, Germany, 1990.

Fig. 6.14a

Fig. 6.14 Articon: four masted cluster supporting office building extension, Bunnik, Holland, 1990.

a. (left) general view.

b. (opposite top) ground floor and first floor plane.

Fig. 6.14b

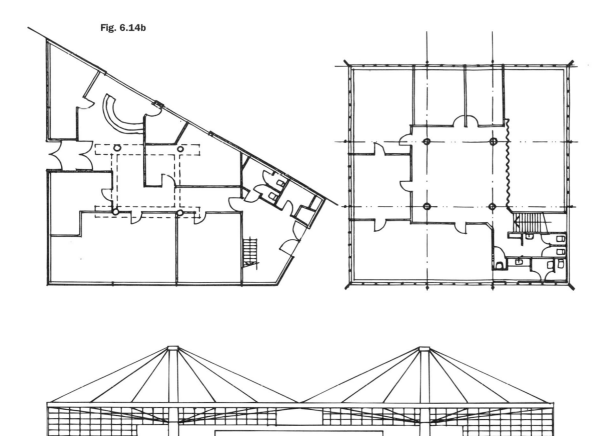

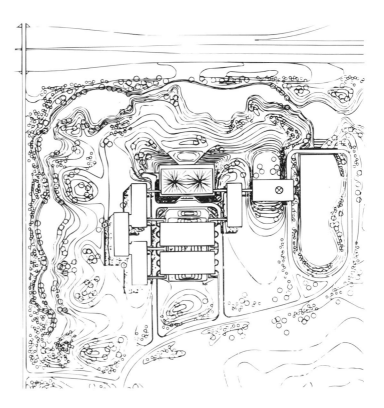

Fig. 6.15
Skidmore, Owings and Merrill: central facilities building, Baxter Travenol Co., Deerfield, Illinois, 1977; cross section.

Canada uses this four-mast cluster principle on an even larger scale. This is a group of three structures, rather like oil rig platforms, which straddle an access bridge across a shallow lake. The square, upper level structures are set diagonally to the line of the bridge and have a group of four masts at their centres. These form the principal supports of the tension system, whilst other cables pass across the outside walls to support perimeter beams. Each platform is on four levels: a lower and a topmost exhibition level, with a pedestrian access level and a mechanical services layer in between.

put into two groups: those with masts located inside the space which is supported, which involves piercing the roof in some way, and those with masts positioned on its perimeter.

Fig. 6.16
As above, site plan.

6.2
ONE-WAY REPETITIONS OF SINGLE MASTED CELLS

Several masted structures consist essentially of linear repetitions of a basic, single masted space. These examples show variations in form, in terms of square or rectangular modules, vertical or inclined masts, and flat or sloping roofs. They also differ in the position of the mast, which can be located within the basic space or on its perimeter. The variations can be expressed in a variety of materials and components of the basic building elements. These multi-cellular structures can be

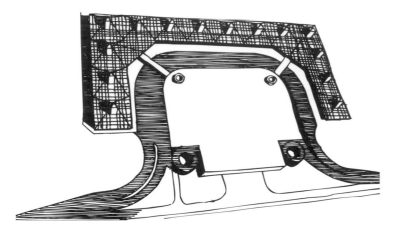

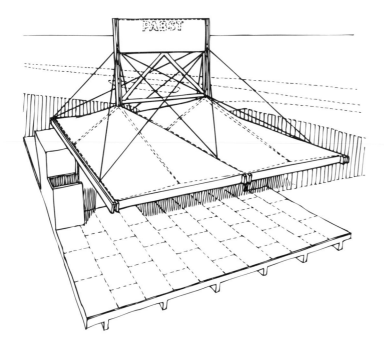

6.15, 6.16). Although the structural logic is simple, it has been applied in a complex building which is large in scale and has two storeys, including a basement and a multiple cable system. The two 13.4m square modules each have a central mast, 10.7m high above the roof, giving an easily recognisable identity to the complex from the nearby expressway. Each mast supports an incredibly large number of thirty-two cables; the twenty-four longer ones run to the edges of the module, whilst the eight shorter ones pick up loads at inner intermediate points on the roof surface. A second set of cables stiffens the roof from below, the 7.3m height of the upper floor making the resulting height restriction acceptable.

The largest example of a block of square modules, each with a central mast, is the 1965 project for an East End Terminal for the former La Guardia Airport, New York. The proposal took the form of a series of fourteen 61m square modules, arranged in a 'U' shape to partially wrap around three sides of its associated multi-storey car park – a beautifully clear and logical concept, the size of which demanded a space deck solution for its roof framework. However, this project, did not proceed to actual construction (Fig. 6.17).

When we consider buildings based not on square but on rectangular modules we find that these too vary widely in form, scale and construction. At one extreme are small 'canopy' structures – a timber shelter to an open stage, and a dealing room ceiling. At the other are two railway station canopies, one a gull-wing form, the other a barrel vault. In each case, the structural logic is the same but the buildings themselves can only be compared by being described in sequence and in detail.

The Pabst stage canopy is a unique example of a timber-framed masted construction on a small scale (Fig. 6.18). Its roof structure consists of three parallel dual timber beams which cantilever over the stage and support the warped planes of the timber roof surfaces. The two vertical masts also consist of timber posts, with timber diagonal bracing, and high level cables criss-cross to the

Fig. 6.17 (top)
William Pereira and Associates: East End Terminal project, La Guardia Airport, New York, 1965.

Fig. 6.18 (above)
Chrysalis East: Pabst Stage canopy, Milwaukee, Wisconsin, 1978.

Structures with internal masts

An example of the simplest possible multiple arrangement, that of two square modules, is represented by the central facilities building of the Baxter Travenol pharmaceutical company in Illinois (Fig.

Fig. 6.19
Heery Architects: Interior dealing room canopy, Victoria Plaza development, Victoria Station, London, 1986.

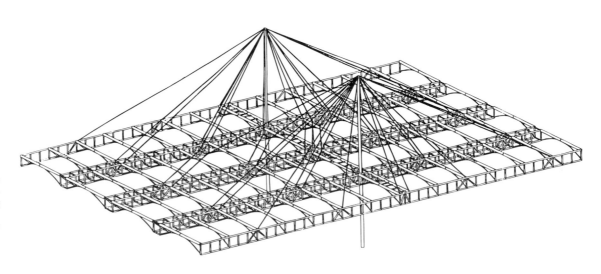

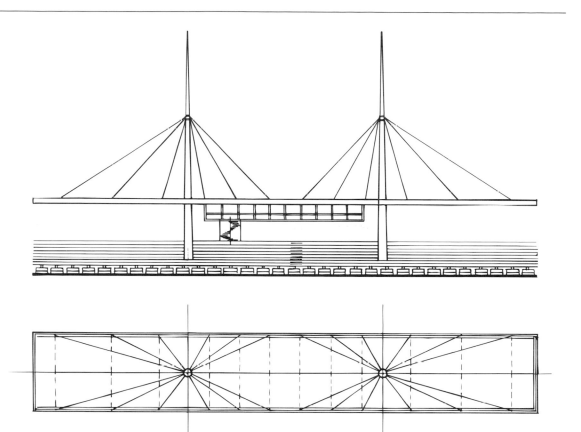

Fig. 6.20
A. Riege:
grandstand roof
and press box,
Marl, Germany,
1967.

mid-points of the cantilevers to provide additional support.

The Pabst canopy's pattern of two centrally masted rectangular modules also forms the basis of the cable-stayed canopy over the dealing room of the Victoria Plaza development, above Victoria station in London. The form of the structure arose out of the need to locate the minimum number of dealing room columns over a line of existing foundations; to limit the depth of the canopy to that of the surrounding floor beams and to keep the weight of the structure to no more than the 134 tonnes capacity of the foundations. Three longitudinal vierendeel box girders form the main structure and the bases of access gangways; two coincide with the lines of the masts, with the third positioned midway between them (Fig. 6.19). The two CHS masts run through and support the girders at that point directly. Elsewhere, they are supported indirectly by rods running from layered anchorages at the tops of the masts. In such an enclosed situation wind effects do not apply and lateral support can be provided by the enclosing side walls. The reference source noted in the Gazetteer provides useful scale and isometric drawings.

A far more substantial structure is the Stadium Stand by A. Riege (Fig. 6.20). This comprises two rectangular modules placed end to end rather than side by side. Their internal masts are brought closer together than the true centres of the modules so as to provide better support for a 'gondola' type Press Box which is suspended from the roof framework. This framework is supported along its edges by twenty-four cables running from the tops of the two elegantly tapered masts. There is a classic simplicity about the whole structure, but it is by no means small – the masts are 1. 6m in diameter at their base and over 31m

Fig. 6.21
P. Zoelly with A.
Wildberger:
exhibition railway
station, Swiss
Expo, 1964.

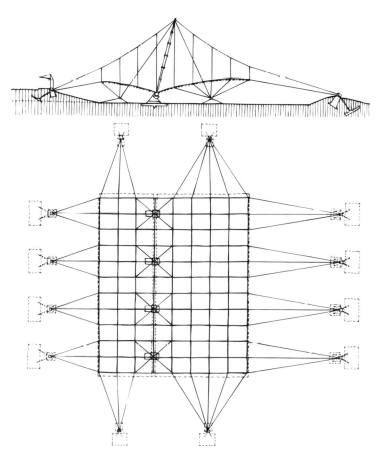

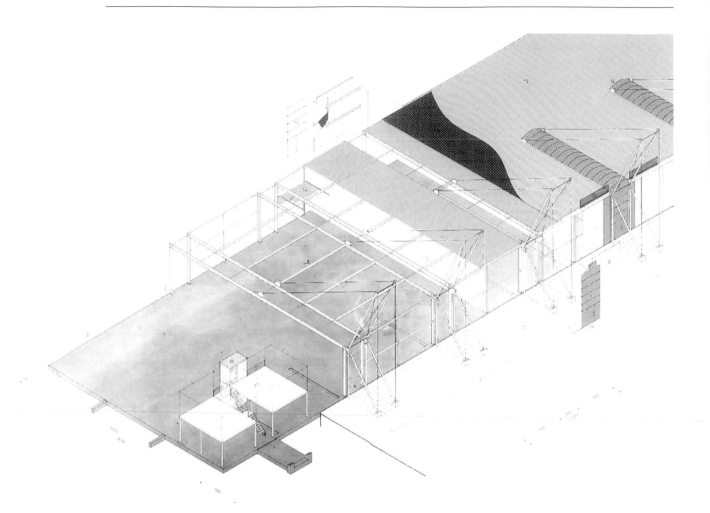

Fig. 6.22
Cepezed Studio:
industrial units,
Rotterdam,
1986; analytical
isometric
drawing.

Fig. 6.23
As above:
elevations.

high; the roof itself is 10m x 67m. The reference source in the Gazetteer again provides full constructional details.

On a much larger scale again, but delicate and breath-taking nevertheless, was the shallow gull-wing canopy to the concourse of the 1964 Swiss Expo railway station (Fig. 6.21). The structural logic was based on four articulated rectangular modules, each having an inclined central mast, 29.7m high made up of four 229 mm tubes. The

masts supported the four main cables of the suspension system, which were anchored into embankments on each side. From points on the main cables, triple diverging hangers descended to pick up selected intersection points on the rectangular steel framework of the roof shells. These points were also tied down by cables radiating from two further ground anchorages, whilst the edges of the roof were tied across to the main embankment anchorages. The overall area of the

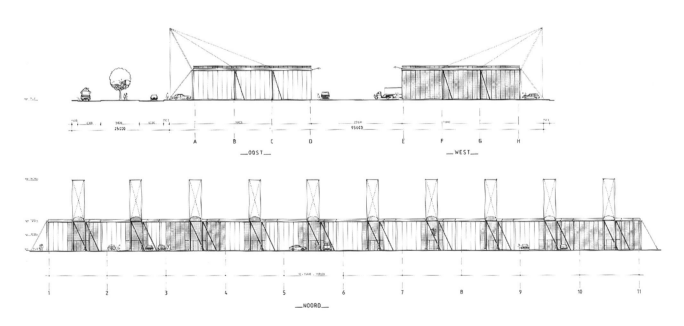

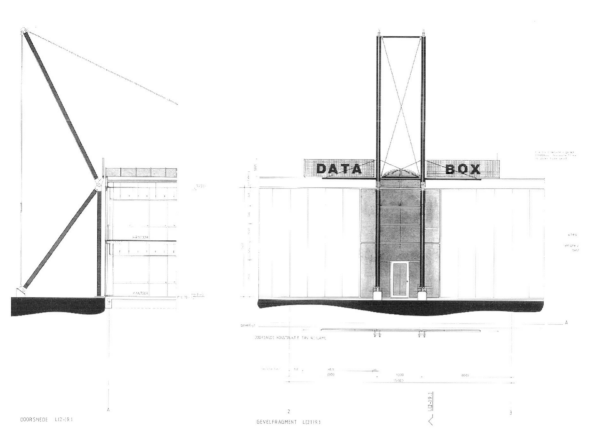

Fig. 6.24
As previous:
eaves and
perimeter wall
detail.

gull-wing roof was 66.7m x 53.6m and its lattice framework was of IPE 22 steel beams forming, in effect, a series of flat facets on two shallow curves. The roof covering of corrugated fibro-cement was drained to a box gutter at the junction of the two wings.

Structures with external or perimeter masts

The primary disadvantage of a centrally masted structure is, of course, the internal obstruction of the mast itself. Locating the mast on the perimeter avoids this problem in principle and one sophisticated way of doing this in practice can be seen in the series of industrial units proposed for N. W. Rotterdam by the Cepezed Studio (Figs. 6.22, 6.23). The unobstructed 30m width of the building is achieved by a structural system of pairs of cable-stayed main beams, 3m apart, supported at their mid-spans by cables running, not from vertical masts, but from a carefully detailed system of pairs of inclined and vertical struts and cable ties focused about an eaves-level junction (see Fig. 6.24). The series of minor modules defined by the dual structural system locates the openings for roof lighting and access point and the position of the controlled signage system. In this way, the compartmented masted system arises out of the functional patterns of the constituent industrial units and the functional needs of their users. It has produced an elegant

design of high architectural quality. In principle, it is a lateral repetition, on a small scale, of the 'Homebase' concept, being of an end-located single perimeter mast (twinned in this case) related to a single, major volume.

Fig. 6.25
A. Ferra and
I. Seignol:
covered cattle
market,
St Etienne,
France, 1973.

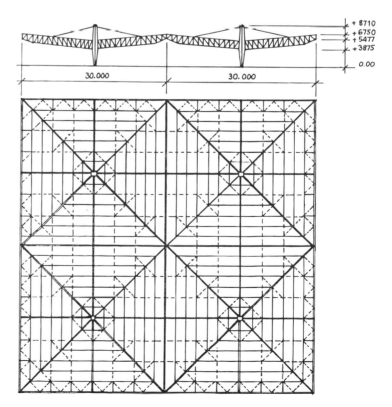

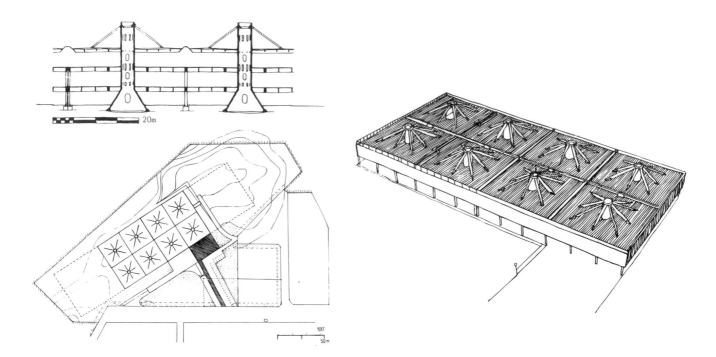

Fig. 6.26
A. Ruusvuori:
printing works,
Tapiola, Finland,
1965.

6.3

TWO-WAY REPETITIONS OF SINGLE MASTED CELLS

The extension of a square, centrally-masted structural unit along two dimensions has formed the basic pattern of several large rectangular structures. They vary in structural material and function and in forming open and enclosed volumes. We shall deal with them in order of numbers of modules: firstly those in which the cells border each

Fig. 6.27
W. Stevens and
J.P. Trimp:
covered market,
Almere, Holland,
1990.

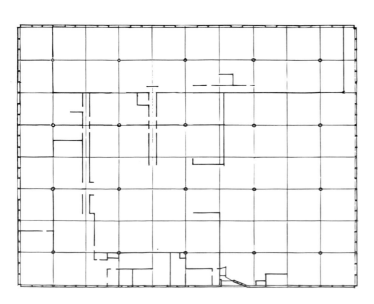

other and, secondly, those in which the cells are separated by an intermediate module, i.e. an articulated or 'tartan grid' pattern in plan.

The covered market at St. Etienne in France (Fig. 6.25) represents a simple group of four individually masted cells, each 30m square. The central masts support eight radiating lattice beams, inclined upwards to form shallow inverted pyramids and cable-assisted at their midpoints from the mastheads. The structure covers an open stockyard, 60m x 60m in area.

More extensively, the printing works at Tapiola in Finland (Fig. 6.26) is a group of eight 26m square structural units, each based on a central, reinforced concrete tubular tower which acts both as a mast and as a service duct. Eight tensile stays radiate from tension rings formed just below the tops of the towers. This structure satisfies the need for column-free work areas with high loading capacity on the upper floor of the building.

On a smaller scale architecturally, the covered market at Almere in Holland (Fig. 6.27) consists of an assemblage of twenty structural and spatial cells, in a five by four arrangement; each cell having a central mast from which square roof pyramids are suspended. Each roof functions as an extract hood for ventilation and smoke removal. In this instance, masted structure was chosen so as to reduce the proportions of the market in relation to the surrounding buildings. The relatively small span of 12.0m between the supports – on a 6m x 6m planning grid to suit the size of the shop units – reflects this criterion.

Discontinuous assemblages of centrally-masted cells

It is invariably useful to articulate particular building elements by a minor module of space and structure.

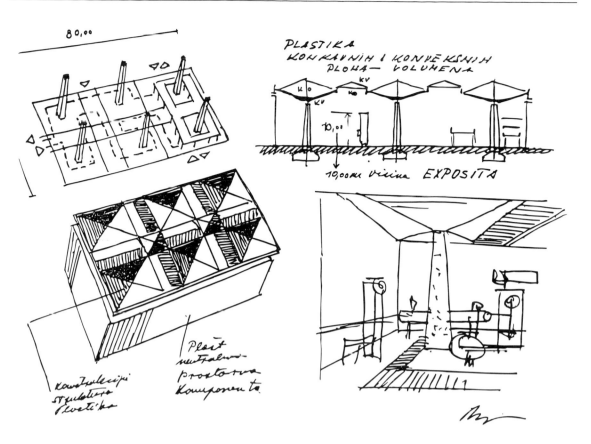

Fig. 6.28
B. Rasica and K. Poltz: German pavilion, Zagreb Trade Fair, 1968, conceptual sketches

Separating elements in this way can not only increase the clear span by using the minor module as a bridge between the major elements, but can also provide integrated openings for roof lighting and access, and enable the significant formal elements to appear visually distinct. Masted structures are no exception to these general principles. For example, the German pavilion at the Zagreb Trade Fair of 1968 (Figs. 6.28, 6.29) comprises six 20m x 20m major modular cells separated by a 10m minor module to enable two substantial roof lights to be located at their intersections. The structural system comprises concrete pylons, which taper from their bases, surmounted by massive concrete inverted pyramids, each 20m square! Above the pyramids, stubby concrete masts form the anchorages for eight tensile stays which run to the corners and mid-points of the roof units.

Concrete was also used for the completed first section of the Max Burren A G vehicle manoeuvering area in Bern (Fig. 6.30). The rectangular concrete roof structure is in essence a group of six

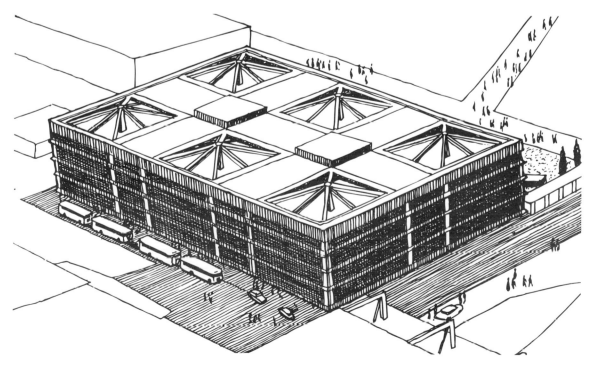

Fig. 6.29
As above: general view.

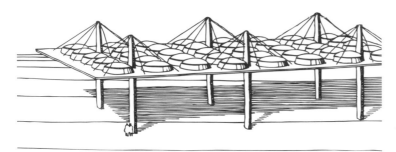

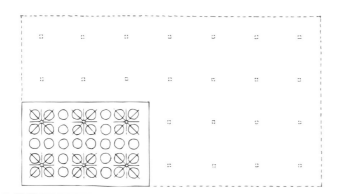

20m

Fig. 6.30
Atelier 5: covered storage area, Max Burren AG, Flamatt, Switzerland, 1962.

structural modules, each with a central mast and eight radiating cable stays. Each module has four circular roof-lights, whilst a minor module of similar rooflights separate each major module from its neighbour.

A more extensive, and structurally more com-

plex design is that of the Tesco supermarket in Bristol. The masted form, and its structural geometry, was the result of several influences: the need for engineering economy, particularly in the efficient resolution of the load effects on poor ground conditions; the need to create a flexible space for the roof-mounted chilling and air-handling plant; the avoidance of internal down-pipes; and the appearance of the roof of the building from the adjacent, elevated section of the M32 motorway (Fig. 6.31). The building consists of ten square, centrally-masted cells, arranged in the shape of a stubby 'T', with half-module intervals between them. But this relatively simple underlying structural pattern in plan is then developed, in section, to produce four raised roof elements combining several modules within octagonal outlines. Cut-aways in the sloping faces of these elements allow input and extract openings to the air-handling plant in the flexible roof-space.

This building demonstrates several 'cautionary tales', viz: the structural concept is visually ambiguous because the extensive pilastered brickwork is clearly capable of supporting the roof elements without the need for masts – (even if a continuous glazing strip were desired); the high level cable connections, and the masts themselves are more clumsy than comparable examples, and the insertion of an off-the-peg flat internal ceiling leads to a bland, conventional interior which fails to do justice to the structural excitement above it. Regrettably, it seems that the building is a somewhat disappointing realisation of an initially exciting intention.

The largest project of this type is the Rotaprint Factory competition entry by the Richard Rogers Partnership (Figs. 6.32, 6.33, 6.34). The design envisages a building 460m long, providing

Fig. 6.31
D. Daw and partners: Tesco supermarket, Bristol, 1986.

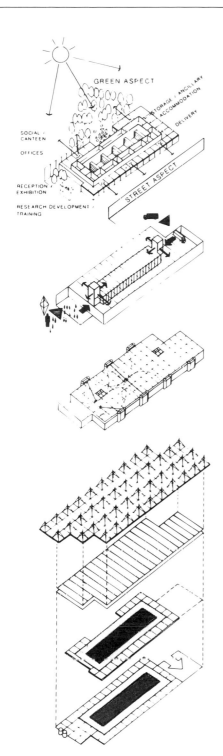

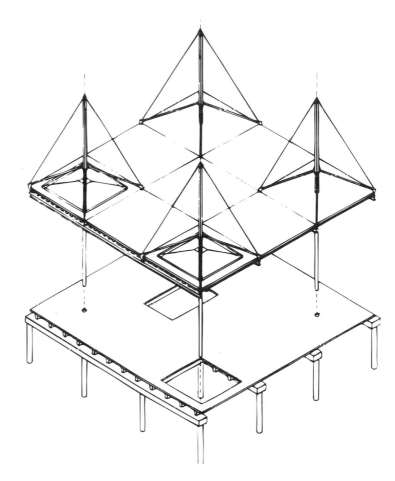

30,000m² of space. It was costed at between £330 and £350 per square metre in late 1988. The spatial/structural system consists of a rectangular assemblage of 20m square cells, seven cells by nineteen, with some omitted at each end for the entry of people and goods. The internal height of 14m allows two major floors at a ground and an upper top-lit production level, with the option of introducing two mezzanine levels around the perimeter. The vertical masts, each with four cable stays supporting continuous span beams, occur in alternate cells, resulting in clear spans of 40m x 40m on the production floor; which is separately supported in concrete. It is interesting to note that the difficulty of incorporating travelling cranes in a masted structure is avoided by using radial crane jibs located against solid portions of the external envelope. ■

Fig. 6.32
(far left)
Richard Rogers
Partnership:
entry for the
Rotaprint factory
competition,
Berlin, 1989;
functions,
servicing,
escape, zoning.

Fig. 6.33 *(above)*
As above:
structural
module.

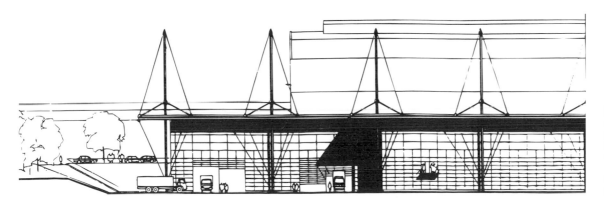

Fig. 6.34
As above:
detail of part
of south-west
facade,
'spinal' mast
locations
(not to scale).

7

TWO MAST STRUCTURES AND ASSEMBLAGES OF TWO-MAST CELLS

Following the analysis of the various ways in which single mast cellular structures can be expressed in architectural terms we can now turn our attention to structures characterised by two masts or multiple two-masted cells. In arrangements of this kind, the spatial/structural cell has so far always been rectangular in plan. In relation to this seemingly characteristic proportion of length to width the two masts have been located in four generic positions: that is, at opposite sides, at opposite ends or at adjacent or opposite corners of the basic rectangle. The first three basic arrangements can each be translated longitudinally and laterally, so as to generate differing families of structures of two mast origin (Fig. 7.1). Typical roof plans of structures based on these principles are shown in Fig. 7.2. We shall discuss, firstly, some examples of side mast arrangements, and an example of a longitudinal translation. Next we shall review some buildings with masts at opposite ends, and at adjacent corners of the basic cell, and then conclude this chapter with some unusual examples in which the twin supports are located inside the main enclosed spaces rather than on their perimeter.

Fig. 7.1
Topological variants of two mast structures and assemblages of two mast cells.

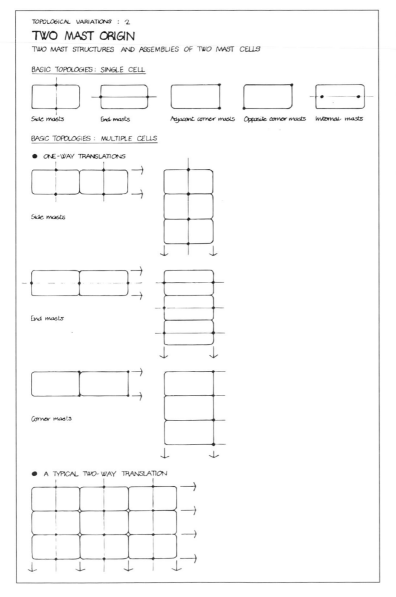

7.1

TWO MAST STRUCTURES WITH SIDE MASTS

The simplest arrangement of two masts located on the sides of a rectangular volume is represented by two, otherwise entirely different projects. The most ponderous, the exhibition centre at Bahia in southern Brazil (see Gazetteer), consists of a massive concrete slab balanced, and tension stayed, about two high concrete pylons containing the vertical circulation. The centre includes a 60m x l0m main hall and has a 50 seat amphitheatre at one end balanced by a high, truncated pyramidal rooflight at the other. This cumbersome composition has been said to 'characterise Brazilian exuberance' but the result seems somewhat elephantine in comparison with other examples of concrete structures in Brazil.

In complete contrast in scale and delicacy is the delightful factory gatehouse canopy in Rotterdam (Figs. 7.3, 7.4, 7.5). The architectural concept is that of a tubular 'H' frame which straddles the midpoint of an elegant steel and glass box containing offices and toilets. This relatively simple idea is developed structurally in terms of two masts with a horizontal pin jointed tubular connector, from which are suspended three long tubular supports above a roof plane which is poised in turn over the accommodation. The masted framework is tension-stayed longitudinally by two pairs of inclined rods to the extended bases of the masts. A tubular outrigger forms a vehicular entrance portal at right angles to the main block. The elements in this elegantly balanced composition are kept visually distinct by the most careful attention to detail. The design is highly successful in marking the entrance control point, and in identifying the company by a structure which has appropriate scale, balance and authority. It is one of the classic designs in architectural masted structures.

One-way repetitions of cells with side masts

It was noted earlier that rectangular modules can be repeated either along their short or their long axes, that is, laterally or longitudinally. As we shall see, the lateral extension of such an initial spatial/structural module forms the basis of several examples. Firstly, however, we will deal with one example of a longitudinal repetition.

The Wakita Hi-Tecs office building (Fig. 7.6) is a perfect example of the repetition of a side-masted cell along its long axis. Two, two-masted cells are placed end to end to form a structural/spatial system consisting of two pairs of tubular masts between which a long, rectangular box of accommodation is slung at first floor level. The floor and roof planes are formed by pre-cast concrete T beams spanning across the building on to longitudinal edge beams. These are primarily supported by short cross beams from the free-standing masts. Their lines continue beyond the masts as short, back-stayed outriggers. The main tensile rods from above, and the wind-bracing rods from below, criss-cross over each other symetrically, across the planes of the side walls (Fig. 7.7). Visually, this produces rather too many lines and a somewhat over-designed appearance. This, of course, is because the concept of the 'floating box' with its minimal supports and inherently long, cable-stayed cantilevers imposes heavy penalties in the terms of structural provisions.

The lateral repetition of a side-masted rectangular cell produces a form whose length depends on the number of repeated modules and which has a row of mast columns down the interior – centrally or off-centre according to the particular design. The buildings representing this basic arrangement fall into three groups: open canopy structures; enclosed volumes with a row of interior columns, and two examples which have masts down the

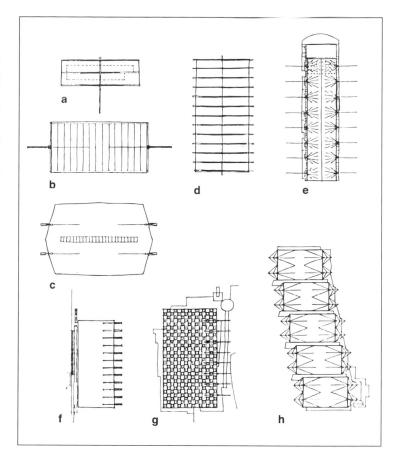

Fig. 7.2 (above) Comparative roof plans of typical two mast based structures (not to scale).

a. Factory gate lodge, Rotterdam, 1984.

b. Oxford Ice Rink, Oxford, 1983.

c. Arosa Ice Rink, Arosa, Switzerland, 1978.

d. Industrial units, Nieuwegeyn, 1986.

e. West Japan Exhibition Centre, Kitkayushu, Japan, 1977.

f. Swimming Pool, Woking, England, 1989.

g. Sports Centre, Charlottenburg, Berlin, 1991.

h. Darling Harbour Exhibition Centre, Sydney, 1988.

Fig. 7.3 (left) Cepezed Studio: Ret factory gate lodge, Rotterdam, general view.

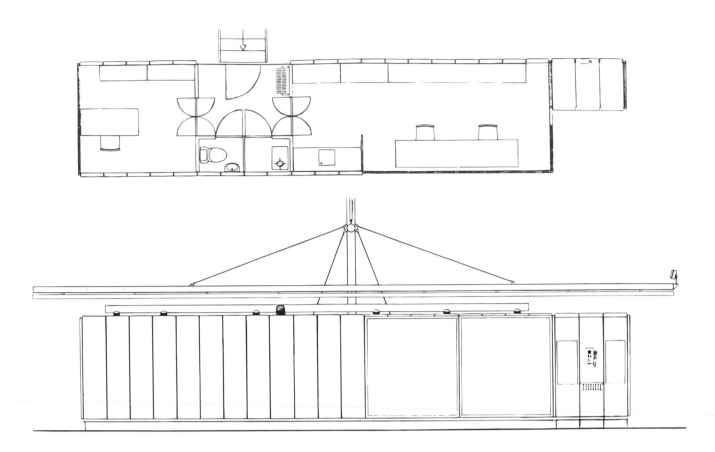

Fig. 7.4
As above:
roof plan, end
elevation.

side of the building because they are located at the adjacent corners of the originating basic cell, rather than on its opposite sides.

Two of the masted canopy structures are similar in form, having been designed for the Italian OM Company to shelter its prototype railway coaches at the Milan Fairs of 1948 and 1950. In the initial

architectural concept, the weather shelter was provided by a thin, sloping roof plane which floated above the exhibit, supported by cables from inclined masts which pierced the roof through circular openings (Fig. 7.8). In the later design of 1950, the masts lost their direct relationship with the roof by being moved to a position outside it. This freed

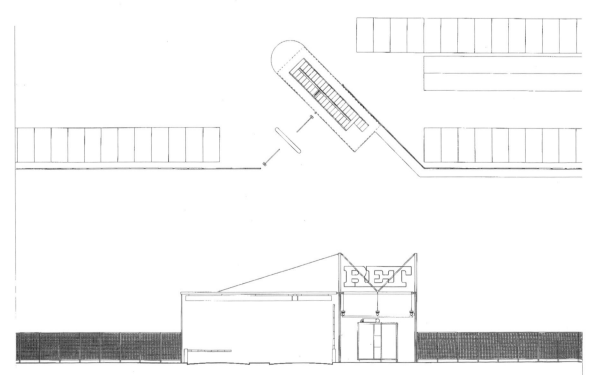

Fig. 7.5
As above:
plan, end
elevation.

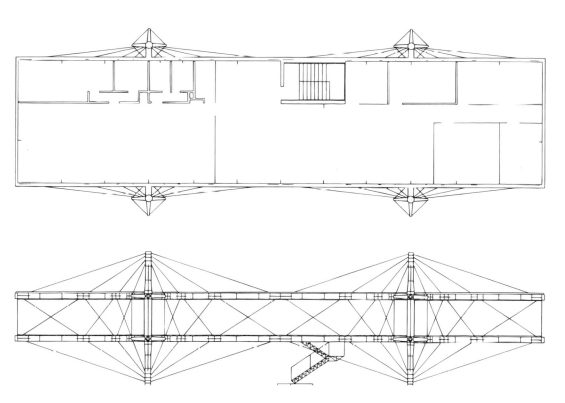

Fig. 7.6
*Shoei Yoh +
architects:
Wakita Hi-Tecs
office building,
1990; plan and
elevation.*

the interior of any structural element and led to an
even more dynamic and 'exhibitionist' configuration
of masts, cables and a floating roof plane.

A more conventionally orthogonal, four-module
canopy is that of the tourist information point on the
A15 autoroute near Le Havre in France (see
Gazetteer). The canopy, of 825m^2, covers a vehicle
pull-in on one side and two box-like sets of accommodation on the other. This difference in function
leads to an off centre location of the quadruple tube
masts, and to differing systems of support on alternate sides. Cables from an intermediate point on
the masts support a trussed system over the road-
way, whereas masthead cables run to the ends of
the roof beams over the accommodation.
Restraining ties against wind up-lift are located
along both sides.

Moving on from open canopies to enclosed volumes, we begin with 'La Rampe', a community hall
and entertainments centre at Echirolles, near
Grenoble (Figs. 7.9, 7.10). The underlying structural concept here is of three spatial/structural modules defined by four masts located off centre along
their sides. The architectural concept is a simple
exercise in solid geometry: a sector-shaped volume containing ancillary rooms intersects oblique-
ly, with the rectangular volume of the main hall. The
two concepts are brought into correspondence by
the square modular grid of the over-sailing roof
framework. This grid controls the alignment of the
internal walls and the four tubular masts. The result
is a beautifully integrated fusion of architecture and
structure in a volumetric, transparent, yet robust
building.

Four very much larger modules form the basis of
the SNECMA factory at Le Creusot in France (Figs.
7.11, 7.12, 7.13, 7.14). The design arose out of the

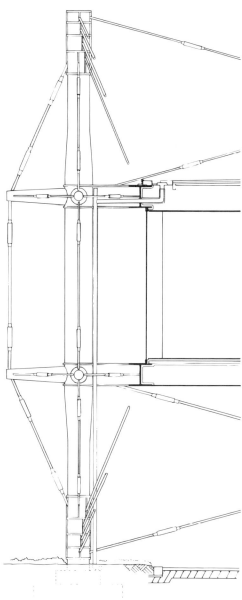

Fig. 7.7
*As above;
detail of
mast supports.*

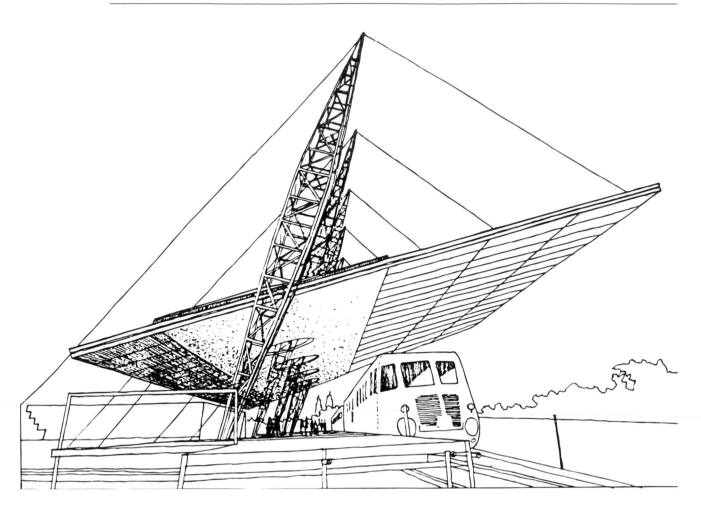

Fig. 7.8
R. Zavanella:
OM pavilion,
Milan Fair, 1948.

need to satisfy three main provisions: flexible manufacturing space with a minimum of obstructions; ease of future extension, and an attractive roof appearance when viewed from the surrounding hills. The structural system is based on three 120m span lattice beams, cable-stayed to masts at their centres and ends. These major beams are exposed above the roof which is hung from them at the intersection points of its two-way, lattice girder framework. This zone contains all the overhead servicing to the plant. Unusually, the main masts, though 34.5m high, are cross-braced only at a relatively low level by a further substantial lattice girder running between them.

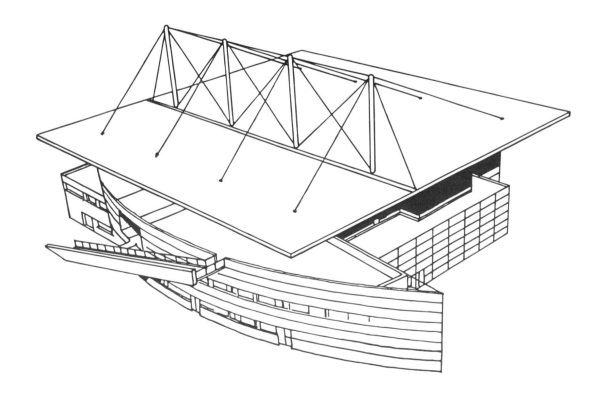

Fig. 7.9
F. Confino and
J.P. Duval:
'La Rampe',
Echirolles, Isre,
France, 1988;
aerial view.

In such a group of four modules with side masts one would expect to see the modules defined by five masts and main beams. In this case, however, the two outer systems are omitted, the roof spanning on to outer wall frames at the ends. As a result, the 91m x 116m manufacturing space is interrupted only by the three, centrally placed masts. Roof lighting to this extensive area is provided by a series of north lights occupying alternate modules of the roof framework. They run parallel to the main beams and are carried down the walls as triangular projections. Functionally, the building is simply a 'big shed' but the triple-masted configuration and the modelling of the rooflights achieves a modest level of architectural quality in an appropriate context.

Two further examples of laterally extended, two-mast modules need to be mentioned. The two buildings, which are identical in cross section (Fig. 7.15), are the factory at Haarlem of 1985 and the industrial units at Nieuwegeyn of 1987 (Figs. 7.16, 7.17). Both buildings are by 'Cepezed' the architects of the factory gate lodge described earlier in this section. The architectural concept is again that of an elegant rectangular box inserted beneath a strongly expressed tubular structure. The basic structural module is of 30m x 5.4m, with masts at the mid-points of the long sides. Repeating this module laterally produces a building 30m wide with only a central row of 355mm diameter masts at 5.4m intervals. This cross-section is identical in both buildings. The main roof beams are also of 355m tubes pin-jointed to the masts and tension-stayed to them by 40mm diameter rods. They are tied down by 100mm CHS to the ground slab. The roof beams have stub hangers to support the internal RHS framework of the roof; this falls shallowly to a central box gutter between two inclined rooflights which are carried down as window slits at the ends of the building. The two buildings consists of sixteen and eleven modules respectively. Their identical cross section is classic in its structural elegance and refinement and it forms the armature of an architectural form of great distinction. A detailed account of this building appears in Brookes and Grech, 1990.

Multiple accretions of rectangular cells defined by balanced cantilevers form the bases of two fur-

ther projects mentioned earlier. The Transcon Lines loading bay canopy is based on a one-way, lateral repetition of the basic cell to produce a twelve bay structure with two lines of masts (see Fig. 5.12). The Parker Square development project took the form of a two-way repetition of the basic cell to produce an overall grid layout of 108 rectangular cells (see Fig. 5.11).

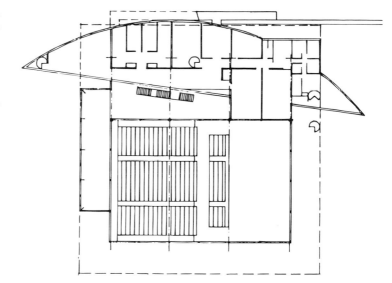

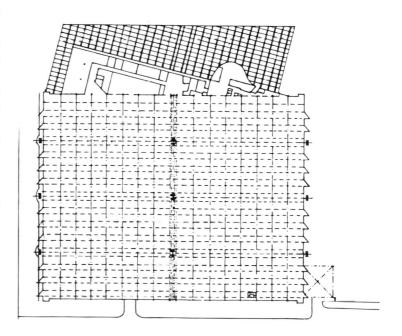

Fig. 7.10 (top) As above; plan.

Fig. 7.11 (above) A. Constanin and P. Rice: SNECMA factory, Le Creusot, France 1987; plan.

Fig. 7.12 (below) As above: longtitudinal section.

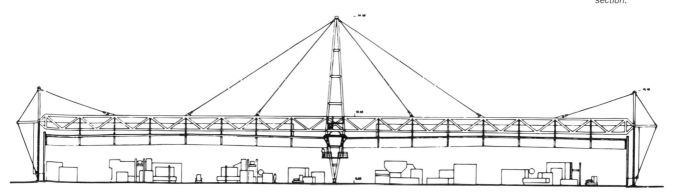

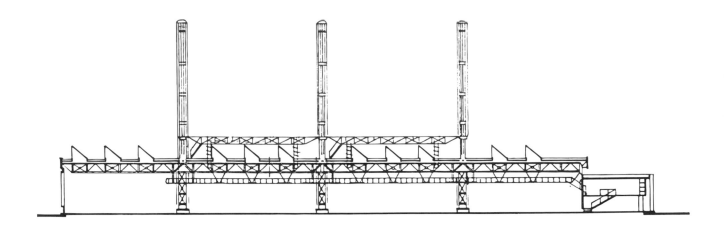

Fig. 7.13
As above: cross
section.

7.2

TWO MAST STRUCTURES WITH END MASTS

The principal alternative position for two masts in relation to a rectangular cell is at the centres of the short ends. This basic arrangement can also be extended laterally, by adding modules side by side, and also longitudinally by placing additional modules end to end. In this section, examples of all these possible configurations will be described. We shall begin with examples of the basic, single volume arrangement and continue by describing some lateral and longitudinal repetitions.

We begin with an interesting comparison of three buildings of similar function: the ice rinks at Braunlage, Arosa and Oxford, built in 1972, 1978 and 1984 respectively. They are of relatively similar area, although their internal height varies from 9m to 17m. Two of the structures have a simple arrangement of two masts at the ends of a rectangular or octagonal volume spanned longtitudinally by a cable-stayed main roof beam, whereas the Arosa building has two sets of masts and primary

Fig. 7.14
As above:
eaves detail.

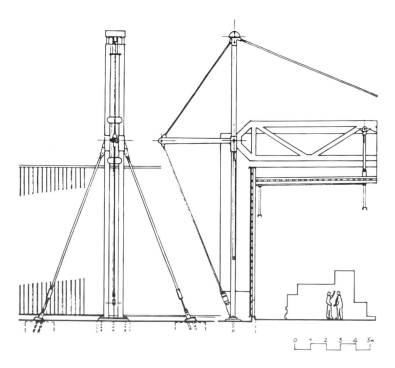

roof beams, spaced apart to allow a long roof light to be provided between them.

In the first example, the ice skating stadium at Braunlage in Germany (Fig. 7.18), the octagonal form reflects the plan of the bleacher seating which allows a natural, unobstructed view of the rink. The structural system comprises two inclined end masts and cable supports to a box section, double-pitched main beam spanning 82m. The resulting roof takes the form of four sloping surfaces on timber secondary framing, partially supported by four concrete perimeter columns. The tapered box section steel masts stand on neoprene pads designed to be stressed only in compression.

The Oxford Ice Rink (Figs. 7.19, 7.20) is slightly smaller, 72m x 38m overall, and is a more sober, but nevertheless striking composition of vertical masts and a horizontal roof line. A masted structure was chosen partly to avoid a 'warehouse' appearance, partly to provide a recognisable visual identity, but most importantly to concentrate the main foundations on to four sets of piles on a poor site. These sets comprise the two foundations for the masts and the two groups forming the tension piles of the main anchorages. The perimeter columns carrying the remaining 20% of the roof load are on shallow pile footings. The structural system is based on a main, longitudinal spine beam comprising two RHS members spanning up to 15m between the overhead supports. An unusual feature is that the two 33m high masts are each in three pin-jointed sections to simplify the structural analysis and avoid the need for site welding. The roof cross beams are of 457mm x 191mm members at 4.8m centres. They are continuous over the spine beam but pinned at their ends. The use of the very high masts in relation to an elegant main volume produces a majestic and somewhat nautical effect of very high architectural and structural quality.

The third ice rink, at Arosa in Switzerland (Fig. 7.21) embodies several of the formal characteristics of the two previous examples, and for similar reasons: structural economy, reduction of volume in a sensitive locality, and visual recognition. The main volume is 74m x 55m but in this case two sets

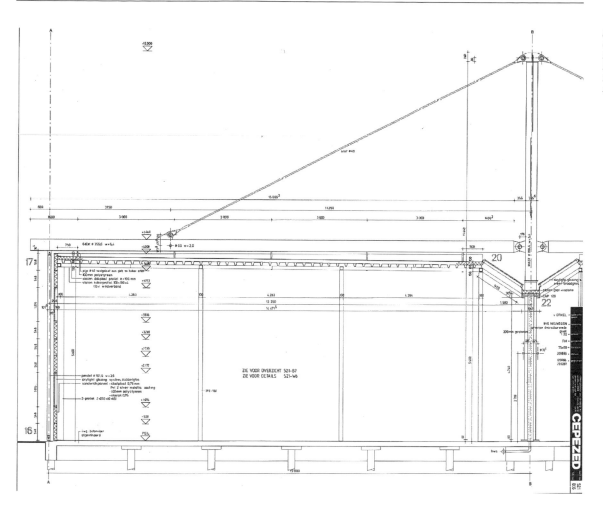

Fig. 7.15
*Cepezed Studio:
industrial units,
Nieuwegeyn,
1987; part cross
section.*

of vertical masts, with back-stays to their founda-tions, and shallow, double-pitched main beams, are spaced approximately 20m apart, enabling a long rooflight to be located between them. The

general similarities with the Braunlage rink are very striking.

A wider version of this dual roof beam principle can be seen on a far larger scale in the State Sports

Fig. 7.16
As above: plan.

Fig. 7.17
*As above:
elevations.*

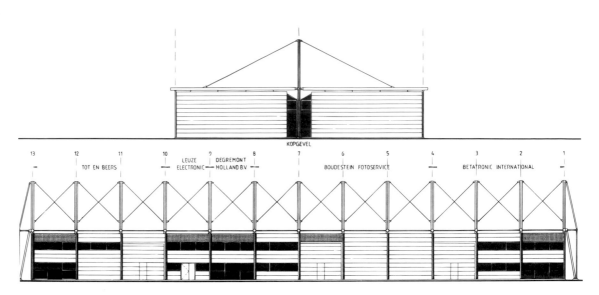

Fig. 7.18
*Westermann
Architectual
Office: Ice
Skating Stadium,
Braunlage,
Germany, 1972.*

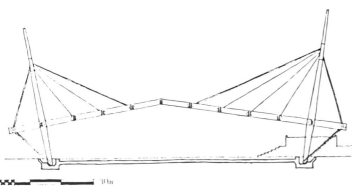

Centre at Homebush, a suburb of Sydney, Australia (Fig. 7.22). The mast and cable-stayed structure of the 5,600 seat main hall consists of two box beams, 3m deep x 3m wide, spanning the 80m of its long dimension. These beams are each supported by two pairs of 130mm tie rods from the 600mm x 400mm twin box section masts at each end. Secondary trusses of the same depth span across the hall and cantilever out 16m from the main beams on the long sides. The tops of the masts are tied back vertically at the ends of the building. The outward inclination necessary to do this means that they make most of their visual contribution internally: in fact, externally the masts are set so far into the main volume that any real correspondence between the two is lost – an unfortunate result in architectural terms.

One-way repetitions of end-masted modules

The lateral translation or repetition of end-masted modules has formed the organising principle of two very large projects. The first of these is a simple accretion of identical spatial/structural cells: the second is a larger and more complex combination of groups of paired, end-masted modules. Both are major exhibition centres.

The former, the West Japan General Exhibition Centre (Fig. 7.23) is a rectangular volume, 230m x 50m in area, comprising two halls with ancillary facilities located in a narrow band around the perimeter. The structural system is based on eight identical modules, 42. 7m x 21.6m, each with four main beams 42.7m long and 600mm deep, and six cross beams. This framework is suspended from each of the 711.2mm CHS masts by eight, 60mm diameter spiral cables taken to the intersection points of the grid. To avoid the problems of aggregating such a large number of cables on to one mast, they are separated into four levels, 900mm apart. On the opposite side of each mast, four backstay cables descend in parallel to an anchorage point located 25m from the building (Fig. 7.24). In this extensive structure, the total lift

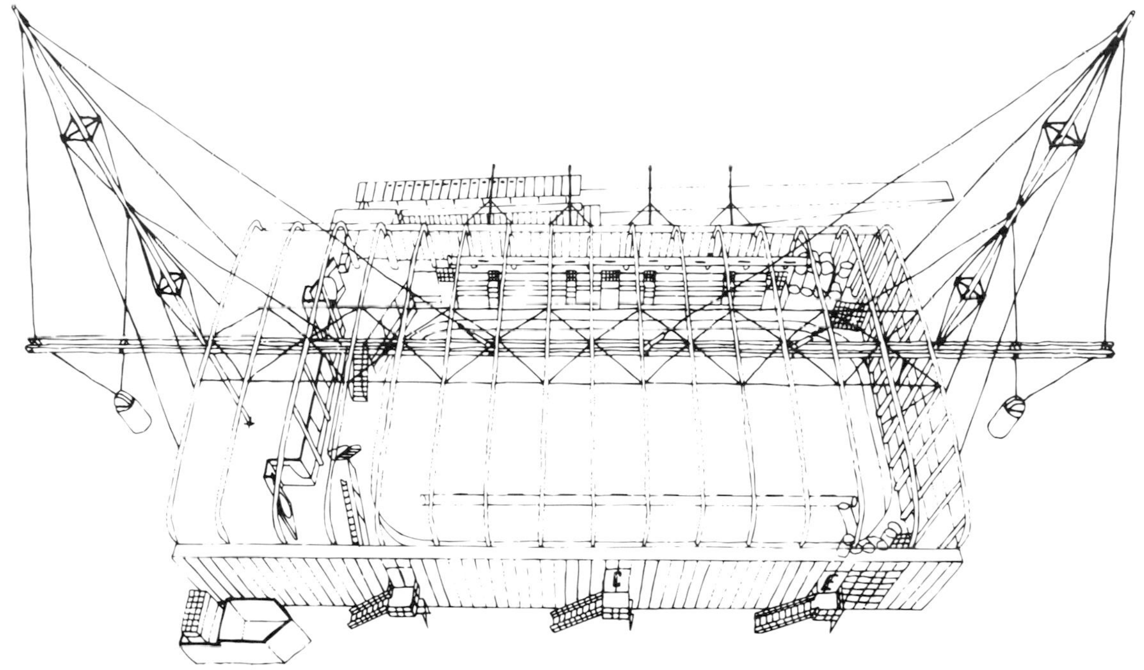

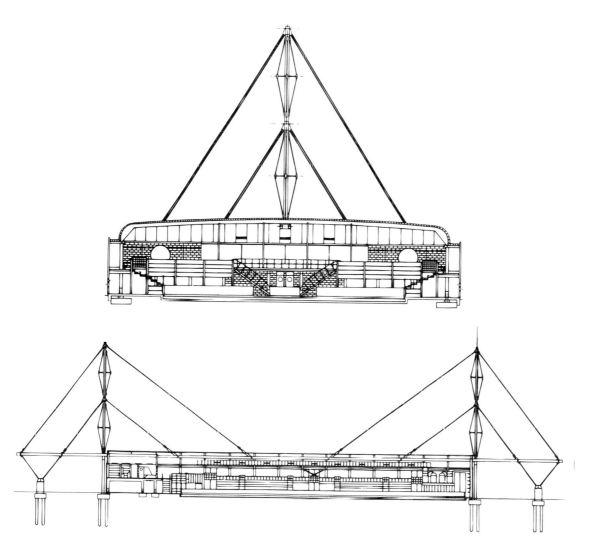

Fig. 7.19
N. Grimshaw and Partners: Oxford Ice Rink, Oxford, England; 1983; analytical drawing.

of the backstays is normally 89 tons, increasing to 108 tons under snow loading. The 74 ton mass concrete anchorages are reinforced by four poured concrete piles, 11.4m deep and l.0m in diameter, to provide a 1.5 safety coefficient. This unusually complex diagonal suspension configuration presupposes a hinge at the base of each mast orientated in the span direction. In this case

Fig. 7.20
As above: analytical drawing and long section.

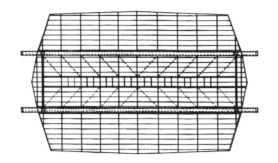

Fig. 7.21
*A. & A. Rocco:
Ice Skating
Stadium, Arosa,
Switzerland,
1978.*

a vertical steel plate performs that function, supporting an axial load of 180 tons with an elasticity range at the tops of the masts of plus or minus 100mm.

The waterside location of the West Japan Centre is similar to that of the second, and even larger complex of two-masted modules, that of the Darling Harbour Exhibition Centre in Sydney, Australia (Figs. 7.25, 7.26). This is the country's largest and most innovative exhibition facility, completed for the Bicentenary in 1988. The 25,000m² Centre consists of five exhibition halls, each 84m by 60m, staggered in plan and connected by quarter arc vaults at roof level. These halls can be used as a single space, or sub-divided into self-contained, independently serviced units.

The underlying basis of the structure is quite simple: each hall consists of two end-masted modules, arranged side by side. The two modules are sub-divided into four half modules by five longitudinal roof beams in the form of triangular lattice trusses designed to resist the horizontal compression forces introduced by the tension stays. Two pairs of similar cross trusses complete the grid of the roof framework. The masts are located centrally at the ends of the modules. They are 33m high and built up from four 406mm CHS steel sections battened together to form vertical, vierendeel

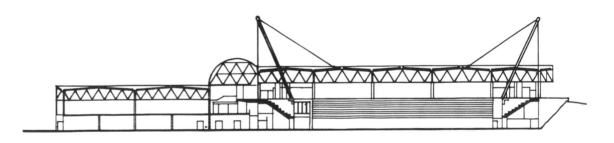

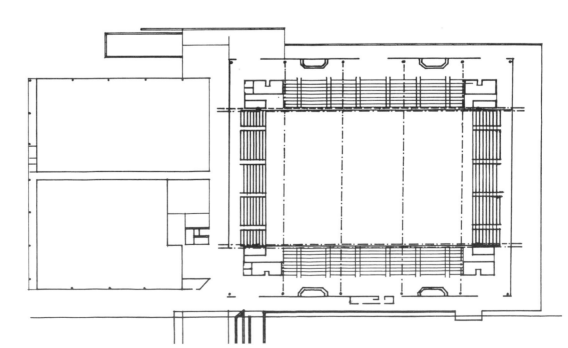

Fig. 7.22
*NW Government
Architect with
Philip Cox and
Partners: State
Sports Centre,
Homebush,
Sydney; plan and
longitudinal
section.*

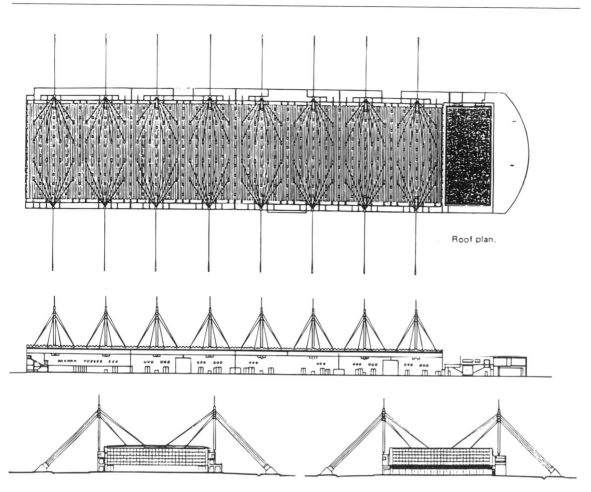

Roof plan.

Fig. 7.23
*Arato Isozaki:
West Japan
Exhibition Centre,
Kitakyushu,
Japan, 1977;
roof plan and
elevations.*

box trusses. Extending from the tops of the masts are mild steel tension rods, supporting the truss grid at approximately one-third span. Back-stays also run from the mastheads, via outriggers, to tension pile anchorages. As in the West Japan Centre, this form of structure satisfies the spatial and functional requirements and reflects the mar-

itime themes of a waterfront environment.

Lastly, a similar pattern of repeated end-masted modules characterises the galleria roof of the Park Plaza shopping centre built over the A1(M) motorway at Hatfield in England. The shallow-vaulted roof of this galleria is supported by twenty-one curved lattice trusses. These define twenty struc-

Fig. 7.24
*As above; mast
and anchorage
detail.*

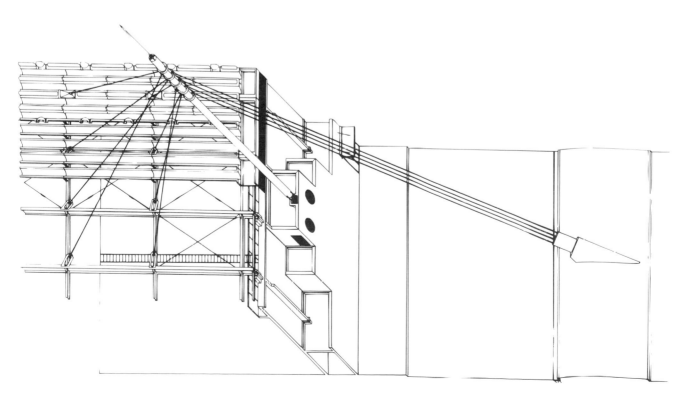

Fig. 7.25
Philip Cox and Partners: Darling Habour Exhibition Centre, Sydney, 1988; part analytical axonometric from above.

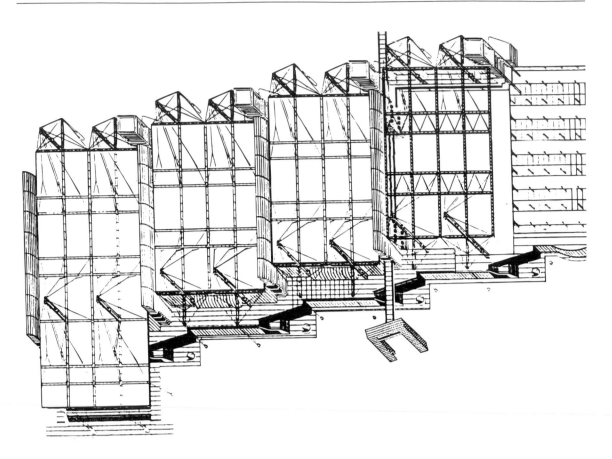

tural bays, each pair of which has an outwardly sloping mast at each end, on the centre-line between them (Fig. 7.27).

A main suspension rod, plus two similar but diverging 50mm rods run from each masthead to connect with the ends of 163.8mm CHS members which in turn support each of the main roof trusses at about one- and two-thirds their span. In this way, each mast supports three trusses. A horizontal cross tie and in-plane and divergent tie-down rods also intersect at the main suspension rod/CHS member connection. This system is thus able to support the roof structure and resist any wind up-lift (Fig. 7.28).

The Galleria roof is supported by the main retail buildings to the East and West of the tunnel at about 13m above the tunnel lid. Along the West side, the roof is fixed, but on the East it is supported on sliding bearings to allow for East-West movement.

The end walls are clad in Pilkington Planar glass

Fig. 7.26
As above: mezzanine level plan.

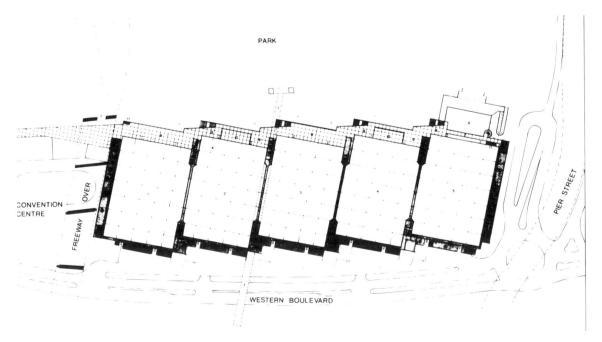

supported by CHS lattice truss mullions at 3.6m centres spanning vertically with transoms at 2.0m centres. The end wall trusses are supported by a spreader system directly on the tunnel roof. The overall East-West stability of the end walls is achieved by the framework cantilevering vertically from the tunnel roof, using vierendeel action between transoms and mullions. The trusses are restrained in a North-South direction by the Galleria roof via specialist bearings.

7.3
TWO MAST STRUCTURES BASED ON MASTS AT ADJACENT CORNERS

The third generic alternative position of two masts in relation to a rectangular spatial cell is to locate them at its adjacent corners. We have not come across any building in which a single volume is structured by just two masts in this way. However, there are several multi-cellular buildings which embody the principle of the lateral repetition of this arrangement. This produces a structure consisting of a series of bays defined by tension-stayed beams supported from a line of masts down one side of the building. We will describe two examples of this arrangement.

The first of these is the major element of the Woking Pool complex. It consists of twelve, corner-masted modules enclosing the principal swimming facility (Fig. 7.29). A masted structural system was chosen to reduce the depth of the main beams, and also to respond to a parallel avenue of existing mature trees. Laminated timber members were chosen for internal environmental reasons. The roof structure consists of twelve pairs of doubly-curved laminated timber beams, 600mm x 165mm, spanning approximately 23.5m and resting on concrete corbels at one end. At the other, the beams are pin-jointed through the raked 219mm x 8mm CHS masts. Tension stays from intermediate points along the beams run to the tops of the masts which are tied back, via the projecting ends of the beams, to ground anchorages (Figs. 7.30, 7.31). This

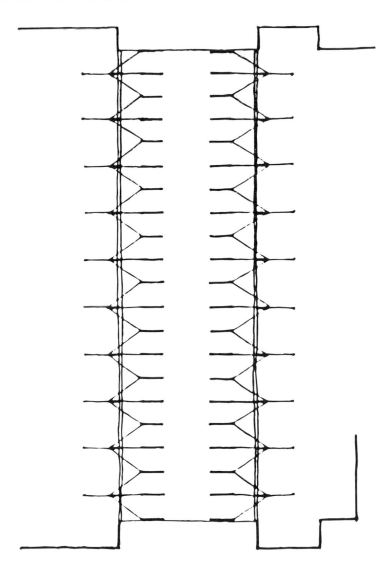

structural system is clear and direct, but the combination of raking masts, curved beams and verticals elsewhere is, perhaps, not an entirely happy one in visual terms.

The Berlin Sports Centre in Charlottenburg by Christof Langhof (Fig. 7.32) is totally different in cross-sectional form. It represents a novel interpretation of a method of resolving the abrupt conjunction of compressive and tensile forces which occurs at the top of the masts in a masted structure. The sports hall itself is roofed by a

Fig. 7.27
Aukett
Associates:
A1 Gallerias
shopping centre,
Hatfield,
England, 1991;
outline roof plan.

Fig. 7.28
As above:
cross section
of masted
roof structure.

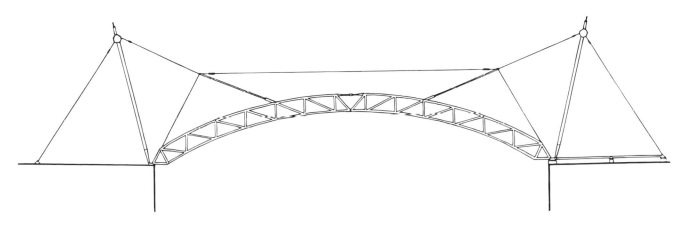

series of asymmetrical trusses, supported on the side walls and also on an intermediate tubular beam which runs the length of the rectangular hall. It is this beam which derives additional support from cables running, not from masts as such, but from the tips of a series of 'fingers' which serve to describe a 180° arc of force from the points of support on the roof down to the ground anchorages. This unique structural mataphor has produced an interesting, if perhaps not generally repeatable design. It should be noted that, in plan, the end masts of the series have been omitted (see Fig. 7.32).

7.4

SOME INTERNALLY MASTED AND LONGITUDINAL DERIVATIVES

We conclude this section by grouping together three projects which can be understood by analysing their forms in terms of rectangular cells with internal rather than perimeter masts. One complex project is essentially based on two such modules side by side: the remaining two are of two modules placed end to end. A fourth and final project is a delightfully *ad hoc* temporary canopy which uses a unique method of support.

The first project, the new railway station at

Fig. 7.29
Faulkner Browns: Woking Pool complex, Woking Pool Complex, Woking, England, 1989; general view.

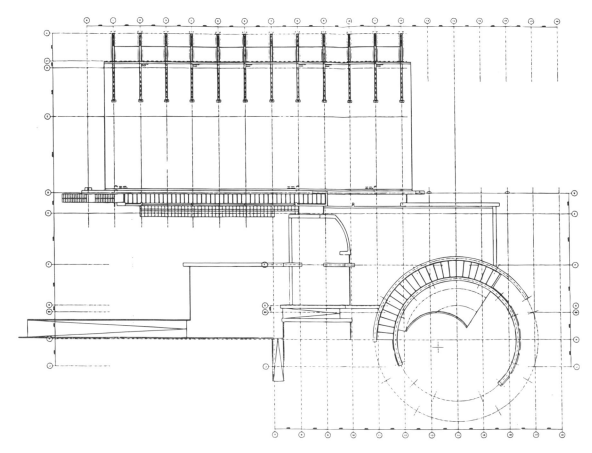

Fig. 7.30
As above: roof plan showing lines of masted supports.

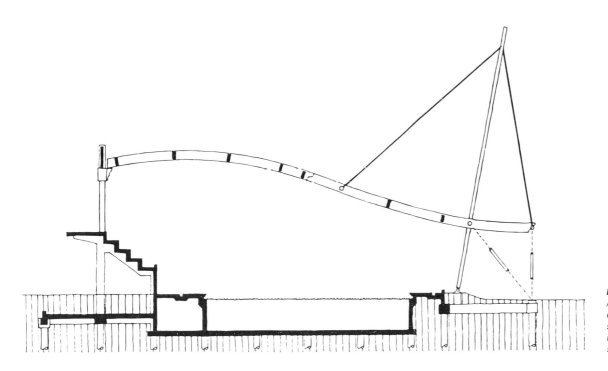

Fig. 7.31
As above: outline cross section of masted structure.

Poole, England (Fig. 7.33 and Fig. 1.6), is at first sight simply a charming architectural exercise of five barrel vaults. However, the relationship of the vaults to the masted support system is not immediately apparent from general views and demands careful study and explanation. The structure is based on two notional structural modules, each 30m by 8m, spaced 4m apart at right angles to the line of the vaults. Each module has a central main beam, made up in fact of two channel sections which pass on either side of two further pairs of battened channels forming the internal masts, and cantilever beyond them. These pairs of primary beams are stayed by tension rods to the tops of the masts using a system of inclined and vertical hangers. They are also tied down at their ends against wind uplift. Across the two primary beams run six

equally spaced secondary UBs from which spring the five bays of the stressed skin plywood vaults. The side thrust of these vaults is resisted by horizontal girders formed between the outer secondary beams on each side and small cantilevers at right angles to them. Overall stability in both directions is provided by the portal action of the beams and columns. This is a delightfully scaled, unassuming, yet appropriate design. The gentle rhythm of the arched vaults complements the verticals and diagonals of the masts and cables in a modest but minor classic fusion of architecture and structure.

The remaining examples are based on two internally masted modules placed end to end but not easily recognisable as such. Both examples have externally expressed lattice spine beams supported on internal masts and cable-stayed from them.

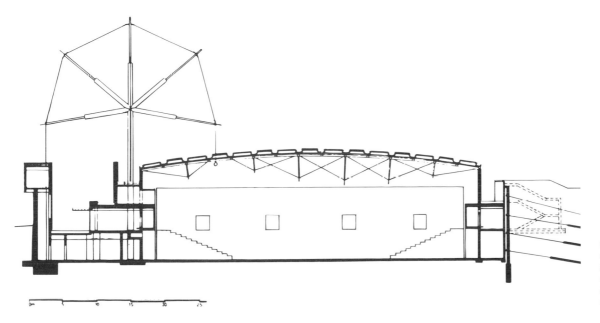

Fig. 7.32
Christof Langhof: sports centre, Charlottenburg, Berlin, 1991, cross section.

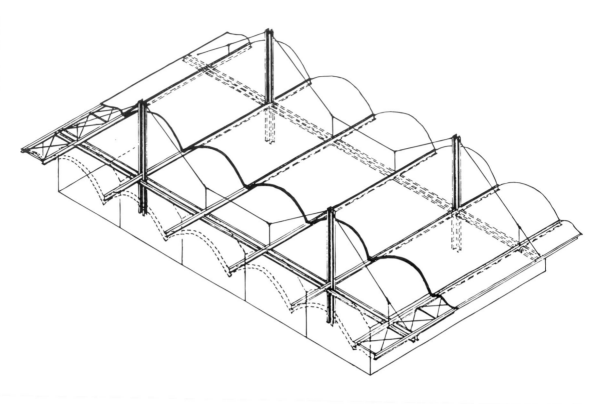

Fig. 7.33
N. Derbyshire:
railway station at
Poole, Dorset,
England, 1988;
isometric
projection of
roof structure.

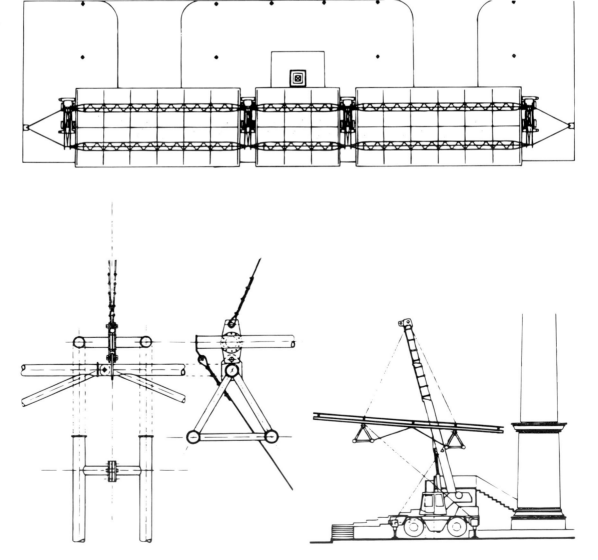

Fig. 7.34
F. Soler:
temporary
canopy to the
Presidential
grandstand,
Place de la
Concorde, Paris,
1986.

In the Paco Rabanne factory of 1986 (see Gazetteer) this primary lattice beam spans the length of the building, which is intended to be the first of a series of similar units to be positioned across a connecting walkway. The beam is supported by pairs of masts, except, unusually, for one end which has a single mast at the hub of a semi-circular end feature. Cable stays run to the intersection points on the lattice.

The Hannover Convention Centre of 1990 (See Gazetteer) is larger than anything we have seen so far, involving 28,500m² of floor space. It is an extensive complex of circular conference and seminar rooms with ancillary facilities 'plugged in' to a long, internal street and public foyer. Above the foyer, at roof level, a large-scale rectilinear space frame is supported on groups of four masts at intermediate points, and on pairs of masts at the ends. These masts and cables support the major spaces whilst other such systems support smaller circular meeting rooms. The main level of the whole complex is supported from below on concrete foundation columns from which spring steel-framed, inverted mushroom capitals.

Finally, we come to the three modules comprising the temporary suspended canopy to the Presidential grandstand erected at the Place de la Concorde in Paris in 1986 (Fig. 7.34). This is an engaging example of *ad hoc* design in which the canopies, two of six bays and one of three, are supported by triangular section beams, the ends of which are slung from cables attached to the jibs of four mobile cranes! The cross-ties to the jacking points of the cranes are particularly interesting in this novel and amusing design. ∎

8

FOUR MAST STRUCTURES AND ASSEMBLAGES OF FOUR AND EIGHT MAST CELLS

In the two preceding chapters we have shown that buildings based on spatial/structural cells supported firstly by single masts and secondly by pairs of masts, together with their patterns of multiple repetitions, can typify distinct families of masted structures. We have seen too, that although two or more examples may embody the same structural logic, this is no guarantee of an immediately recognisable similarity in appearance. The differing configurations of masts, tension members and roof beams can be expressed in a variety of forms and materials according to the demands of function and scale, and as influenced by the architectural and structural concepts put forward by the designers.

We now come to the third, and equally extensive class of masted structures: those based on arrangements of four masts, and on multiples of four-masted and eight-masted cells. The structural logic of this group of buildings involves two important, defining characteristics; the first is that the four masts may be located, in plan, either at the corners of a square spatial/structural cell or at the centres of the four sides. No four mast structure based on this latter principle appears to have been built, but an eight mast arrangement based on the same principle will be described later in this chapter.

The second characteristic is that in rectangular four mast arrangements, the masts may be located not only at the corners of the spatial/structural unit but at any symmetrical, intermediate positions along the two opposite sides. In fact, the positions of the masts can vary continuously from being located at the extreme corners of the basic cell, to being as close together on each side as the demands of function and structural stability will allow.

We have selected three representative mast positions to typify this pattern of continuous variation: firstly, 'corner' mast locations; secondly, 'intermediate' locations and, thirdly, 'spinal' mast locations; this latter term relates to the fact that when a closely-spaced mast arrangement is extended laterally it produces a pattern of pairs of masts down the centre of the building. These topological variants are shown in Fig. 8.1 *(opposite)*; some typical plans are shown in relation to the sub-groups in which they occur, in Fig. 8.2 *(opposite)*.

The third characteristic is that in structural terms, the suspension system extending outwards from the mastheads may be two-way, i. e. in opposite directions on each side of the masts, forming a series of planar frames down one long axis of the building, or two-way, along both axes of an orthogonal planning grid, forming a mat of structural umbrellas.

In this section we shall discuss single volume structures first; continue by dealing with one-way repetitions, and conclude the section by a review of two-way repetitions, distinguishing between cells of square and rectangular proportions.

8.1

FOUR MAST STRUCTURES WITH MASTS LOCATED AT THE CORNERS OF THE BASIC SPACE

Typical plans of structures based on this arrangement and its one-way and two-way repetitions are shown in Fig. 8.2. Only two structures are representative of the basic, 'masts-at-four-corners' space. The first of these, and the earlier in date, consists of a series of temporary training pavilions for the Nat West Bank. However, these were tented, fabric-roofed structures and will therefore be discussed in detail in Chapter 9 (Fig. 9.5).

The remaining example is the new East Croydon Station, completed in 1991 (Plan, Fig. 8.2b). The corners of this long, rectangular building are defined visually and structurally by four pairs of tubular lattice masts of ladder form, set 55m apart (Fig. 8.3). Two major lattice box girders, slightly sloped from mid-span, define the edges of the

building and are cable-stayed to the mastheads. These main girders support the new glazed roof over the central concourse and its flanking shops and offices. The lines of the main structure are continued outwards as short, tapered outriggers, tied back to the bases of the masts (Fig. 8.4). A masted structure was chosen so as to limit the foundations needed to eight points on the existing bridge deck and to minimise disturbance to the ten million passengers who use the station every year. The expressive vestibule through which they pass is as potent a symbol in 20th century technology as was the Doric portico of the former Euston Arch in the stone masonry of 1836.

One-way repetitions of four mast cells

The lateral repetition of a basic four-masted cell with masts at its four corners produces the archetypally simple form of a rectangular building with masts down each side. It is perhaps not surprising, therefore, that this type of structure occurred quite early in the development of masted structures. Two examples, of 1958 and 1960, make a particularly interesting comparison: these are the gymnasium of the Central Washington College at Ellensburg, Washington State, USA, and the Winter Olympic Stadium at Squaw Valley, California. Architecturally, these buildings represent respectively the tectonic and the organic approaches to virtually the same problem. The former is a simple box on the ground, to which masts and cables are attached; the latter concept is essentially that of a shallow, double pitched roof poised over a moulded ground surface (see Fig. 5.13).

The Nicholson Gymnasium covers an area of 119m x 45m. Supporting its almost flat roof are fourteen pairs of pre-stressed concrete masts, 24.3m long, cast in two halves and located at 9.14m centres. From the mast heads, two shorter cables run to the quarter points of the span and, surprisingly, continue externally along the plane of the roof to meet the two longer cables at a combined central anchorage and beam end connector at mid-span. This tension system supports 660mm x 280mm glulam roof beams, joined at mid-span, with concrete purlins on metal hangers. The whole structure is post-tensioned from continuous underground anchorages, each of which takes cables from two masts in a 'V' arrangement at a point just above ground level. The Progressive Architecture reference noted in the Gazetteer shows a set of clear details.

The Squaw Valley Olympic Stadium covers a smaller arena of 91m x 71m. Its main structure consists of seven bays, defined by eight sets of tapered steel masts and box girders at 9.75m centres. Twin cables run from the tops of the outwardly raked masts to the one-third and two-third points on each half span and these act independently. The main box girders are set close to the solid embankments of the seating and continue down the reverse slope, as outriggers, to mass concrete piled anchorages. There are virtually no external walls as such, only a ground-hugging, low profile roof form in keeping with its position in the landscape.

In contrast to the relatively simple structures just mentioned, the Plant House at the Royal Botanical Gardens in Edinburgh is a more complex exercise in intersecting triangulations, also based in essence on repeated four-masted cells (Fig. 8.5). The Plant House consists of a main building which is extremely long in proportion to its width – that is, 128m long by only 19m wide – and a shorter Orchid House at right angles to it (see Fig. 8.2e). The enclosures are divided into five distinct climatic zones. These greenhouses are basically steel portal framed structures of 'mansard' form set on a concrete perimeter beam foundation. At one end of the greenhouse, the lower ground level means that this beam becomes a string course supported on concrete struts and wall units.

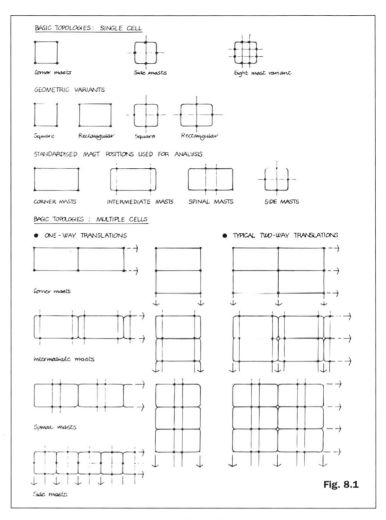

Fig. 8.1

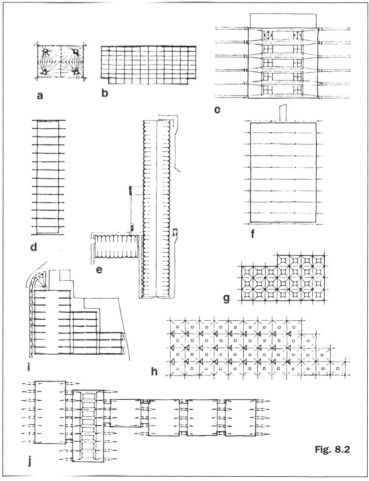

Fig. 8.2

Fig. 8.3
Alan Brookes Associates: East Croydon station, 1992; front elevation.

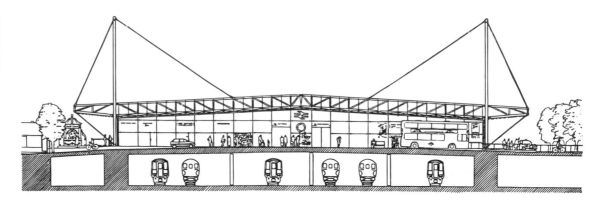

Fig. 8.4
As above: roof structure.

Fig. 8.5 *(below) G. Pearce et al. MPBW Scotland: Plant houses, Royal Botanical Gardens, Edinburgh, 1967; general view, cross section and part roof plan of the main greenhouse.*

From the bottom of each lower member of the portal frames a series of diamond shaped tubular steel pylons inclines slightly outwards, strutted from their high points back to the portal frame at the 'eaves point' of the mansard. Thinner struts run from the angles of the diamonds to the mid-point of the lower member of the portal frame. This whole system forms, in effect, a series of boat shaped space frames which constitute the 'masts' of the tensile structure. On the shallower, upper slopes of

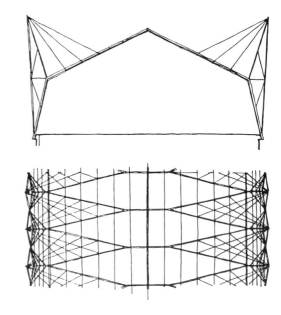

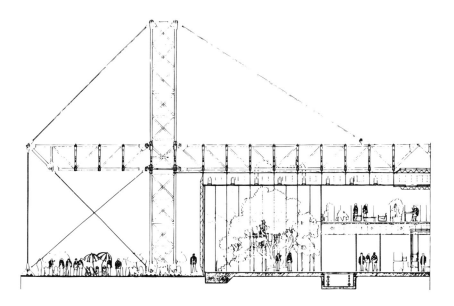

Fig. 8.6
Richard Rogers
and Partners:
entry for Napp
Laboratories
competition,
Cambridge,
England, 1979.

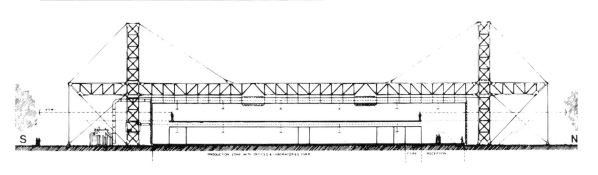

Fig. 8.7 (below)
L. Savioli et al.:
wholesale flower
market, Peschia,
Italy, completed
1981; general
view.

the mansard, the portal frame becomes two Y-shaped members to which are attached five rafters on each side. The prongs of the Y start at eaves level and its stem extends only one rafter bay down from the ridge. Six cables diverge from the tops of the space frames to support the roof framing at the three lowermost rafter positions.

This is a complex structure with a great many difficult connections between members of different form, and at awkward angles. Its sheer length – there are forty-two space frame pylons on each side of the main structure – and its 'cat's cradle' nature make it a *tour de force* in tensile structures of such a comparatively early date. It is an intricate structure which seems to have been meticulously assembled, and these qualities probably make the costs and effort worthwhile.

To conclude this section, two further buildings, completed in 1979 and 1981, need to be described. They show that, by that time, mast architecture was able to be expressed in very large structures, and it is interesting to note that both use the same structural principle; the central section of the roof spans between the ends of two masted cantilever structures running down each side of the main volume.

The smaller of the two examples is the Richard Rogers competition entry for Napp Laboratories in Cambridge, England (Figs. 8.6). The two major design objectives were to provide the maximum

Fig. 8.8
As above;
cross section.

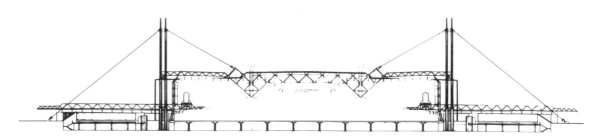

Fig. 8.8
As above;
cross section.

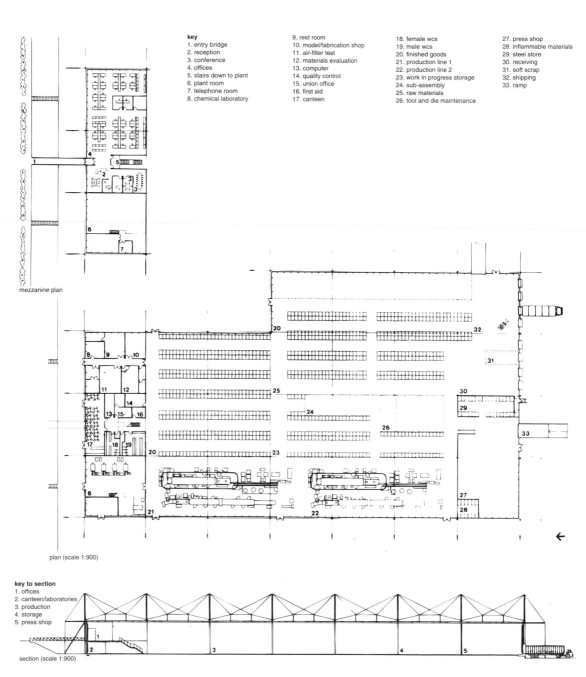

Fig. 8.9
Richard Rogers
and Partners:
Fleetguard
factory, Quimper,
Britanny, France,
1978; plans and
cross section.

key
1. entry bridge
2. reception
3. conference
4. offices
5. stairs down to plant
6. plant room
7. telephone room
8. chemical laboratory
9. rest room
10. model/fabrication shop
11. air-filter test
12. materials evaluation
13. computer
14. quality control
15. union office
16. first aid
17. canteen
18. female wcs
19. male wcs
20. finished goods
21. production line 1
22. production line 2
23. work in progress storage
24. sub-assembly
25. raw materials
26. tool and die maintenance
27. press shop
28. inflammable materials
29. steel store
30. receiving
31. soft scrap
32. shipping
33. ramp

mezzanine plan

plan (scale 1:900)

key to section
1. offices
2. canteen/laboratories
3. production
4. storage
5. press shop

section (scale 1:900)

degree of internal flexibility in plan and section, and to identify the site both in itself and as one of the 'gateways' to Cambridge. The design envisaged a long rectangular volume, 350m by 70m and 8.4m high to accommodate an interior mezzanine floor. The fourteen bays are defined by 25m high tubular lattice towers, with twin tension rods to the one-third points of the external roof beams from which the roof of the building envelope is hung. The lines of the

beams are continued as outriggers, stayed vertically to ground anchorages. This structural form was chosen for its functional and structural clarity and economy. However, from the model, its undeniably clear and rational concept does have a rather 'lumpen' shipyard look about it. Perhaps because of this, the design was unsuccessful in the competition.

The Flower Market at Pescia in Italy (Figs. 8.7, 8.8), is one of the largest, fully-enclosed masted

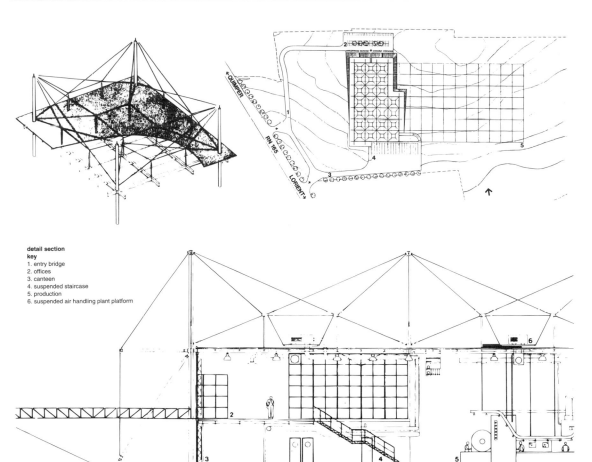

Fig. 8.10
*As above:
typical structural
module, site
plan, part cross
section in detail.*

**detail section
key**
1. entry bridge
2. offices
3. canteen
4. suspended staircase
5. production
6. suspended air handling plant platform

structures to have been built, although the largest – the Benneton factory at Treviso in southern Italy – is about four times its floor area. The project began with a competition, set in 1949, but the winner's initial scheme bore no relation to the final building. This is an enormous structure covering an area of over 10,400m² devoted to the delivery, display and sale of some 400 million flowers per year, together with the associated offices, restaurant and bar. The central space is covered by a roof structure in five bays, each 107m by 19.5m, defined at each of their corners by not one, but a cluster of four tubular masts. The central part of each module consists of a 110m by 20m space frame hung from the innermost masts in each cluster by only four tension rods in each bay. The two outer masts in each cluster of four are back-stayed to ground anchorages. The outer margins of the roof are formed by a series of square frameworks made up of triangular lattice girders. These rest at one end on two major longitudinal beams supported by the cables and, at the other, on a tubular perimeter beam which is threaded through the mast clusters. This side framework forms the horizontal member of the cantilever system on each side, and resists the horizontal forces involved. This is a complex building structurally and visually, but its level of detail and intricacy succeeds in reducing the huge bulk of the accommodation to a human scale – and with an inspirational feel to it. It is almost a 'cathedral to flowers' in modern technology.

Two-way repetitions of four mast cells

Masted structures of this type, that is, those based spatially and structurally on multiple repetitions of a basic, corner-masted unit in two dimensions, are of two kinds depending on their arrangement in plan. One group consists of relatively simple aggregations of adjacent square or rectangular cells, the roof beams of which may be tension stayed in one or two directions from the corner masts. The second group is based on the concept of parallel 'bands' of space and structure, separated by minor modules, forming an alternating rhythm of wide and narrow bays. We will discuss examples of these two concepts in turn.

The first category includes four exemplary buildings of high architectural quality; indeed, the two earliest structures set such high standards of design and innovation as to be largely responsible for the subsequent worldwide interest in mast architecture. These are the Fleetguard Factory at Quimper in France, by Richard Rogers, and the Renault Warehouse at Swindon, by Foster Associates.

The Fleetguard Factory (Figs. 8.9, 8.10, 8.11) is a manufacturing and distribution centre for a range of heavy-duty engine filters. A suspension structure was chosen so as to provide internal flexibility and ease of extension and, by keeping the structural elements outside the building envelope, to allow the perceived height of the building to be reduced

Fig. 8.11
*Foster
Associates:
Renault parts
distribution
warehouse,
Swindon,
Wiltshire,
England.*

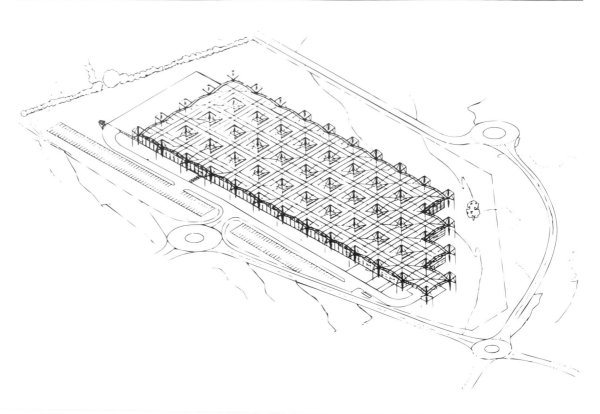

thus minimising its impact on the Breton landscape (see fig. 13.4). The building consists of twenty-five modules, each 18m square, defined by 356mm diameter tubular steel columns which project 8m above the roof. To these are attached the mild steel tension rods which support the roof beams at 6m intervals, four ways, along two axes. A secondary set of rods is provided to counteract the upward wind loads, and a third set is located on the line of the columns to limit deflection and control the reaction of the roof to repeated asymmetrical loading. Most of the structure consists of elements which need little prefabrication and which can be connected simply on site by bolted or pinned connections (see also Fig. 13.5).

The Renault parts and distribution centre (Figs. 8.11, 8.12 and see 12.1 to 12.4) is a larger and

technologically more innovative structure, although it lacks the classic spidery elegance of the Fleetguard building. The brief was for 20,000m² of warehouse space with potential for future expansion, plus a training school, showroom and offices. The initial design was based on cells with a single central mast with radiating beams slung from the top, each four-way 'umbrella' conceived as an independent structure. However, because of the scale of the building, and the consequent need to provide internal bracing and expansion joints, it was decided to develop the design as a series of two-directional portal frames.

The building as completed is organised in a series of 24m square bays, the corners of which are defined by 457mm diameter tubular steel masts, 16m high. In essence, the structural system

Fig. 8.12
*As above:
detail elevation
of typical bay.*

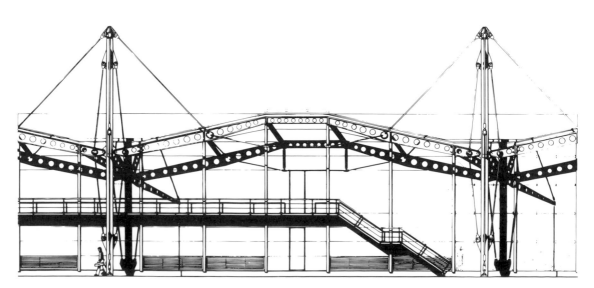

consists of unbraced portal frames, defining the sides and diagonals of the square modules, of which the masts are the vertical members. Additional ties, 7m out from the masts, stiffen the tubes and provide beam/column fixity. The pin-jointed arched beams are supported by pre stressed tension rods at quarter points and provide the inverted catenary to resist wind uplift (Fig. 8.12). The interdependence of the structure means that loading on one bay affects the performance of adjacent bays, the whole roof absorbing the loads without expansion joints or structural connection with the walls. Whereas at Fleetguard an elegant simple box is hung, inert, inside a mast and rod cobweb, at Renault the assertive structure reflects the upward forces of the tension rods – a more restless and active aesthetic. The building is discussed in detail in Chapter 12 and its structure is shown in Chapter 13.

A development of the Fleetguard aesthetic characterises the Magazin d'Usine shopping centre at Nantes in France, also by Richard Rogers (Fig. 8.13). The rectangular building, housing 80 low cost 'factory shops' on two floors, demanded rapid, inexpensive construction and a distinct visual identity. Customers are encouraged to pass round the U-shaped shopping mall past all the shops on both floors before returning to the double height entrance foyer at one end. The plan consists of a group of twenty-seven modules in a 9 x 3 arrangement; each module is 28.8m by 14.4m, with its corners again defined by tubular masts, in this case 28.8m high. Each line of four masts across the building forms a three-span frame, set in sequence at 14.4m intervals down the building. At mid-mast height, transverse and outrigger booms are pin-jointed to the masts, together with longitudinal booms connecting adjacent frames. Thus an overall, tubular roof framework is built up (see Fig. 13.5). The rods and vertical struts support the booms from the mast heads, forming a truss system to resist wind uplift. Sway stiffness is provided by ties on the ends of the outriggers whilst longitudinal stability is achieved by cross-bracing the two bays containing the service cores of goods lifts and toilets. Vertical hangers puncture the roof to support its mild steel section beams; these carry steel decking, insulation and felt. Plant rooms above the central spine wall provide heating and ventilation via ducts about the shopping malls leading to mesh panels above the windows of each shop. This is an exceptionally neat and lucid structure in the Fleetguard aesthetic, but its structural concept is based on laterally-spanning frames rather than centralised 'cellular' modules – an important structural distinction. The shopping centre at Epone is similar in its structural concepts but has an irregular perimeter and is over twice the size (Rice, Thornton and Lenczner, 1989).

The second group of structures in this category consists of buildings and projects in which minor modules occur between major bands of space and

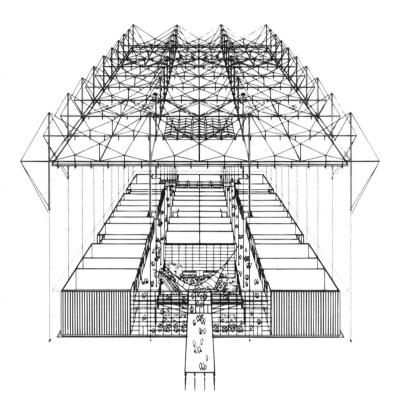

Fig. 8.13
Richard Rogers and Partners: Magazin d'Usine shopping centre, Nantes, France, 1986; expanded perspective.

structure. The end elevation of the 1987 EBC Aerospace building at Delta, British Columbia in Canada shows clearly one possibility in the sectional implications of this planning concept (see Gazetteer). A double-banked system of perimeter masts is separated by a minor module along their adjacent sides. Tension rods from the masts support an inverted catenary framework. The adjacent pairs of masts define the minor module and are cross-braced together above it.

Two parallel bands of space and structure, set slightly apart, also formed the basis of Ian Ritchie's entry for the Reference Collection Building competition at Kew Gardens in London (see Figs 9.14 and 9.15). A larger block of square modules, 15 long by 3 wide is flanked by a smaller block, 6 modules long by 3 wide, the outer modules in that case taking the form of open pergolas. This membrane-roofed design will be described more fully in Chapter 9.

The same pattern of alternate wide and narrow

Fig. 8.14
Ahrends Burton and Koralek: Sainsbury supermarket, Canterbury, Kent, England, 1984; site plan.

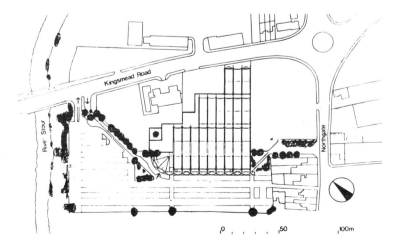

Fig. 8.15
*As previous:
general view.*

housed in three parallel bands of space and structure in lengths of three, six and nine bays respectively, the bands being separated by two minor modules of 3m width. The structural units are defined by four corner masts, each of two CHS tubes, 406mm in diameter. From these, twin 60mm tie rods support the mid-points of the main 356 x 112 universal beam roof members, spaced at 7.2m centres. Tubular outriggers are stayed down to points at the bases of the masts, and also support a delicate external canopy. The structure is an example in which the roof is deliberately made heavier to counteract any tendency to lift under wind uplift. A masted structure was chosen to relieve the visual anonymity of a supermarket, to minimise the bulk of the building in relation to the cathedral and, perhaps, to respond to the verticality of its gothic spires. In all these respects, this beautifully detailed building is extremely successful.

Finally in this group we need to note the Theme Building of the Wonderworld Theme Park proposed for Corby in Northamptonshire, England (Figs. 8.16, 8.17). This is probably the largest masted complex so far designed, although its construction has not yet begun. The design envisaged a structure over a quarter of a mile long covering an area of 38,500m², well in excess, for example, of the otherwise comparable Darling Harbour Exhibition complex of 25,000m².

The intention is that the six main themes of the park will be presented in six parallel bands of accommodation, each band to be 64.8m wide and separated from its neighbours by an 8.1m minor module of circulation and structure. Each band consists of a number of rectangular modules, 62.4m by 6.2m, side by side, at the edges of which

modules orders the space and form of the Sainsbury's supermarket at Canterbury (Figs. 8.14, 8.15). The architectural brief generated the plan, and its architectural expression determined the choice of structure. The three principal functions of a supermarket: delivery, storage and sales are

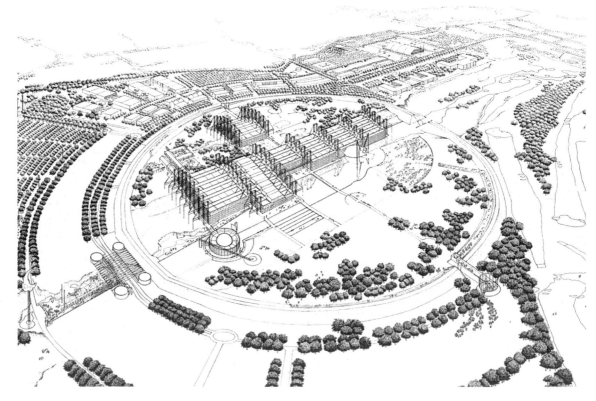

Fig. 8.16
*Derek Walker
and Associates:
Theme Building,
Wonderworld
project, Corby,
Northants,
England, 1982;
aerial view.*

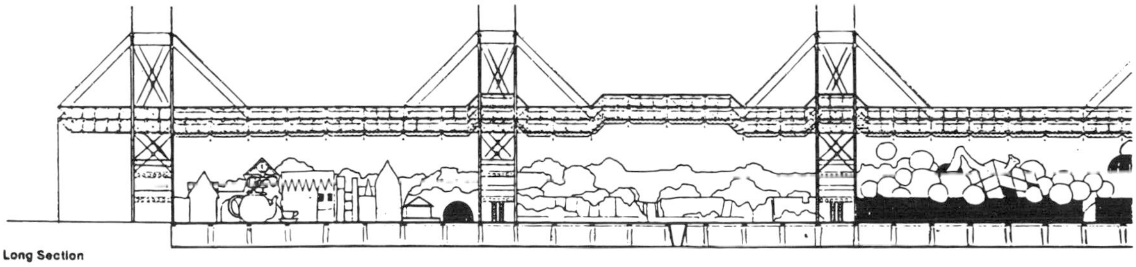

Fig. 8.17
As previous:
part section.

Long Section

the roof planes set down 2.7m to follow the slope of the site. The corners of the modules are identified by high masts in ladder form, from which tension stays run to the quarter points of the main lattice beams. The masts of adjacent modules are braced together above the separating module to form 8.1m wide frameworks. The end masts have the main beams continued out from them to form long outriggers. The reasons for the choice of this form of structure included the ability of cable assistance to reduce the large spans necessary, the speed of erection, ease of phasing and general economy, and its obvious ability to produce a visually exciting and easily recognisable form.

8.2
FOUR MAST CELLS WITH INTERMEDIATE MASTS

We noted in the general introduction to four-mast cells that the masts may be positioned at intermediate points along opposite sides of the cell instead of at the four corners. Moving the masts away from the corners has two advantages: first, introducing what are in effect double balanced cantilevers ought to make the structure more efficient. Secondly, when such cells are repeated laterally, the masts form a spatial and structural pattern of 'nave and aisles' which can be functionally useful: the main central space can be used at its full height whereas the side spaces may incorporate a mezzanine to provide two floors of smaller spaces (Fig. 8.18). In other circumstances, however, the internal columns may constitute obstructions, particularly if the building is a small one. For this reason we would expect structures of this kind to have fairly large spans, and this is in fact the case.

The key to understanding this category of structures lies in the characteristics of the plan and the section. In plan, the examples illustrated are of three kinds: a single-celled building, a three-celled canopy structure which is not immediately recognisable as being of this kind because it is wider than it is long, and other examples of a more normal proportion. The interest in these buildings lies in the sectional implications of the different positions of the masts in plan in relation to the length of the sides of the original spatial and structural cell, i.e. their location across the width of the building. We will deal with the examples in the order described,

which is also roughly in order of increasing size of the building as a whole.

A perfect example of a single volume with four masts positioned at intermediate points along its sides is the airport building at Bundaberg on the mid-Queensland coast of Australia (Figs. 8.19, 8.20). In this structure, a gently curving rectangular vault is suspended over a transparent space, supported by four strong, 400mm diameter tubular columns. These main supports occur at the centres of the second and sixth bays of a seven bay system defined by eight, equally spaced, vertical perimeter ties which restrain the roof shell against wind uplift. The masts are tied together across the building above roof level, and from each masthead four cables run, longitudinally, to the tops of the vertical ties, whilst a fifth cable extends out, laterally, to the ground. In this way the structure is supported and stabilised from the mastheads to the ground anchorages in both directions. In a small airport, this is a system of struts and cables which seems to echo the delicate structure of early biplanes; its poise seems to suggest the lightness of flight, and it is a classic piece of mast architecture on a small scale.

One would expect that laterally repeated rec-

Fig. 8.18 (below)
Comparative roof plans of typical four mast based structures with 'intermediate' mast locations (not to scale)

a. Transcon lines terminal, USA, 1953.

b. Shopping centre, Craigavon, Northern Ireland, 1975.

c. Liquid ink factory project, Milton Keynes, England, 1983.

d. ADT car auction viewing area canopy, Manchester, England, 1989.

e. Terminal 2, Nice Airport, France, 1987.

f. McCormick Place exhibition complex, Chicago, 1988.

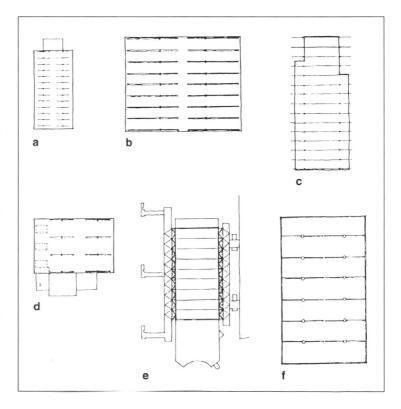

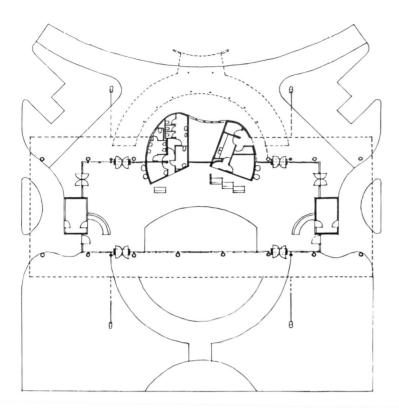

beams spaced 25m apart. These beams take the form of double cantilevers, extending 18m each side of the two masts, spaced apart by a 12m central section. The masts consist of twin CHS members, 18m high with twin, tubular section tension stays on each side. Tubular lattice rafters, slung below the main beams on short hangers, span the 25m between them at 6.0m centres. They carry cold rolled purlins supporting a high performance roof cladding system. The structure is not entirely symmetrical as one end of the roof is extended over the auction rooms and supported by an additional line of four columns at that end (Fig. 8.18d).

The second, wide-proportioned building is the shopping centre at Craigavon in Northern Ireland, a relatively early example of 1975, and the first true masted structure to be erected in the UK. The structure is a straightforward arrangement of eight bays defined by main beams of universal column section, at 12m centres (Fig. 8.18b). Each beam is a double cantilever, supported by tension rods from two 'ladder' form masts in weathering steel. Across the building, the beams span the 48m wide central space between the masts, and continue a further 36m outwards to backstay stanchions on each side. The ratio of the spaces between the supports is 1:1.3:1. An interesting feature is that wind uplift was counteracted by deliberately adding a layer of washed gravel to the Butyl sheet roof covering.

The remaining examples in this category are similar 'nave and aisle' arrangements, of various sizes and proportions.

First, Nicholas Grimshaw's design for a liquid ink factory at Milton Keynes (Figs. 8.23, 8.24), is a clas-

Fig. 8.19
Bligh, Robinson Architects: airport terminal building, Bundaberg, 1989; plan.

Fig. 8.20 (below)
As above: general view.

Fig. 8.21
(below right) Glendinning and Hanson: ADT Group, car auction viewing area canopy, 1989; general view.

tangular cells would form the bay system of a building which was longer rather than wide. That this is not necessarily so as is shown by the plans of two structures in this category. The first of these is the ADT Group's vehicle viewing canopy at Belle Vue, Manchester (Figs. 8.21, 8.22). The main roof covers an area of 106m x 75m. The logic of its structure reflects the functional logic in the architectural brief, coupled with the need to establish a recognisable identity for the building related, perhaps, to the circus tent which once occupied the site. The canopy was required to cover three long blocks of parked cars, each block related to its own auction room at one end. In response to this, the roof consists of three masted cells, 106m long, defined by four triangular section main lattice

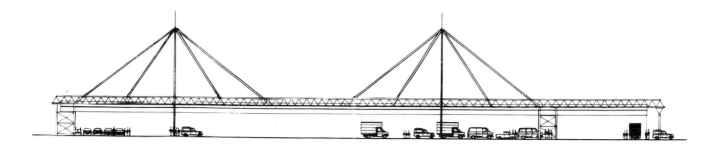

sic example. The building consists of a central, 39.6m wide production space with a 7.4m working height. On either side are 10.8m wide bands of two-storey space for ancillary purposes (Fig. 8.18c). The cross section is sober and rational; masts and roof beams form double cantilevers, with a rafter length of 15m between them; the vertical backstays are positioned just outside the external walls; as the roof decking is located above the structure an awkward eaves detail would have had to be designed if the building had proceeded to construction.

Secondly, in this remaining group, the Aerogare at Nice Airport, is unusual in two respects: firstly, the spaces on each side of the central space are surprisingly narrow in relation to the main space, i.e. in the ratios of 1:7:1 (Fig. 8.18e); secondly, the ten masts and cables support an unusual form of lens-shaped roof with sloping clerestory glazing along its sides (Fig. 8.25). This is a large building, over 18,000m² in total area.

The last building worthy of note in this category is the McCormick Place exhibition complex in Chicago. This is a massive development; the architectural problem was to provide almost 140,000m² of space for exhibition and ancillary purposes, on a restricted site and partly over a network of railway tracks. The solution was to provide a two-storey podium, the top of which forms the floor of the main exhibition hall; this has an internal height of 12.2m. The hall is covered by a seven-bay, double-cantilever masted structure, straightforward in form, but very large in scale. The twelve masts are spaced on a grid of 36.6m x 73.2m, with 36.6 outside cantilevers tied down externally on the East and West sides (Fig. 8.18f). The scale of this structure is such that the tapered concrete masts extend to a height of 18.3m above the roof and are wide enough to act as extract and input ducts at higher and lower levels respectively; the reference in *Progressive Architecture* includes a cross section of these ducts. The tension system, too, is

Fig. 8.22
As above: long section.

Fig. 8.23
Nicholas Grimshaw and Partners: projected design for a liquid ink factory, Milton Keynes, 1983; plan.

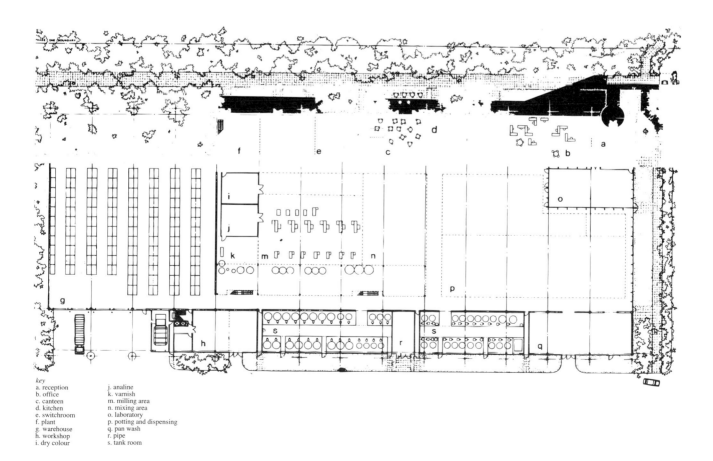

key
a. reception
b. office
c. canteen
d. kitchen
e. switchroom
f. plant
g. warehouse
h. workshop
i. dry colour
j. analine
k. varnish
m. milling area
n. mixing area
o. laboratory
p. potting and dispensing
q. pan wash
r. pipe
s. tank room

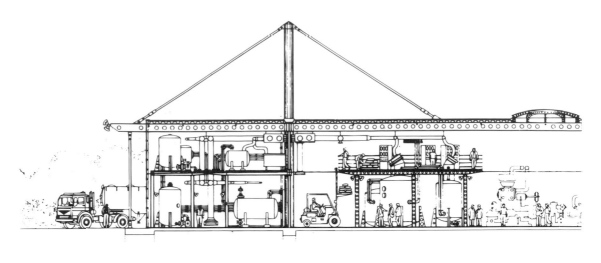

Fig. 8.24
As previous: part cross section.

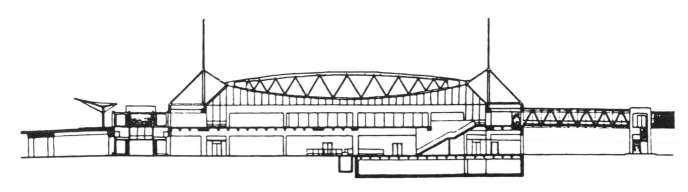

Fig. 8.25
P. Andreu: Terminal 2, Nice airport, Nice, France, 1987; cross section.

unusual in consisting of parallel cables in a 'harp' pattern, rather than the more common radiating form (Fig. 8.26).

8.3
FOUR MAST CELLS WITH 'SPINAL' MASTS

We now come to structures which are based on the principle of two pairs of closely spaced masts positioned on the opposite long sides of a basic rectangular spatial/structural cell. When repeated laterally, this arrangement results in a long building with pairs of masts defining a 'spine' along its centre line. This is not only useful for movement and servicing but also as the armature of an 'open form' for future extension. The buildings noted fall

into two groups: firstly, six buildings comprising an 'Inmos family' (although the Inmos factory was not the first instance of the basic idea), and secondly, structures in which the masts are set much closer together in forming the series of vertical frames of buildings which lack the horizontal spread of the members of the Inmos group. We will explore each of these categories in turn; some typical roof plans of the buildings mentioned are shown in Fig. 8.27.

Buildings making up an 'Inmos family'

The six buildings in this category are variations on the common organising concept just mentioned, i.e. that of using pairs of masts to define a 'spine', usually used for movement and servicing, along the centre-line of the building. From the tops of

Fig. 8.26
Skidmore, Owings and Merrill: McCormick Place exhibition centre, Chicago, 1988; cross section.

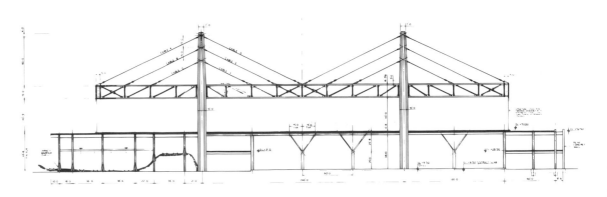

the masts, tension stays are used to reduce the spans of the main beams on each side of the spine. In relation to the width of the spine, the outward cantilevers of the main beams are larger than usual so that their end support and stiffening requires careful consideration. The first four examples are comparatively similar in form and scale, whereas the remaining two are altogether larger. The best-known example of this organising concept is the Inmos microchip factory at Newport in South Wales, completed in 1982. However, the idea first appeared earlier in the form of the Tosho printing works at Haramachi in Japan, in 1961 (Fig. 8.28).

For this building, designed by Kenzo Tange and his team, the architects' brief was to provide an unobstructed space with constant temperature, lighting and colour conditions for a critical production process. In fulfilling these requirements, the building consists of a central movement and servicing spine, with a 30m wide manufacturing area on each side. Between the masts which define the spine, and occupying the whole of its width above roof level, is a reinforced concrete box girder, carried by the lower part of the masts. At the bottom edges of this continuous box are the supports for the main, triangular lattice girders which span outwards to perimeter columns. The main beams are tension-assisted by CHS tubes from two masts in a 'V' formation and the effect of this pattern of dual supports is to locate the main beams between the cross axes of the masts rather than in parallel with them – a most unusual arrangement which does make some contribution to stiffening the roof framework. The complete design, though an innovative and interesting masted structure in its own right, seems to have attracted only a minimum of attention in 1961.

In contrast, its close formal successor, the Inmos microchip factory at Newport in South Wales (Figs. 8.29, 8.30, 8.31), became the focus of considerable interest and admiration after its completion in 1982. The architects, Richard Rogers and Partners, faced a more demanding brief but, in collaboration with Tony Hunt, the engineer, produced a classic example of mast architecture.

Inmos required a building for microchip manufacture, research and development, together with offices and a restaurant. Most importantly, the brief specified a Class 100 clean room, implying a higher servicing intensity and maximum flexibility both during installation and thereafter. In response to this, the key feature of the plan is the location of the 3,000m², unobstructed clean room on one side of the movement and servicing spine, balanced by the other accommodation, (separated by one open, landscaped bay) on the other. The main plant loads along the length of the building are carried by a multi-level spine formed by pairs of twinned masts, cross braced in both vertical planes. Replacing Kenzo Tange's box duct

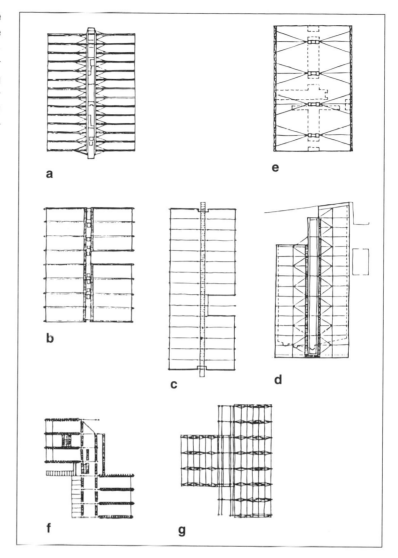

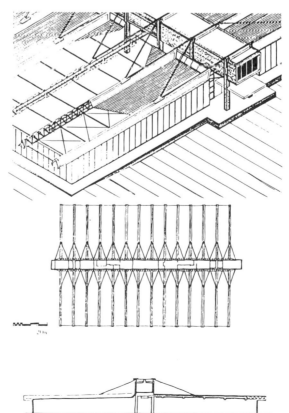

Fig. 8.27 (above) Comparative roof plans of typical four mast based structures with 'spinal' mast locations (not to scale).

a. Tosho printing works, Haramachi, Japan, 1961.

b. Inmos microchip factory, Newport, South Wales, 1982.

c. Patscenter, Princeton, USA, 1983.

d. Sainsbury, Canterbury, England; competition entry, 1982.

e. British pavilion, Osaka Expo, Japan, 1970.

f. Liverpool Garden Festival pavilion, England; competition entry, 1982.

g. Liverpool Garden Festival pavilion, England; competition entry, 1982.

Fig. 8.28 (left) Kenzo Tange and ERTEC: Tosho printing works, Haramachi, Japan, 1961.

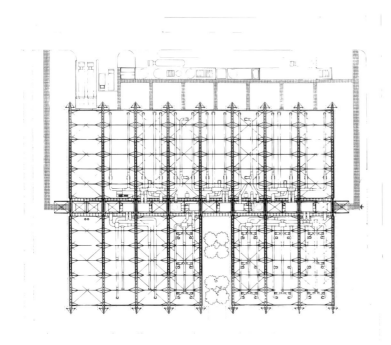

by openly exposed major servicing elements gave the required servicing flexibility and enabled significant savings to be made in the building envelope and in total construction time. On each side of the spine, the 36m span prismatic trusses are tension-assisted at the one-third and two-third points along their span. This exposed lattice roof structure is the upper services distribution zone, and supports an underslung roof system. The structure was designed for simplicity, both in fabrication and erection, by the use of repetitive structural elements and by designing a family of simple, elegant connections in high strength stainless steel.

Kenzo Tange's original concept of a twin-mast 'spine' also formed the basis of a third project, published concurrently with the Inmos design in 1982. This took the form of an entry, by MacCormac, Jamieson and Pritchard, for the Sainsbury supermarket competition (Fig. 8.32). Their design is for a relatively modest building, with a gaiety and lightness unknown in most supermarkets. Twin masts define a central spine to the building, along which runs a concrete first floor to provide two hours' fire

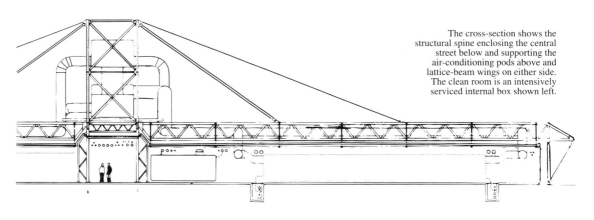

Fig. 8.29 (above) *Richard Rogers and Partners: Inmos microchip factory, Newport, South Wales, 1982; plan.*

Fig. 8.30 (right) *As above; part cross section.*

Fig. 8.31 (below) *As above; detail of central circulation and servicing spine defined by the masted structure.*

The cross-section shows the structural spine enclosing the central street below and supporting the air-conditioning pods above and lattice-beam wings on either side. The clean room is an intensively serviced internal box shown left.

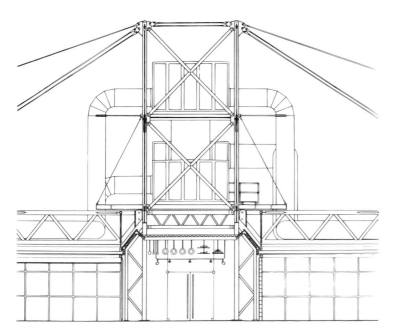

resistance for the upper level offices, and to take up the horizontal compression component of the roof framework. Each mast supports three cables which run to the mid-points of the cranked roof beams. This is a natural and human scaled building. It is interesting to note that although this entry was unsuccessful, the winner of the competition was another masted structure, that of ABK described earlier (Figs. 8.14, 8.15).

The fourth example of the 'Inmos concept' is the first phase of the research and development facility of Patscenter International completed in 1983 on an industrial park near Princeton, New Jersey, USA. The client is an American offspring of the company for whom the Richard Rogers Partnership designed a facility of similar function, but non-masted form, in England in 1975. Their Princeton building has a morphology which is similar to that of the earlier Inmos design in that it uses a suspension structure to enable unobstructed space to be provided on each side of the move-

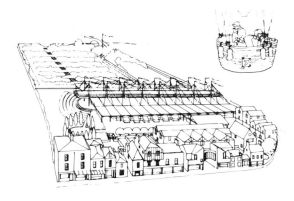

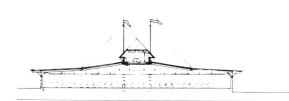

Inmos, and Peter Rice, of Ove Arup and Partners, was in charge of the engineering of the Patscenter building.

A comparison of two masted competition entries

The remaining projects to be noted in this section are two surprisingly similar entries, by the Napper Collerton Partnership and Nicholas Grimshaw and Partners for the competition, held in 1982, to design a major exhibition building for the Liverpool Garden Festival (Figs. 8.34, 8.35).

The designs had to reconcile the rather general but still exacting demands of the festival exhibition spaces with the more precise requirements for long term recreational use once the festival had closed. Both design teams combined the English traditions of the glazed arcade and the particularly appropriate conservatory and winter garden, with the dramatic effect of a successful exhibition structure.

Each of the two proposals comprises two, twin-mast spines spaced some distance apart to define a much wider circulation spine similar to that of a shopping 'mall', but neither design uses all the possible 'served' space available on each side of the

Fig. 8.32 (left) MacCormick, Jamieson and Pritchard: entry for the Sainsbury supermarket, Canterbury, competition, 1982.

Fig. 8.33 Richard Rogers and Partners: Patscentre, Princeton, USA, 1983; cross section.

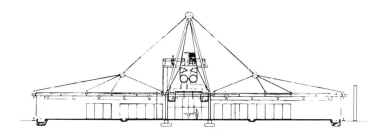

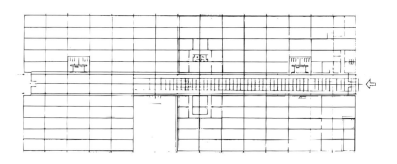

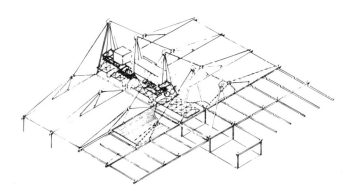

ment and serving route. However, there are significant differences between the functional constraints and the architectural forms of the two designs. For example, the Patscenter's laboratory and office space did not need the high levels of cleanliness, servicing and security demanded by a micro-chip facility such as Inmos, and the later building had to be simpler in construction because in the US construction industry unconventional construction is costed heavily. Moreover, Patscenter is smaller: the main beams span 25m rather than the 40m at Inmos whilst their floor areas are 40,000m^2 and 85,000m^2 respectively.

There are equally significant differences between the suspension structures, most noticeably in that the cross-braced lattice mast frames of Inmos are replaced by simple tubular A-frames with prominent, flat washer connections at the main nodal suspension points (Fig. 8.33). This structural system has four elements:

i)   The four parallel cable-stayed beam systems comprising the A-frames, the two main beams on either side, and their quadruple hanger.

ii) The portal frame on which the A-frames rest.

iii) The outer ties which restrict the up-lift of the roof.

iv) The suspended service capsule supports comprising longitudinal lattice trusses, the hangers of which are used to stabilise the tops of the A-frames.

It should be noted that Tony Hunt and his associates were the engineers collaborating on

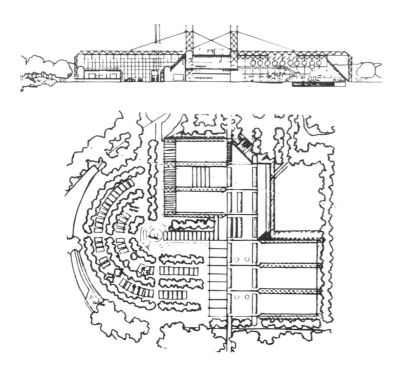

*Fig. 8.34
Napper,
Collerton,
Partnership:
competition
entry, Liverpool
Garden Festival
pavilion, 1982.*

main movement area. The former uses two groups of three bays on alternate sides, separated by an entrance bay, whilst the latter simply provides a smaller volume located centrally on one side and a larger one extending the whole length of the other. Both designs are sufficiently large in scale to enable mezzanine floors to be provided in the spine and in the narrow flanking spaces.

In the Napper Collerton entry, the roof structure over the main volume appears to be more direct, comprising conventional prismatic lattice girders, supported at their mid-points from the mastheads, running from the masts at one end to lattice columns at the other (Fig. 8.34). However, the true cross section, i. e. with a large volume on one side of the spine and smaller units of accommodation on the other, responds more specifically to the three sets of spatial and functional circumstances by using three different structural systems. This somewhat 'tailored' Napper Collerton approach thus makes an interesting comparison with the typical Grimshaw approach of two 'big boxes', identical in cross section, attached to a linear circulation structure. Although the total estimated costs were identical at £2,250,000, this related to relative floor area costs, at the time of £313.20m^2 for the Grimshaw entry and £234.064m^2 for the Napper Collerton scheme.

In structural terms, in the Grimshaw scheme the twinned masts support a triangulated system of upper ties and lower level struts to support one end of the main horizontal roof beams. These take the form of 356mm CHS spars, stabilised by cross trees and tension rods in the same way as a yacht mast. The outer ends rest on 457mm CHS columns, and the whole system defines a 38m clear span space on each side of the central spine. This exoskeleton of masts, struts, ties and spars supports a series of barrel vault roofs comprising polycarbonate sheet on curved metal rafters over the plant spaces, pool hall and spine, and insulated sheeting with a pvc membrane over the main hall (Fig. 8.35).

It is interesting to note that although the competition entry was unsuccessful, its roof spanning system was actually used, almost identically, in the Ladkarn (Haulage) Ltd office and workshop building designed by the Grimshaw Partnership a year or two later and erected on the London Docklands in 1984 (see Gazetteer). The shining, profiled steel cladding, with its soaring masted structure, 23m high and picked out in red, fulfilled the client's requirements for a highly visible headquarters building. However, it was taken down in 1987, re-erected in Alpine Way, Beckton, London EC6, and sold on to another company.

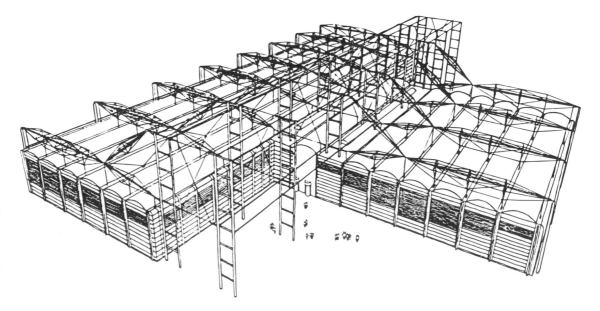

*Fig. 8.35
Nicholas
Grimshaw and
Partners:
competition
entry, Liverpool
Garden Festival
pavilion, 1982.*

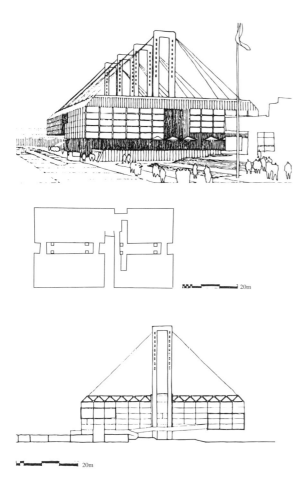

Fig. 8.36 (left)
P. Powell and H.
Moya: British
pavilion, Osaka
Expo, Japan,
1970; general
view, sketch plan
and section.

Structures characterised by vertical masted frameworks

We continue the exploration of this concept by the analysis of three projects characterised by a twin-mast, spinal layout, but which lack the wide, flanking spans of the Inmos model. In the following examples, the pairs of masts perform a somewhat similar spatial and structural function, but they lack any centralised servicing element and are more

modest in their spans – although the first example was a sizeable building.

In this case, the British Pavilion at the Osaka Expo of 1970 (Fig. 8.36), the essential formal idea of the building envelope was that of an empty box, turned upside down and supported clear of the ground by cables from a series of vertical frames which project through the roof top, i.e. through the bottom of the inverted box. The building had two important features: first, the four pairs of masts did not define a usable circulation space, but an unusable void between what are, in fact, four 'boxes' of gallery accommodation connected at high level by a diagrid roof structure; secondly, the masts were of major visual importance because, being completely unstayed, four pairs of substantial box sections connected at their highest points were required to achieve the necessary stiffness. This was a large structure of some power, but with a subtle Japanese quality in the enclosing walls.

The remaining projects in this category are much smaller: the first is a small house at Kamakura, in Japan (Fig. 8.37). Here, the idea of a vertical masted spine is externalised in the form of a long, cross-braced framework, to form an exposed walkway. Attached to this connecting deck system are a number of curved and eccentrically sloping roofs which project beyond their 'caboose' type individual rooms. In total, the house is an architectural version of a Russian Constructivist composition of great tension and dynamism to which the mast and cable system makes a major contribution.

Lastly, the Bognor Regis station project (Figs. 8.38-8.40) by Weston, Williamson, uses the basic concept in two forms of open canopy structures, re-interpreting the lightness of Victorian cast-iron construction. In the former, closely-spaced vertical frames have a metal diaphragm between the masts at mid-height forming a canopy with the twin butterfly roofs on either side. Upper and lower ties run

Fig. 8.37
Riken Yamamoto
and Field Shop:
house at
Kamakura,
Japan, 1989;
general view.

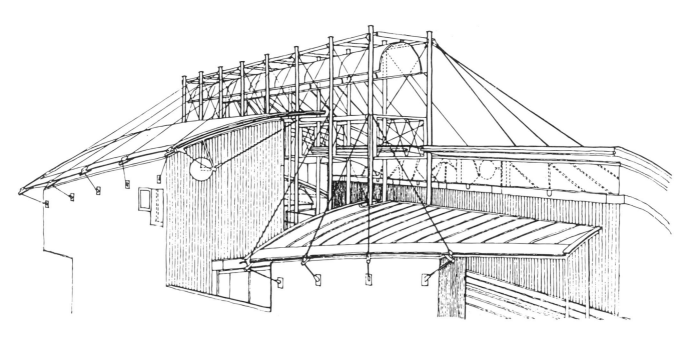

Fig. 8.38
Weston,
Williamson
Architects:
canopy
structures for
Bognor Regis
station, England;
section.

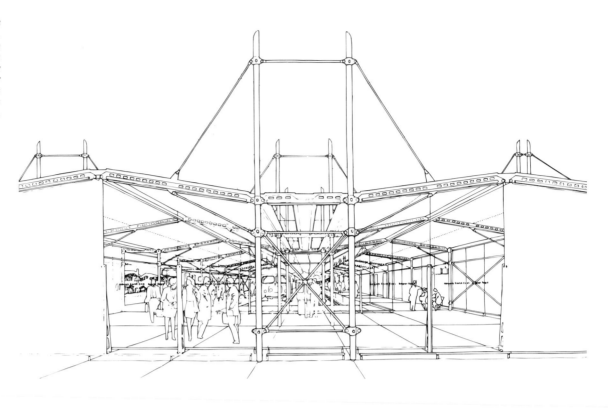

to the mid-spans of the sloping cantilevered rafters which span across the tracks. The connectors of the system slip on to the columns like rings on a finger, and are welded in position. This design promises to be one of the lightest and most delicate pieces of mast architecture if it proceeds to construction.

Fig. 8.39
As above:
joint detail.

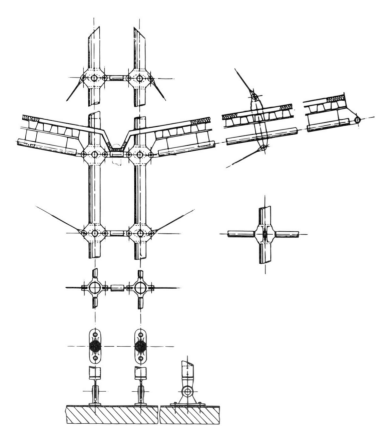

In other locations in the same project, a second type of structure brings the two masts even closer together, with only a valley gutter between them (Figs. 8.39, 8.40). At this point, therefore, we reach the most extreme position possible of a four-masted spinal type of arrangement, where the spine has been reduced to an absolute minimum width for constructional and functional viability.

8.4

FOUR MAST AND EIGHT MAST CELLS WITH SIDE MASTS

All the three types of four mast configurations described in the previous sections have originated in one of the two primary mast location strategies, that is, positioned at the corners of a basic spatial/structural cell. The alternative generic strategy is to position the masts not at the corners of the cell but centrally on each of its four sides. This strategy can be effected using four or eight masts, as we shall see, and in theory at least the arrangements can be extended in one or two directions as shown earlier in Fig. 8.1. Not all of these abstract possibilities have so far been realised in actual buildings. However, those which we are aware of will be reviewed in this section, together with a further example which has five masts on each side, used in conjunction with a central tower rather than achieving major spans across an unobstructed space. Outline roof plans of the buildings mentioned are shown in Fig. 8.41.

The originating arrangement, that of a single space with four mast supports each at the centre

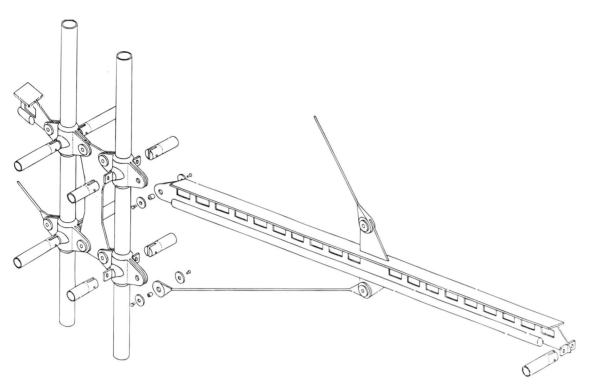

Fig. 8.40 (left)
As above:
component
system.

Fig. 8.41 (below)
Comparative roof
plans of typical
side mast
arrangements
using four or
more masts (not
to scale).

a. Leisure centre,
West Swindon,
Wiltshire,
England, 1985.

b. Warehouse,
Hannover,
Germany, 1986.

o. Tilburg railway
station, Tilburg,
Holland, 1964.

d. Hall 7,
National
Exhibition Centre,
Birmingham,
England, 1980.

of one of the sides, is one configuration of which no examples seem to have been built. However, that it is possible to extend the concept linearly is shown by the Tilburg Station structure (Fig. 8.42). This consists of three square spatial/structural cells, each having four points of support at the centres of the sides in the way which we are discussing. However, the structure does not correspond completely to the masted model we have in mind because only those supports on the long sides are in the form of masts; the remainder consist of double or quadruple concrete pillars positioned centrally on the Island platform of the station. Each of the three cells is roofed by four hyperbolic paraboloids separated from each other by narrow sloping bands: the overall area of the whole structure is 63m x 21m.

The eight mast version of the side mast strategy we are considering, i.e. involving two masts equally spaced on each of the four sides of an uninterrupted space, is shown in two buildings of widely different scale and nature, one of which is square and the other slightly rectangular.

The smaller of the two, but later in date, is the warehouse at Hannover, completed in 1986 (Figs. 8.43, 8.44, 8.45). In this case, a firm trading in dental products needed a clear, high space to accommodate a semi-automatic shelving system together with a small area of office space and a loading bay. The resulting building is 30m square. Its roof is supported by cables from the tops of the eight masts which are equally spaced around the four sides. At the four intersecting points of the cables, short hangers support the flat roof framework, their upper parts forming the vertical members of a

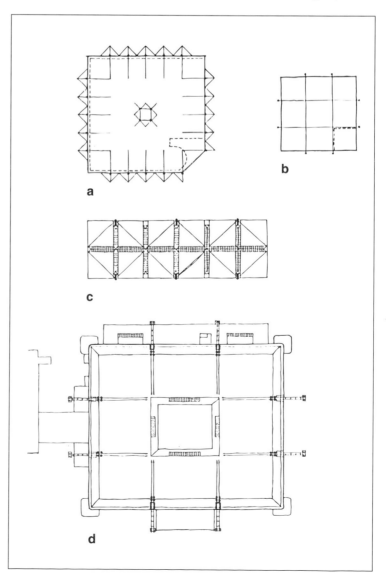

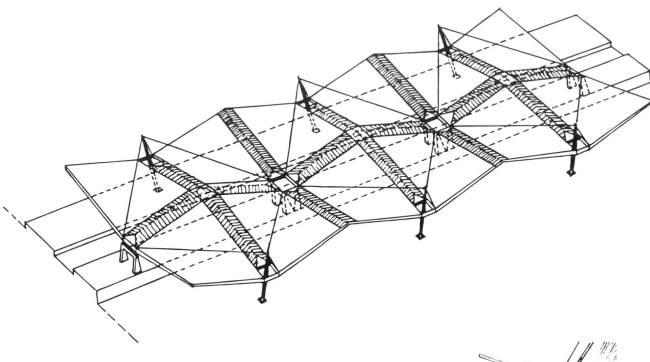

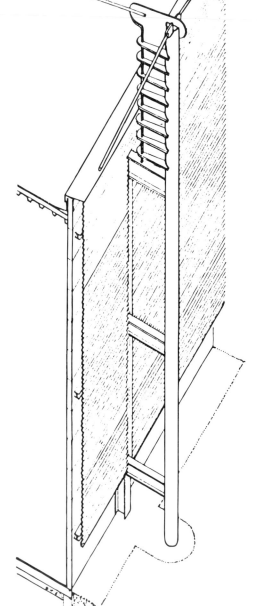

Fig. 8.42 (above) K. van der Gast: railway station canopy, Tilburg, Holland, 1964.

Fig. 8.43 (below) K. Schuwirth and E. Erman: dental products warehouse, Hannover, Germany, 1986; plans and section.

Fig. 8.44 (right) As above: axonometric detail of external column.

stress-reversal bracing system. The steel tube masts are concrete filled for fire protective and statical reasons. Protection for the structure in general is effected by the fire proofing of the interior shell.

An interesting and unusual feature of this building is that there are no outriggers or backstays to tie back the tension forces produced by the suspended roof structure. This obviously has implications for the design of the vertical elements of the structure which are, in fact, vierendeel stanchions of unusual design. The innermost member, positioned in the plane of the external wall, is an I section beam which runs to roof level only. This beam is connected by other stub beams to the outer main member, an externally

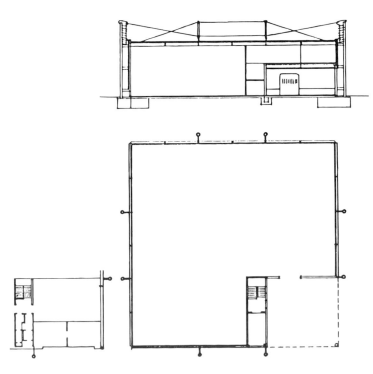

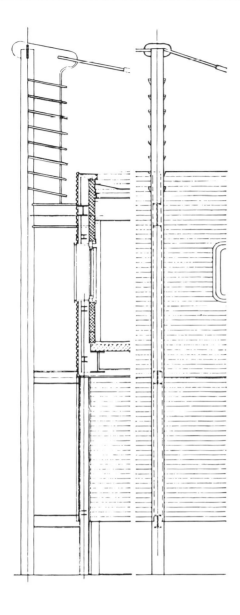

A similar structural logic underlies the very much larger Hall 7 of the National Exhibition Centre in Birmingham (Fig. 8.46). The architectural brief for this building required a design for a public arena and column free exhibition space of 10,000m², together with ancillary accommodation, all to be provided within a short time-scale. The clear space eventually provided measures 108m x 90m. Masted structures of this size have to compete with several other forms of structure. However, initial feasibility studies showed that single-span trusses would need to be so deep as to be difficult to transport, space-framed domes would have taken too long to assemble and erect, and the material for a fabric roof would not be supplied in time. Weight comparisons, too, showed that a masted structure needed less steel than a deep truss scheme.

The completed building needs only eight supports for the whole roof. It consists of nine, virtually equal sized Nodus space frames supported by four tubular steel lattice box trusses, two in each direction, which were, incidentally, delivered in 30-34m lengths. The trusses intersect at the one-third points where they are supported by the tension stays (Fig. 8.41d). These consist of pairs of steel tubes which pass over the tops of the eight 36m high masts to outriggers and thence to the ground tension piles. The masts themselves are in the form of four-post vierendeel lattices. Around the main volume, a 3m wide perimeter zone is defined by further 12m high vierendeel frames at 6m centres, providing overall stability and accommodating the enhanced range of environmental services. The space frames were assembled at ground level with sprinkler and lighting systems installed, whilst the central unit is at a higher level for clerestory lighting and increased headroom.

In practical terms, this building satisfied the requirements of the brief well, and was designed and constructed in sixteen months. Architecturally, it is a major landmark amongst the uninspired and uninspiring group of halls making up the main NEC complex which falls somewhat short of its continental forerunners.

Lastly in this group of side mast orientated struc-

Fig. 8.45 (left)
As previous: eaves detail.

expressed steel tube which runs to the full height required as a cable anchorage. To provide the substantial additional stiffness which this tube requires, a rather Art Deco composition of vertical and horizontal welded steel flats extends inwards from the tube above roof level (Fig. 8.45). This produces a series of decorative finials around the perimeter which is unusual, attractive, and of functional origin!

Fig. 8.46
Edward D. Mills and Partners: Hall 7, National Exhibition Centre, Birmingham, England, 1980.

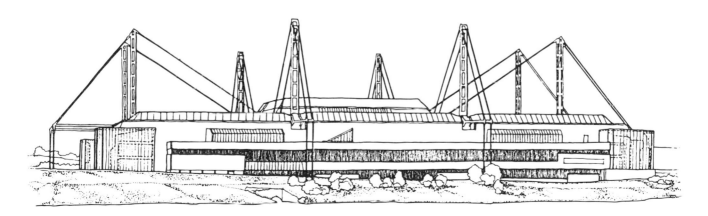

Fig. 8.47
*Thamesdown
Borough
Architects with
Anthony Hunt
Associates:
Leisure Centre,
West Swindon,
Wiltshire,
England, 1985;
engineer's
conceptual
sketches.*

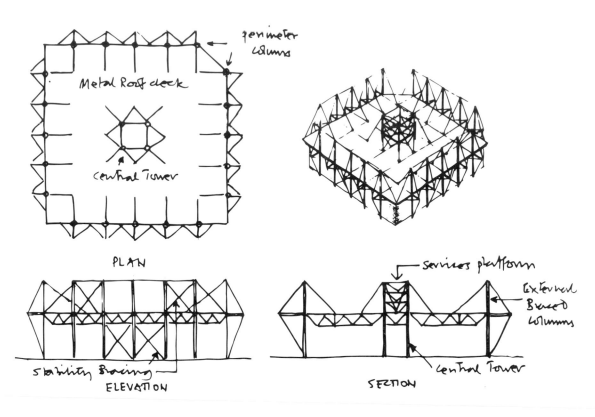

Fig. 8.48
*As above:
sketch of
exterior, outline
plan and part
cross section.*

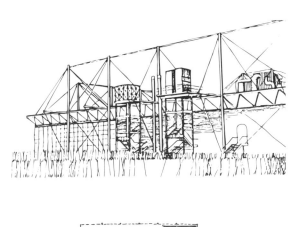

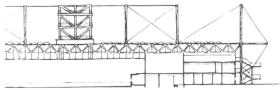

tures we need to note the West Swindon Leisure Centre in Wiltshire (Figs. 8.47, 8.48). The Borough of Thamesdown required a leisure centre to house an extensive set of recreation facilities for the increasing population of West Swindon. The facilities to be provided included a 25m swimming pool, a sports hall, library, drama studio, health suite, youth club, community centre, squash courts, snooker rooms and associated eating and drinking facilities. A square plan with inherent multi-axial and neutral properties acknowledged the island site and allowed a flexible response to the different surrounds on each face. This geometry enabled a strong identifiable umbrella of a roof structure to be designed independently of the resolution of the interior requirements.

The roof structure of the building takes the form of a two-way grid of tubular steel lattice girders, 2.5m deep and spanning 93.6m. These are exposed on the interior and supported externally by tension rods from four sets of five masts at 14.4m centres along each of the four sides of the building. A secondary grid of lattice rafters supports the flat roof decking. Stability around the perimeter is provided by conventional cross bracing in selected bays. Architecturally, a prominent and unifying 'cornice' denotes the thickness of the roof zone in the form of a triangular lattice girder at eaves level which also stiffens the top of the profile steel wall cladding. The clarity of this well detailed building is mainly the result of the major contribution made by its masted structure to unifying the variety of elements in the accommodation.

This concludes the main part of our taxonomic analysis of masted structures. Not all the examples cited in the Gazetteer have been illustrated, or mentioned specifically. Nevertheless, we believe that most of the significant and noteworthy examples have been covered. At the outset, we decided to keep separate those structures which incorporate fabric or other flexible membrane roofs, and we now turn to these. ∎

9

MASTED MEMBRANE STRUCTURES

In the totality of masted structures there are two particularly characteristic features which occur in some buildings but not in others: these are roofs which consist of flexible membranes, and cantilevered, grandstand forms of structure associated with raked spectator seating. These features have such significant technical and formal implications as to identify distinct sub-groups of structures and to justify their being treated separately. We shall deal with masted membrane structures here, and with grandstand structures in the next chapter.

How Frei Otto and his collaborators transformed the world of tents and awnings in the 1950s and 60s has been outlined in Chapter 3. In terms of time, the basic research and development work began in 1959 and reached its culmination in the impressive cable-network awnings of the Munich Olympic arenas in 1972. There seems then to have been something of a pause until, in 1982, the Haj airport terminal marked the beginning of a new surge of membrane roof designs. These took the form of more permanent masted structures than the garden festival and exhibition tents of the first phase. The masted membrane structures of the second phase appeared mainly between 1985 and 1988, although there are one or two earlier ones. Examples continue to be completed today, when they are becoming commonplace.

To appreciate the nature and scope of these more recent membrane-roofed buildings, their analysis must be based on a different principle from that used so far. It is not appropriate to use the disposition of the masts in relation to an enclosed space as a basis for analysis because that relatively simple relationship cannot adequately reflect the range of forms that membrane roofs can take; it is more appropriate to use the configuration of the membrane itself, as determined by the means of support and stress induction to characterise and order particular examples. Using this approach, there are three ways, in principle, of suspending a membrane roof from above, in addition to using internal masts to raise it up from below.

9.1

MEMBRANES SUPPORTED DIRECTLY FROM THE MASTS

The simplest method is to attach a warped surface to masts at the four corners of a square planning module. This principle is suitable for small spans and is the basis of the twenty-four square modules which make up the awnings of the Visitors' Centre at the Yulara Tourist resort near Ayers Rock in central Australia (Fig. 9.1).

For larger spans, the warped plane needs to be

Fig. 9.1
Philip Cox and Partners: Visitors' Centre, Yulara National Park, NT, Australia, 1985.

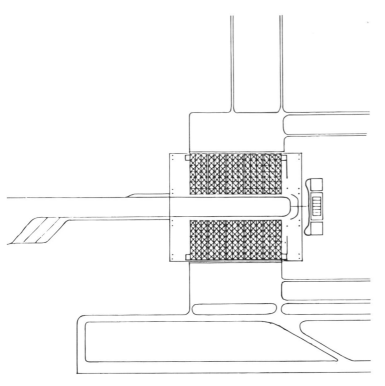

There are two basic ways of thus raising the central parts of a membrane roof: one can either devise a system of cables running from the mastheads, or construct an external framework over the roof and suspend the membrane by short cable ties from it.

9.2
MEMBRANES SUPPORTED BY CABLE NETWORKS

The cable suspension principle has been adopted in a number of buildings and projects. In an early example of 1968, Frei Otto's relatively simple design based on a square module for a building site covering at Southwark in South London was outlined. The cables are of two kinds: the main carrying cables have the primary function of spanning the space from corner to corner, whilst suspended from them are shorter, suspension cables which connect the pick-up points on the roof to connectors on the carrying cables. The design also shows how the outermost corners of the structure can be supported by raking props in the plane of the walls to provide horizontal stiffness and avoid the need for external guys on a restricted site.

Individual pick-up points on a membrane roof inevitably lead to higher stress concentrations around those points. To even these out, single-point suspensions have been replaced by sus-

Fig. 9.2
Skidmore, Owings and Merrill: Haj Terminal, Jeddah, Saudi Arabia, 1982; site plan.

picked up at points across its surface, not only to maintain the curvature and therefore the stiffness of the membrane, but also to produce sufficient headroom for the activities to be accommodated beneath it, and to provide for rainwater disposal near the supports rather than in the centre.

Fig. 9.3
As above; general exterior view.

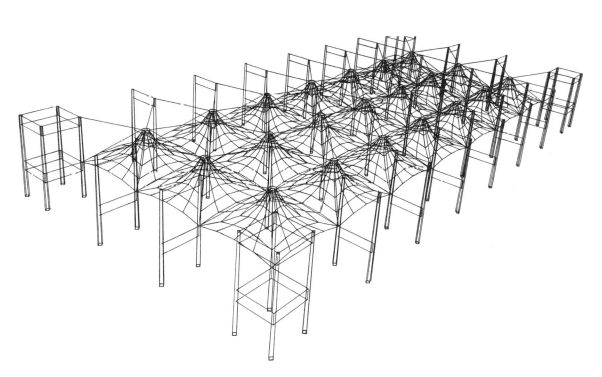

Fig. 9.4
As above;
analytical
drawing of
structural
system.

pended tension rings in two, otherwise widely different structures. The first of these, the enormous Haj Airport terminal at Jeddah in Saudi Arabia (Figs. 9.2, 9.3, 9.4), is classically simple, despite its size. It takes the form of two identical structures separated by an open mall. Each structure consists of five units, each unit being composed of 21 tented roofed modules, 45m square, arranged in a 7 x 3 pattern. The open awning of each module is supported at its centre by an open tension ring, 3.96m in diameter, which not only curves and stresses the fabric but also allows for air circulation in the stifling desert heat. The tension rings are slung from cables running either from internal steel masts, 2.5m in diameter at their bases tapering to 1.0m at the tops, or from external stiffening frames round the perimeter. These provide the overall stability of the structure.

Similar tension rings were used in the temporary tented structures erected for the Nat West Bank in 1987 (Fig. 9.5). Although the structure appears from the outside to be supported only by the four corner masts, this is not so. Conceptually and materially, the standard tent was a four module design in which the central anchorage, normally another mast, was replaced by the top of a hidden internal two-way steel lattice structure, supported at its ends at the mid-points of the four walls. This is an ingenious way of avoiding a central column so as to provide an unobstructed interior, but it will be seen as an unhappy hybrid by architectural and structural purists!

Interesting mast and cable suspension systems characterise the membrane roofs of five further masted structures. The first of these, the competition-winning design for the retail food market at Dubai (Figs. 9.6, 9.7) is a classic example of the

'accented, undulating' tent form developed by Frei Otto. In fact, it is a much larger and, due to the shape of the site, more tapered version of his rectangular tent erected for the Hamburg Horticultural Exhibition of 1963. Despite the tapering

Fig. 9.5
Fisher Park
Architects:
mobile training
centre for the
Nat West Bank,
England, 1987.

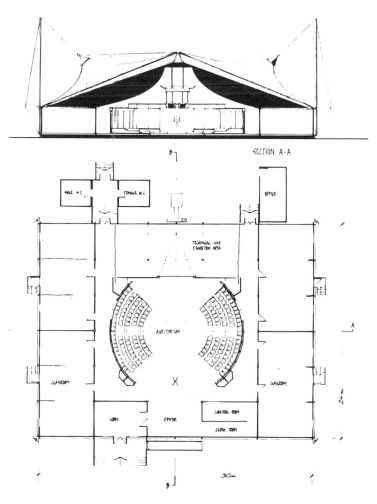

SECTION A-A

Fig. 9.6
GMW Architects:
competition-
winning design
for a retail food
market and
transport
terminal, Dubai,
UAE; view of
model.

roof membranes, the substantial vierendeel lattice supporting towers continue at the same height, and would have signalled an impressive desert landmark. Regrettably, the United Arab Emirates failed to commission the competition winners to construct this design.

The second structure is a barrel vault membrane with high and low points, pierced by masts in a 'nave and aisles' arrangement (Fig. 9.8). This mem-

brane configuration covered the Block A pavilion of the Tsukuba Exposition in Japan, in 1985 – and its fabric demanded even more complex cutting by being curved in plan.

The third structure in this group, the award-winning Schlumberger research and development centre in Cambridge, reaches the highest levels of architectural and structural quality and innovation. In contrast to the mainly square modules seen so

Fig. 9.7
As above; site
plan.

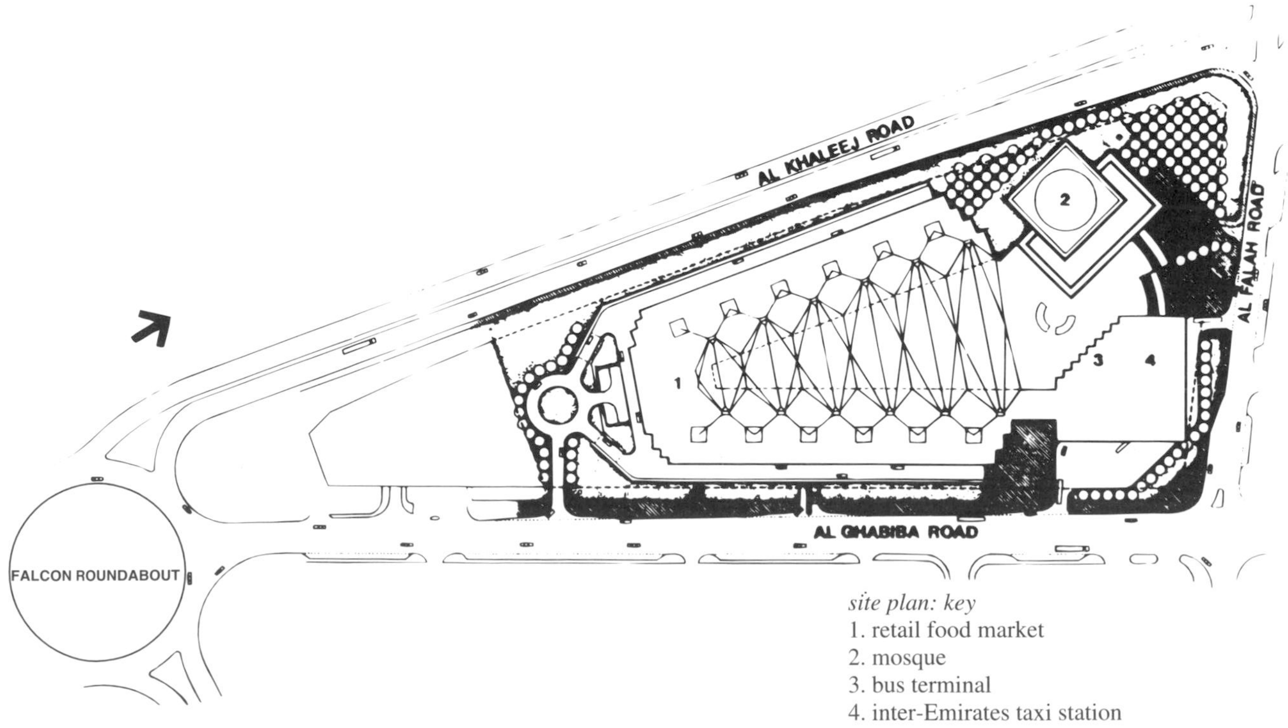

site plan: key
1. retail food market
2. mosque
3. bus terminal
4. inter-Emirates taxi station

AL KHALEEJ ROAD

AL FALAH ROAD

AL GHABIBA ROAD

FALCON ROUNDABOUT

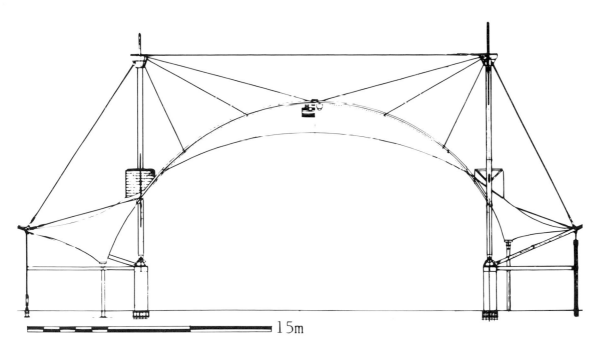

Fig. 9.8
*Fumihiko Maki
and Associates:
Block A pavilion,
Tsukuba
Exposition,
Japan, 1985;
cross section.*

15m

far, the building is centred around a series of three rectangular, spatial and structural cells (Fig. 9.9). Each cell has its own structural and visual identity by the rounded profile of the fabric roof, by its four supporting masts, and by being separated from its adjacent cells by a minor module (Fig. 9.10). This articulating space is occupied by a prismatic lattice framework and rooflight at high level, and defined by a vertical strip of glazing down the walls.

The surface geometry of the major membrane-roofed spaces takes the form of three identical tents, each with dual ridge lines. Spanning laterally between the masts on either side of the building are the main carrying cables, and from these primary elements, secondary supporting cables run to fourteen pick-up points on the surface of the facetted, but roughly bubble-shaped membrane. The plan is shown in Fig. 9.11.

The main raking masts do not continue uninterrupted to ground level: instead, they are pin jointed to the point at which the prismatic roof trusses rest on two vertical CHS members to form the main cross framework of the central modules. Also at that point, another pin joint connects one end of the downward sloping tubular outriggers, the other ends of which meet the main 50mm solid steel backstays of the main structure (Fig. 9.12).

The membrane itself was the first major installation of Teflon-coated glass fibre fabric in the UK. Its technical details are fully described in the *Architects' Journal* of 24 October, 1984 and details of the

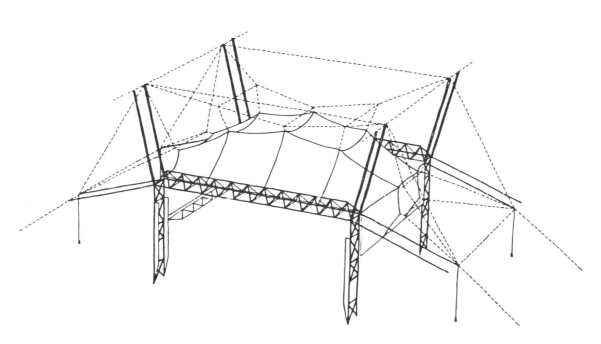

Fig. 9.9
*Michael Hopkins
and Partners:
Schlumberger
Research
Laboratory,
Cambridge,
England, 1985;
analysis of
typical module.*

Fig. 9.10
As above;
exterior view.

building envelope in Brookes and Grech, 1990.

We conclude this series of cable-supported membrane roofs by reviewing two structures in which a basically flat membrane is drawn up into modular 'peaks' by hangers from a cable network arranged above it. The smaller of the two buildings is Renzo Piano's Italian Industry Pavilion for the 1970 Osaka Expo in Japan and it is, therefore, a comparatively early example, whilst the larger is Ian Ritchie's entry for the Kew Gardens competition of 1984.

The Italian Industry Pavilion was a square structure, 38m x 38m, 10m high externally and with an internal height of 6m (Fig. 9.13). From the outside it appeared to be a single volume structure, but in fact it had a single, central mast, implying a four module structural basis. The main carrying cables criss-cross diagonally over the roof, between the sixteen perimeter masts, and between the corner masts and the central column. From the carrying cables, short suspension cables pick up the centres of the square, fabric membranes into high

Fig. 9.11
As above; cross
section.

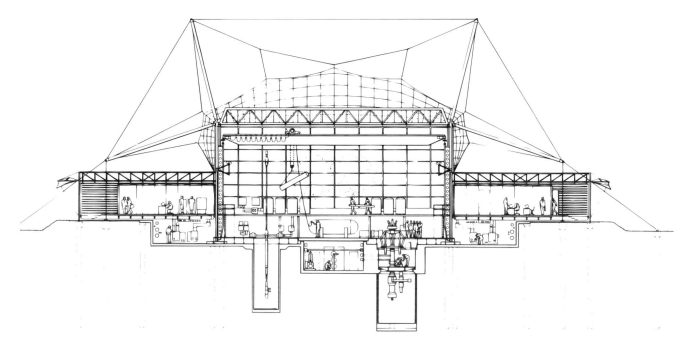

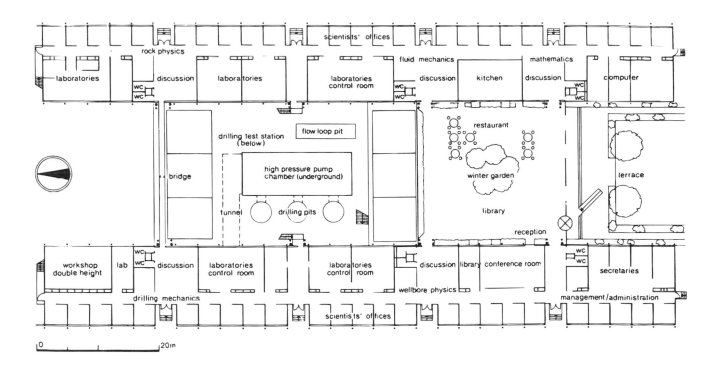

rock physics
scientists' offices
laboratories discussion laboratories laboratories control room fluid mechanics discussion kitchen mathematics discussion computer
wc wc wc wc wc wc
drilling test station (below) flow loop pit restaurant
bridge high pressure pump chamber (underground) winter garden terrace
tunnel drilling pits library
reception
workshop double height lab discussion laboratories control room laboratories control room discussion library conference room wc wc secretaries
wc wc
wellbore physics
drilling mechanics management/administration
scientists' offices

0   20m

points. The fabric is of translucent, reinforced poly-ester, in two skins separated by an air space to avoid condensation and improve the insulation. An unusual feature is that 'peaked' membranes of this kind also form the walls, the high points being ten-sioned by another set of diagonal cables attached to the short outriggers of the wall frames. Subjectively, this building does seem to be too much like a steel and wire cage to be particularly endearing, but much would have depended on the colour of the frame and the fabric.

Last in this series of masted and cable-support-ed membrane structures is Ian Richie's 1984 com-petition entry for the Kew Gardens reference collection and exhibition building. The design envis-aged two blocks made up of square, fabric-rooted modules. Each block is three modules in width but of differing modular lengths (Fig. 9.14). The general spatial and structural concept groups six modules into a structural unit with masts at its four corners. Two main carrying cables span across the three lines of modules, and are drawn together into a rectangular network which passes over their cen-tres. At these points, the translucent fabric mem-brane is picked up by shorter suspension cables. This idea is incompatible with the fifteen module length of the longer block so that its structural logic is inconsistent at one of its ends. The shorter, six module block is, however, consistently structured, but at a lower level, and with the outer line of mod-ules left as open pergolas (Fig. 9.15). Outriggers, set at 45° to the building, and with vertical back-stays, tension the whole system. At the base of the back-stays, the anchorages come and go amongst individually designed, topiary enclosures which ruf-fle the surrounding area into a romantically struc-tured arboreal landscape. Regrettably, this entry was not successful in the competition.

Fig. 9.12
As above; plan.

20m

Fig. 9.13 *(left)*
Renzo Piano and Associates: Italian Industry Pavilion, Osaka Expo, Japan, 1970.

105

Fig. 9.14
*Ian Ritchie
Architects:
competition
entry, Reference
Collection
Complex, Kew
Gardens,
London, 1982;
roof plan.*

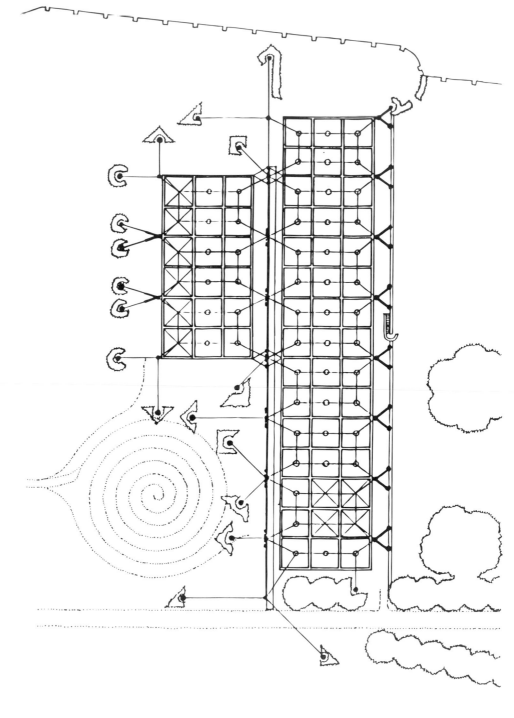

Fig. 9.15 *(below)
As above;
general view.*

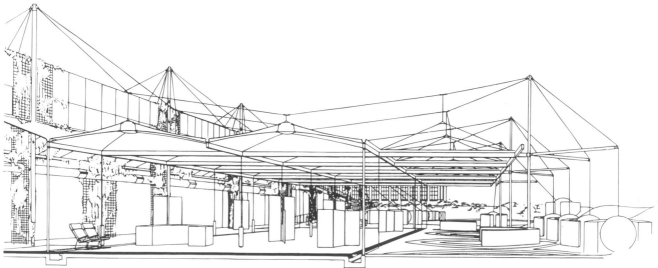

9.3

MEMBRANES ATTACHED TO AN EXTERNAL FRAMEWORK

All the buildings discussed so far comprise either fabric awnings directly attached to supporting masts, or fabric roof membranes supported from cable networks of various kinds above the roof surface – either close to it or at a higher level. The third method of supporting a membrane roof, apart from using a compression arch which is outside the scope of a work on masted structures, is to provide a mast-supported external framework which corresponds relatively closely to the profile of the membrane which it supports.

The pallet handling building in the Air France freight zone at Charles de Gaulle Airport in Paris is an instance of this principle (Fig. 9.16). It has been applied to a covered area of 30,000m² in which the 100m by 300m modular sections are independent of each other. The main structural support is provided by tubular columns at 18.75m centres, linked by straight re-formed I sections. The arches which

define the line of the roof membranes are of 32.3mm steel tubes, articulated at their ends and supported by cables from the 14m high mastheads. In this way, the span of the arched ribs is reduced from 18.75m to 12m. Colour has been used to enhance the visual effect: the structure is canary yellow and the pvc coated polyester is royal blue.

To summarise this group of structures very briefly, there are currently three principal ways of organising a masted membrane roof: one can attach small-scale awnings directly to the mast elements, or one may pick up the larger membranes by cable networks or by an external framework. However, for the middle group, Frei Otto has sketched out many different ways of defining and stressing a tented surface related to his own, very useful categorisations (Roland, 1970), and several built examples have been described. This is an open-ended field for architectural and structural innovation which has hardly been touched. It does overlap with some tented grandstand structures and we will describe these in the next chapter. ■

Fig. 9.16
M.L. Bianchi and M. Malinowski: Pallet Handling Building, Charles de Gaulle Airport, Roissy, Paris, France, 1988.

10

MASTED GRANDSTAND STRUCTURES

Grandstands form a distinct sub-group of masted structures for two main reasons: they are naturally cantilevered and are associated with ramped spectator seating. Beyond these basic characteristics there is a wide variety of forms and materials in the constituent elements: the masts; the cantilevered structural roof; its decking and its tension members. Structures of this kind involve a fairly extensive canopy surface which in most cases is more or less flat but which can be sloped inwards or outwards related to the patterns of shading and rain protection which are to be provided. Moreover, the roof can take the form of a rigid plane, or a flexible fabric membrane. One of the fundamental issues which has to be resolved is whether the roof can be given sufficient weight and stiffness to counteract wind uplift or whether some form of tie-down system will be needed. Examples of both principles can be seen in the buildings described in this section.

The designer's response to the built-up levels of the spectator seating also makes an interesting study. At one extreme we have already noted one instance in which the spectator seating seems to have exerted no influence at all on the form of its associated canopy: this is in the stadium stand at Marl in Germany, designed by A. Riege (Fig. 6.23) which could just as easily stand on a flat site as be associated with an embanked stadium and for this reason is described amongst other extended single mast based structures in Chapter 6.

In all other cases, the seating has exerted a significant influence on the form of the cantilevered roofs and their supporting masts, for example, at its simplest in defining the spectator access route at Vaterstetten, and at its most complex in forming part of the main structure in the stadium at San Juan. To come to terms with this varied sub-group of masted structures we can divide them into three groups:

i)   Canopies covering only a part of the spectator seating.

ii)   Similar canopies incorporating fabric roof elements.

iii)   Complete grandstand structures.

10.1

CANOPIES COVERING ONLY A PART OF THE SEATING

Fig. 10.1
Yeovil Football Club Grandstand, Yeovil, 1990; cross section of grandstand.

Broadly speaking, it is the requirements of stadia in terms of numbers of spectators and the degree of coverage of the roof which provide the key to their cross-sectional form, whilst the economic circumstances of the sporting organisation influence the constructional logic and materials. These principles are well illustrated by the three structures we wish to note in this section.

The new terraced grandstand for Yeovil Town Football Club is a simple and direct design which provides spectators with an uninterrupted view of the pitch at a very low cost. The new roof extends over fifteen bays above the terraces. Its long horizontal plan is counterbalanced, visually and structurally viewed from the opposite side of the pitch, by the verticals of the sixteen tubular masts. On the entrance side, a triangulated system of steel outriggers and tiedowns appears on each side of the main accommodation element. Conventional steel beams form the roof cantilevers, the main stanchions up to roof level, and the raking supports to the precast concrete terracing. This main beam system is braced and strutted with tubular steel masts and ties above roof level, galvanised but unpainted. This constructional system was extremely cost effective and it demonstrates some useful principles for any small sports club wishing to upgrade its terraced accommodation.

At the Bayamon stadium in San Juan, Puerto Rico, the requirements were on a vastly larger scale, in entirely different climatic and cultural

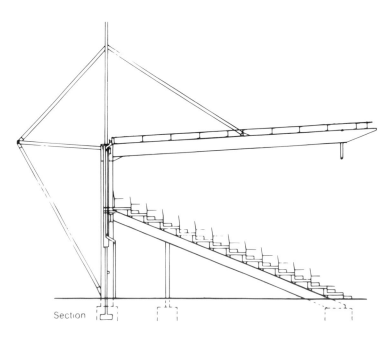

Section

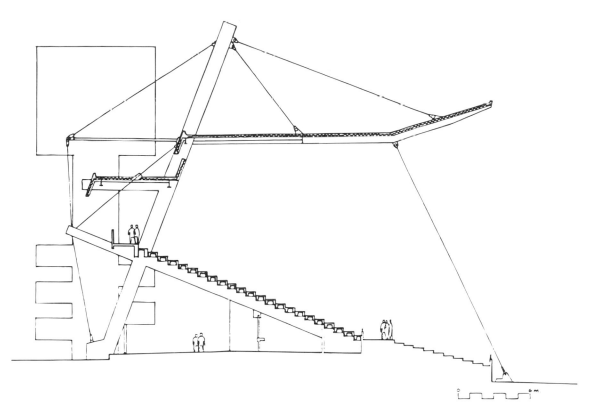

Fig. 10.2
Reed, Torres,
Beauchamp et
al.: Juan Ramon
Loubriel Stadium,
Bayamon, Puerto
Rico; cross
section of
grandstand.

circumstances, but with an equally interesting logic of masted design and construction.

The requirements were for a baseball stadium specifically, with all the seats protected from hot sun and winter showers in a tropical country in which concrete is the most abundant building material. This led to the design of an extensive roof element encircling the more narrowly curved end of a roughly egg-shaped plan. The section shows the useful structural triangulation of the inward-inclined masts and the cast-in-place seating. The leading edge of the roof is tilted up to allow high balls to be kept in view. This tilt was found to have unexpected aerodynamic advantages during wind tunnel tests, and the light and ventilation slots between the roofs at the back of the stand were also increased in size to alleviate roof pressure in high winds. Above the seating, the main masts are twinned, the space between being used for drainage and electrical services. These masts were post-tensioned before erection. There is a clear structural logic to the section, although the tiedowns could, perhaps, have been better aligned (the reference noted in the Gazetteer provides key structural details in outline).

The last of the three buildings in this group, the National Athletics Stadium at Bruce, near Canberra sets a very high standard indeed. The dramatically curved roof plane, tilted inwards at 12°, consists of 100mm of concrete on metal decking, a form of construction chosen to provide sufficient mass against wind uplift. The five 36m high masts are hinged at their feet to rotate in a plane perpendicular to the stand and rest on columns attached to its rear wall. Apart from some minor flaws in detailing

this is an inspired design, light in appearance with slim masts and an elegant roof profile, and the architects, Philip Cox and Partners, with Ove Arup and Partners as engineers, achieved this with minimal fuss, ahead of schedule and at only a modest cost.

10.2

CANOPIES INCORPORATING FABRIC ROOFS

Four recent grandstand structures have combined masted structural designs with striking fabric coverings. One of these uses the flexible covering by stretching it over arches rather than drawing it up

Fig. 10.3
Philip Cox and
Partners:
National Athletics
Centre, Bruce,
Canberra,
Australia, 1977;
cross section of
grandstand.

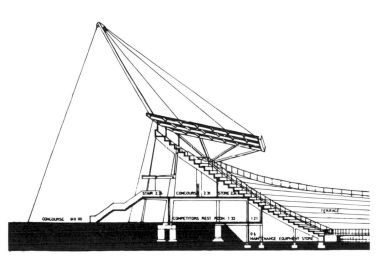

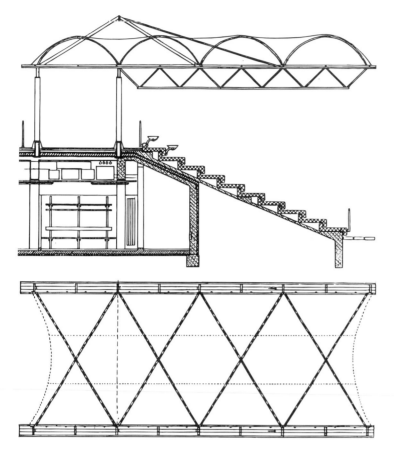

and a parallel line of secondary masts acting as vertical back-stays. Each of the eleven bays has a barrel vaulted membrane roof, formed by intersecting diagonal arches of steel tubes, springing off the main lattice beams. At the base of the vaults, the roof drains into dual valley gutters comprising two steel channel sections connected, toe to toe, by a steel flat and located on top of the lattice booms.

The next two examples in this group set new standards in elegance and clarity of structure through inspired and dedicated architect and engineer collaboration.

The first of these is the refurbished Mound Stand at Lord's Cricket Ground in London (Fig. 10.5). The principle adopted in the refurbishment was to retain and extend the well-liked original brick arch and concrete base structure of 1898-99, and build a new series of terraces on top of it. As part of this concept, the fabric and steel roof is the uppermost layer of a six-decker sandwich of accommodation. Its superstructure is 100m long and 12m wide, of which half is curved in plan.

In essence, the roof comprises six spatial and structural cells, each centred around a 406mm diameter mast with a 12mm fire resisting shell (Fig. 10.6). Tubular booms extend equally towards the pitch and to the rear and both have cable tiedowns, that is, to the front of the upper promenade and to triangulated frames projected from the rear structure (Fig. 10.7). From the projecting tips of the masts, a network of cables carries a series of fabric pick-up rings located at the column positions and at mid-span between them.

The front and rear of the fabric membrane is attached in 3.6m scallops to curved boundary

by tension rings; this is the delicate, kite-like canopy to the sports park at Vaterstetten in Germany (Fig. 10.4).

Here, an eleven bay cantilevered roof is carried on two lines of quite stubby vertical masts: a line of main masts from which the roof is cantilevered,

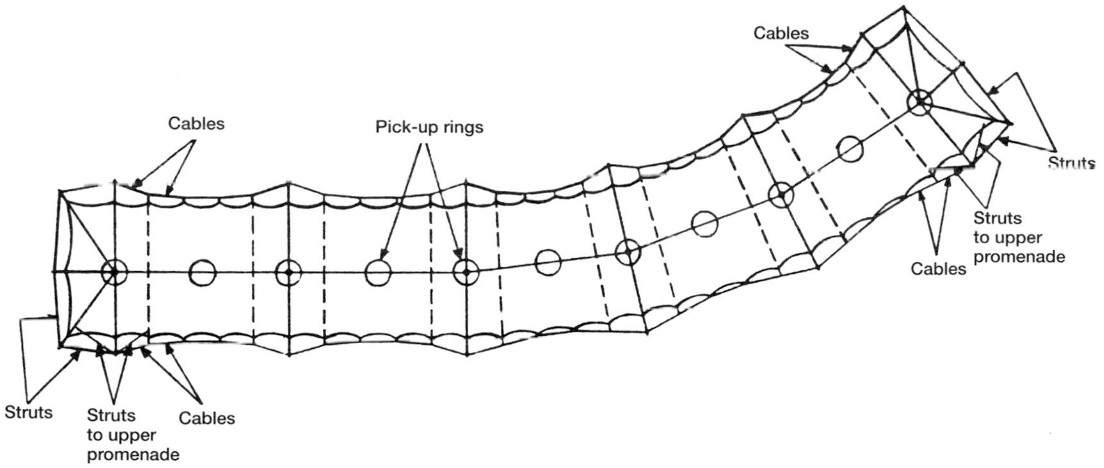

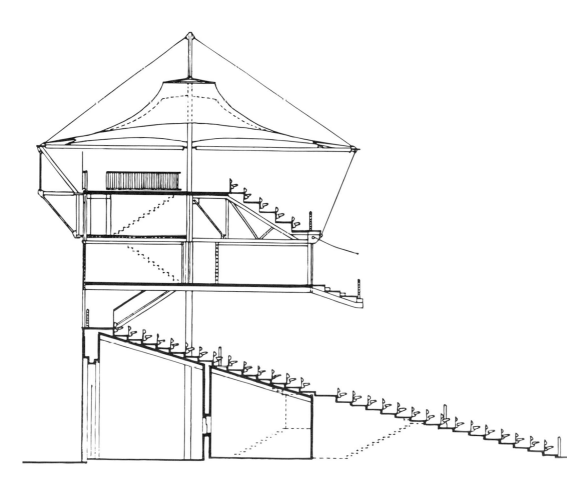

Fig. 10.6
As above; roof
plan.

cables which connect the boom ends. Other arched valley cables draw down the fabric into an undulating form to provide the necessary stiffness. The fabric itself is of pvc-coated polyester, treated with pvdf on the upper surface to improve durability.

It is not possible in a short account such as this to do justice to the sensitivity and the architectural and structural understanding which has been brought to bear in this superb and widely commended design. We can only say that a close study of the references noted in the Gazetteer will be amply repaid.

The Mound Stand established a new aesthetic

for tented canopies and its morphology was continued in the next structure in this section, the new Sussex Stand at Goodwood Racecourse (Fig. 10.8). The roof structure is similar to that at Lord's, not only because structural economy, visual delight and translucency were desirable objectives for both projects, but also because the same engineers, the Lightweight Structures Division of Ove Arup and Partners, advised both Michael Hopkins and Arup Associates. Main tubular mast elements have booms fore and aft but with an inwardly raked, tubular back-stay plus additional tie-downs of solid round tie bars rather than cables (Fig. 10. 9). The polyester-reinforced pvc fabric stretches

Fig. 10.7
As above; cross
section of
grandstand.

between zinc impregnated cables and has a predicted life of fifteen years. The fabric is drawn up around the masts to circular tension rings which are themselves supported by a three collar membrane and tension stay anchorage at the masthead. In the exposed, windy conditions of the Sussex Downs, the structural members needed to

be heavier than at Lord's. Moreover, the structure is shorter and was further reduced from four masts to three for economy. In consequence, the stand looks as if it should have been longer, and is somewhat top-heavy in appearance compared with its predecessor.

The longest and most recent of these partial

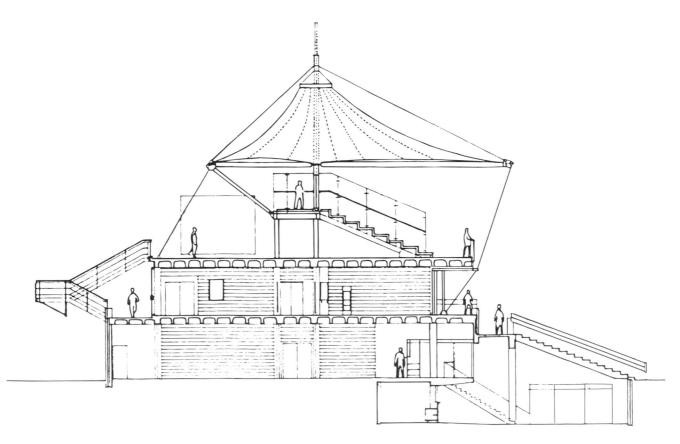

Fig. 10.10
Sheffield Council
Architects: World
Student Games
Stadium,
Sheffield,
England, 1991;
photograph of
model.

canopies is that of the Don Valley Stadium in Sheffield (Fig. 10.10). Its main element is a seven bay structure which has at each end an additional bay continued round the curve of the running track and separated from the main block by an open, 'hinge' bay with its own conical roof. The masts, cantilever booms and rear outriggers all take the same form of tubular vierendeel 'ladders', a highly successful unifying idea which identifies and orders the rhythm of the structure. Dual tension stays, backstays and vertical tie-downs stabilise the tensile cantilever system. The fabric roof covering is stretched between the horizontal vierendeels forming the main booms, and sweeps up to rear arches formed in curved tubes on the line of the masts. The masts rest on the first floor cross bar element of the main grandstand structure to provide an unobstructed space at ground level which is used for changing and practice facilities beneath the stand.

Fig. 10.11
Philip Cox and
Partners: Sydney
Football Stadium,
Sydney,
Australia, 1988;
general view.

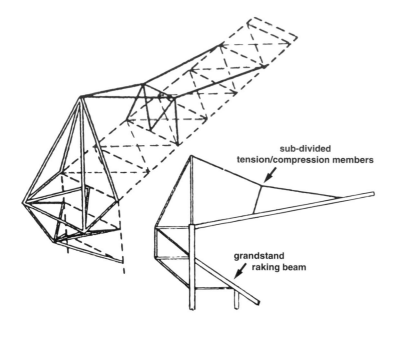

sub-divided
tension/compression members

grandstand
raking beam

Fig. 10.12
*As above;
isometric and
structural
diagram showing
structural
concept.*

This is a straightforward, simply conceived and award-winning structure to which the pairs of masts, booms and ties make a sober, measured contribution.

10.3

CANOPIES SURROUNDING THE ENTIRE STADIUM

The extension of a masted grandstand structure round the entire perimeter of a stadium has occurred at regular intervals in recent years. The most spectacular example has been the Sydney Football Stadium of 1988, a swooping and rising, 'roller-coaster' stand, the form of which springs from the influence of climate, function and aspect. It is pulled down towards adjacent houses to respect their scale and to respond to threatening weather from the south whilst conversely swelling up on the east and the west, providing additional seating in the more important central viewing areas in respect of a north-south pitch (Fig. 10.11). It is a tensile structure which uses 'A' frames rather than masts, but it is nonetheless interesting.

The grandstand roof is a tensile-supported cantilever roof structure extending 30m outwards from the supports. The rear tie-downs pass over two sets of outriggers and are taken back to the structure, thus saving the costs of large, tension foundations. Alternate 8.5m bays in the roof form statically determinate independent structural systems, whilst the infill bays consist only of purlins. Adjacent pairs of suspension systems are inclined together to form stable A-frames and this reduction saved some 300 tonnes of steel. The front stays are bifurcated to provide two points of support for each rafter, and secondary bracing is

provided at that point which this reduces the effective length of the individual members and enables small-diameter, thick-walled cables to be used. There is also in-plane roof bracing (Fig. 10.12). A slot at the leading edge reduces wind loads by up to 25% and is decked with mesh as a maintenance walk-way.

The structural system is completed by space trusses located below the grandstand seating to deal with the slight misalignment of the radial roof beams with the grandstand beams which follow a more gentle curve in plan.

The roof has a perforated aluminium under ceiling. This allows wind pressures to pass through and load the structural cladding above, creates a smooth soffit to the roof and improves its appearance, it also increases acoustic absorption and prevents pigeons from roosting in the rafters. Ingenious detailing of the purlin system enabled both layers of the roof cladding to be installed from above and the entire roof was erected without scaffolding, on time and within budget.

More conventional masts characterise the remaining structures in this group, although one is thoroughly unconventional in its form. This is the King Fahd Stadium in Riyadh, Saudi Arabia. Its roof covers an area of 77,000m^2 and is the largest cable-tensioned Teflon-coated glass/fibre structure so far built.

In form, this is a cantilevered version of the 'accented undulating' type of cable-stayed fabric roof originally outlined by Frei Otto. The 290m diameter translucent roof membrane was post-tensioned. It is drawn up to high level collars around the 60m high masts and formed into doubly-curved surfaces by two sets of cables. Main carrying cables run from the inner edge of the canopy, over the main masts and form cantenary curves to a second ring of lower masts, raked outwards around the perimeter. Between these cable ridges other arched cables draw down the membrane to form deep valleys, and run to ground anchorages. This exotic and staccato silhouette on the exterior provides, translucent daylight penetration in parallel with protection against solar heat gain.

The Thialf Sports Centre at Heevenveen in Holland (Fig. 10.13) is more conventional. It is an enclosed ice stadium of 90m x 200m with two semi-circular apsidal ends. The sixty-two tubular masts surrounding the stadium stand on precast concrete columns. From the base of the masts, inclined rsj struts support a lens-shaped lattice roof framework, tension-assisted from the mastheads by two ties on the arena side and relieved by horizontal outriggers with raked and vertical backstays on the other. The interior is a breathtaking spatial experience, for which the closely spaced supporting structure still seems astonishingly light for its span.

Lastly in this section is the new Stadio

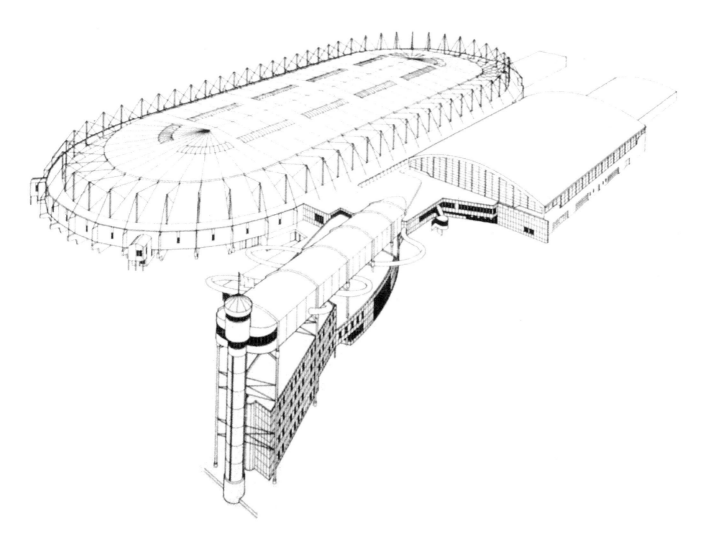

Communale in Turin. This also uses a dual mast arrangement, as at Sheffield and these masts also support the upper level of the stands. The internal tension ring, to which the radiating main cables are attached, is made of eight cables with an 8.5cm cross-section. A second tensile system of additional parallel cables spans across the narrow axis of the elliptical stadium to assist the inner ten-sion rings. The roof covering is of metal sheets with interlocking joints. This is an ambitious structure with which to end this section: its roof overhangs the spectator area by 41m and it can hold its own in comparison with the works by Nervi in the same city, despite some unsophisti-cated minor elements and occasional trivialised details. ∎

Fig. 10.13
Van der Zee and Yberna: Thialf Sports Centre, Heevenveen, Holland; aerial view.

11

ROTATIONAL STRUCTURES

In the introduction to the method of analysis used in this study we cited three generative principles which could be used to describe the assemblages of cells which make up the larger masted structures. We have explained how two of these principles, translation and articulation, form the underlying basis of the majority of buildings analysed so far. In this chapter we deal with a very small number of structures characterised by the third principle, that of rotation.

Several centrally-masted structures of circular form have been designed and built, but these should be seen as geometric variants of the generic, single-mast type of structure already discussed in Chapter 6. The circular, centrally-masted element of the Mercedes Showroom in Vienna is an example of this type (see Gazetteer). The kinds of rotational structures discussed here are based on a different principle: they incorporate masted frameworks which are repeated by being rotated about a point or points so as to generate a building of circular or elliptical form. These structures fall into three topological groups according to whether the masts are located inside the building envelope, form part of it, or are positioned outside it (Fig. 11.1). Comparative roof plans of structures whose origin consists of a rotational transformation are shown in Fig. 11.2.

Fig. 11.1
Alternative topological positions of masts in relation to the building envelope of circular or elliptical masted structures.

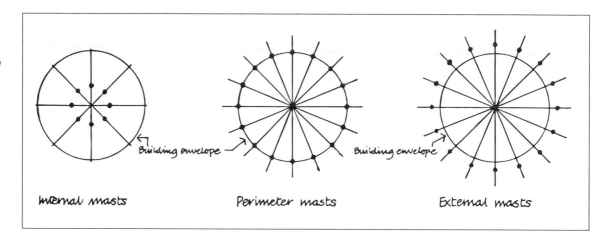

Fig. 11.2
Comparative roof plans of rotational masted structures (not to scale).

a. Pan American passenger terminal, JFK airport, New York, 1960.

b. PTT Telecommunication exhibition stand, Amsterdam, 1986.

c. Travel and Transport Pavilion, Chicago Exposition, 1931.

d. UK Pavilion, Rand Easter Show, Johannesburg, 1950.

e. The Stadium, Wonderworld Project, Corby, England, 1982.

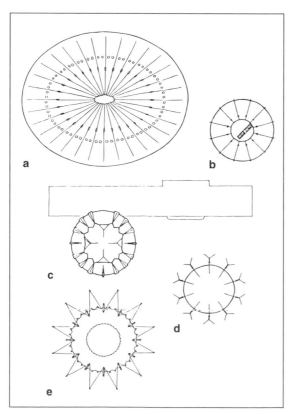

11.1

MASTS LOCATED WITHIN THE BUILDING ENVELOPE

Two structures show entirely different, detailed applications of this principle: the first is a large and elliptical air terminal; the second, a smaller and circular exhibition stand.

The former, the passenger terminal for Pan American World Airways at New York International Airport, was completed in 1960 (Fig. 11.3). The overall planning objective was to provide the most direct route for the passenger to the aircraft, and to allow the aircraft to be parked, radiating nose-on to the elliptical building, under the overhang of the roof and only a few feet from the glass walls of the concourse.

The 33.5m roof overhang is supported by thirty-two radiating girders of pre-tensioned steel, resting on massive concrete piers at their mid-span. The six tension cables of each girder are connected to a central tension ring which is itself tied down by six steel columns fixed to a mass concrete anchorage. The roof deck is of light weight reinforced concrete on 75mm cellular glass panels to form an acousti-

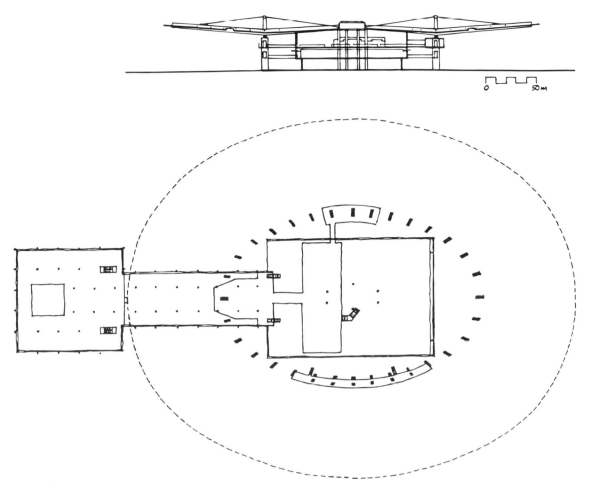

Fig. 11.3
*Tippetts, Abett,
McCarthy and
Stratton: Pan
American
passenger
terminal, JFK
airport, New
York, 1960;
section and plan.*

cally absorbent undersurface to the canopy. It has a series of skylights in addition to the central oculus (Fig. 11.2a).

In analysing this building it must be said that this is not, strictly speaking, a conventional masted structure because the cables run over a central king post rather than being attached to a central mast, making it a cable-stayed cantilever beam structure. However, we have included this example because its general configuration represents a principle which could be interpreted in more conventional masted terms by continuing either the upper or lower supports as a single member.

The second rotational structure of this kind is the smart, well-proportioned display stand for the Telecommunications Branch of the Dutch PTT organisation (Fig. 11.4). The objective was to design a demountable exhibition stand of a distinctive and eye-catching nature which could be re-used at trade fairs around Europe. The structure is based on twelve repetitions of a mast and cantilevered beam system, rotated about a central void as in the Pan American Terminal, but following a circular rather than elliptical path. Moreover, the masts are not equally but unequally spaced in relation to the overall length of the main beams. The resulting potentially out of balance load condition is counteracted by ties taken to the base of the mast so as to avoid obstructing the central ring or the

ground level circulation. The column-to-precast-concrete pad detail was designed as a moment connection to assist in stability during erection. The upper level floor plate is of pvc foam-filled pressed steel sandwich plates bolted to the horizontal frame members whilst the roof is merely of fabric, stretched on springs between the main frames.

Architecturally and structurally this is an appealing design: the ground level can be used as a general product exhibition area whilst the upper level can be used to entertain potential customers in more comfortable and private surroundings; the circular form is eye-catching, the cantilevered upper floor is exciting and the proportions seem well-balanced and attractive.

11.2
MULTIPLE MASTS AROUND THE PERIMETER OF THE BUILDING

The second type of rotational multiple-masted arrangement is characterised by the positioning of the masts externally around a 'rotunda-type' volume. This principle was adopted on several occasions in the early development of modern masted structure. Indeed, two projects of the 1930s which are important chronologically have already been

117

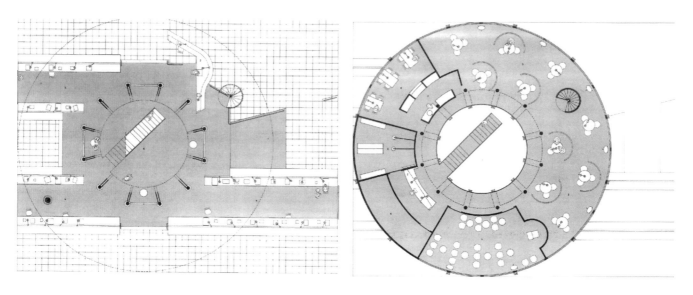

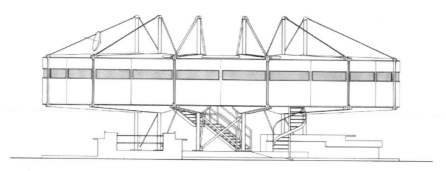

Fig. 11.4
P and P Wintermans: PTT Telecommunications exhibition stand. Amsterdam, 1986; ground and first floor plans; elevation, and half cross section.

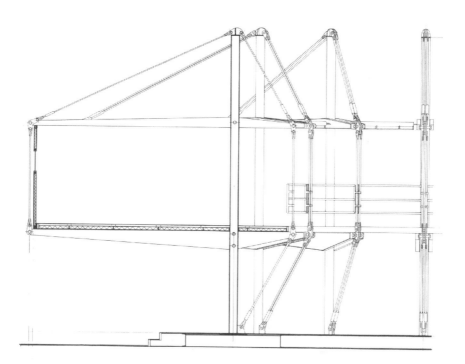

noted in the first part of Chapter 5. They represent distinct structural variations of the basic principle and we will again describe them here.

The first is Nikolsky's design for the Moscow Palace of the Soviets Competition of 1931 (Fig. 5.5). From the rudimentary line diagram this appears to envisage a circular, peaked tent struc-ture, drawn up to a compression ring hung by cables from a ring of fourteen vertical cigar-shaped masts. In the absence of any indication of back-stay cables, the lack of the necessary high level compression ring to hold the masts upright seems to show a lack of structural awareness on the part of the Russian constructivist architects.

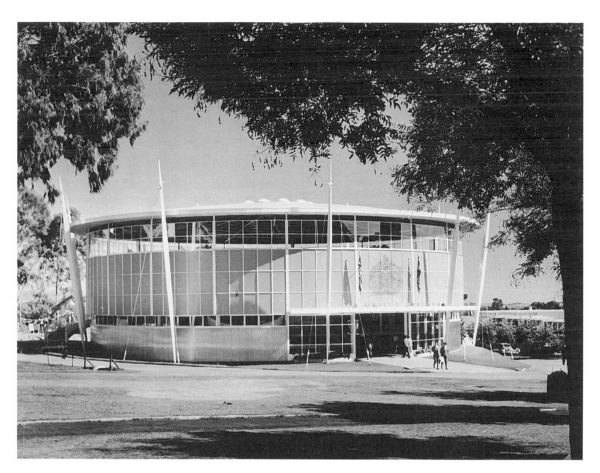

Fig. 11.5
Fleming and
Cooke: UK
Pavilion, Rand
Easter Show,
Johannesburg,
1959.

Two years later, the Travel and Transport Pavilion of the Chicago Exposition of 1933, (Figs. 5.6, 5.7) also adopted a masted, rotunda type form which was 91m in its overall outside diameter and 62.5m clear internally. The masts themselves were in the form of twelve prismatic lattice towers, 46m high, arranged in interacting braced groups of three. The subsequent cladding of the towers produced a series of triangular buttresses, from the tops of which, in each group of three, fourteen cables 54mm in diameter ran to huge mass concrete anchor blocks. Between the four quadrant tower groups, four large windows were inserted, each with a sophisticated 'rising sun' pattern of glazing bars. Elaborate and ingenious precautions were taken to accommodate the rise and fall, and expansion and contraction of this monumental early masted structure.

A more recent building of this kind, and the first permanent British exhibition building to be erected outside the UK, is the British Pavilion constructed for the Rand Easter Show in Johannesburg in 1959 (Fig. 11.5). The formal concept of this building is quite simple: it is a glass-walled cylinder, over which is a 33.5m diameter shallow dome, partially suspended by cables from slender, double-tapered external masts with backstays. From its overall form, its delicate masts and its curtain wall proportions this is a design entirely of its period – none the worse for that, but perhaps a little too good-mannered for some tastes. However, it may be that a permanent exhibition building cannot afford the architectural histrionics which are acceptable and necessary in the frenetic world of temporary exhibition structures!

Our last rotational example could be placed either in this category, or under grandstands or, perhaps, under membrane structures, depending on one's purposes! We include it here because it is truly rotational, which many grandstands are not,

Fig. 11.6
Derek Walker
and Associates:
The Stadium,
Wonderworld
project, Corby,
England, 1982;
elevation.

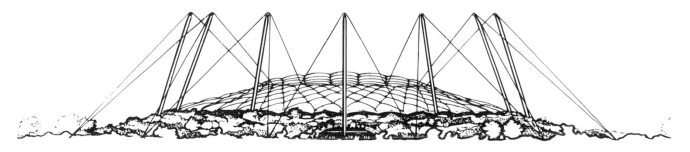

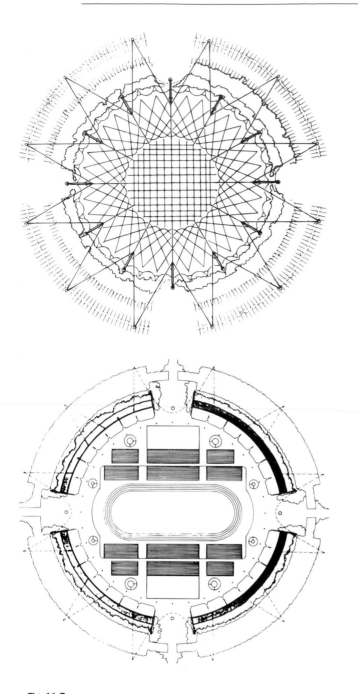

Fig. 11.7
*As above; plan,
roof plan.*

and because it neatly rounds off the present sequence of externally masted rotational forms – albeit not of rotunda form.

The proposed stadium for Wonderworld, in Northampshire (Figs. 11.6, 11.7), is intended to be roofed by a steel cable net, supported by a central steel ring, and hung from twelve steel masts which are stayed back into the surrounding parking areas. The cladding to the lens-shaped main roof is intended to be an inflated double membrane of Teflon-coated glass fabric, to give good natural light internally, acoustic absorption, and insulation against condensation – all for minimal weight. However, its future construction remains uncertain.

This completes our review of the various rotational, curvilinear arrangements and in doing so we reach the end of this formal taxonomic analysis of modern masted structures.

As we stated at the outset, our intention has been to clarify the multitude of masted configurations which have been envisaged and built; to impose a degree of order which seems to be intrinsic to the field, and to enable new examples to be analysed, identified and understood in a way which is authentic and meaningful to all concerned. We can now turn our attention to the structural characteristics and architectural conclusions of these explorations. ∎

STRUCTURAL CASE STUDY:
The Renault Parts Distribution Centre, Swindon

12

This detailed account is included to illustrate the typical factors which influence the design, fabrication and erection of masted structures. The study also shows how a typical hypothetico-deductive design process produced the final form of a major work of architecture. Over a range of major and minor design problems the designers seem to have proceeded by a process of 'conjectures and refutations', to use Karl Popper's terms, in their exploration of the brief and its realisation (Popper, 1963).

12.1

INCEPTION

The nature and architectural quality of this building originated in the beliefs of the central, Paris directorate of the Renault organisation. These beliefs lay in the importance of establishing an overall image of excellence in the Company; in demonstrating innovation in both the product and its manufacturing environment, and in realising the tangible benefits which could accrue from well-designed buildings. All these beliefs proved to be justified in the Swindon project.

In Paris, a 'Comité Visuelle', under a Coordinateure d'Expression Visuelle at the time, M. Sebastin de la Salle, was responsible for the architectural aspects of company policy. He and other senior executives of the parent company carried out a series of interviews and building visits to explore general ways of achieving their environmental

design objectives. After a further series of interviews with the directors and senior managers of Renault UK Ltd, Foster Associates were appointed to prepare a feasibility study for the Swindon project in February 1981.

Renault UK Ltd had foreseen the need for expansion in 1979 and they had acquired the 6.67 hectare site in 1980 and obtained planning permission on the basis of a design and build package for a conventional, bulky warehouse. For this reason, the local planners restricted the building area to a maximum of 50% of the site. However, by their own approach to the general location, arrangement and appearance of the building Foster Associates were able to convince the planners that a less bulky and visually innovative design could justify an increase in the site coverage from 50 to 67%, thus obtaining for Renault a potential commercial gain of 16,350m² of floor space!

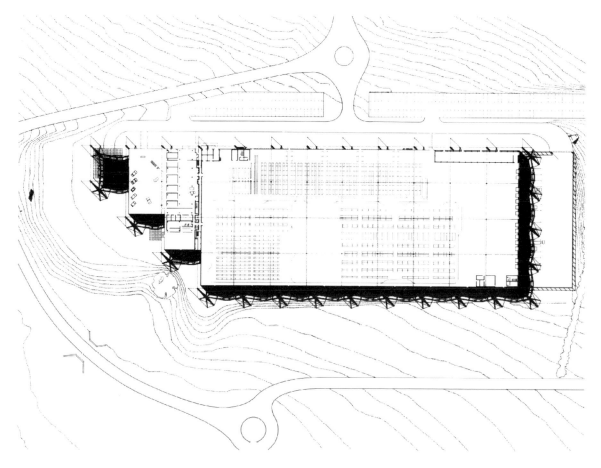

Fig. 12.1
Foster Associates: Renault Parts Distribution Centre, Swindon, England, 1983; ground floor plan.

12.2
DESIGN APPROACH

The building form reflects Sir Norman Foster's basic principles of industrial building design. These are, firstly, that the organic growth of industrial facilities must be reflected not in relatively immutable rectangular buildings but in architectural forms which have the potential for random growth over time. The form of the Renault Centre meets this criterion by being based on modular units extendible in any direction to fill out the irregularities in the site. The suspension structure meets the same criterion by providing connection points for future modules without disturbance of the existing structure.

The architects' second principle is that the depth and scale of the space within which the workers are employed must enable them to have a view outside. This basic human need is only partially achieved in this building by a top light in each module, plus additional north-facing lights in the warehouse. These lights also perform the important function of showing, internally, that the building is a suspended structure. But they were a late addition to the design, and the architect has since said that he would have liked more glazing in the walls had the economic constraints been less stringent. That this could have been achieved to some extent at the time is referred to later.

12.3
FUNCTIONAL REQUIREMENTS

Fig. 12.2
As above; analytical model of the structure, used for computer-based stress analysis.

Renault UK required 20,000m² of warehouse space with training school, restaurant, office and showroom space amounting to about 25,000m² in total (see Fig. 12.1). Because spare parts for cars come in a wide range of sizes, fully automated stor-

age systems were not suitable. Consequently, the warehouse functions partially manually, albeit using re-locatable racking and storage bins serviced by an AGV system. For this kind of installation, and for the showroom and offices, a spatial module of about 24m square and 8m high was found to be optimal. It was to achieve the structural depth for this span and keep its encroachment on the internal space to a minimum that the undulating suspension structure was developed. In fact, the internal height varies from 7.5m to 9.5m.

12.4
THE STRUCTURAL CONCEPT AND ITS ANALYSIS

The initial proposal was for a series of independent structural umbrellas, developed from a single mast with radiating cable-stayed beams. However, a relatively large, two-directional structure of this kind would have required some form of internal bracing and expansion joints, which were deemed to be unacceptable. Consequently, the initial concept of a series of square modules with central masts and radiating beam umbrella structures was replaced by one based on masts at the corners of the modules, with arched cable-stayed beams spanning orthogonally and diagonally between them. This design was then developed as an unbraced, two-directional portal frame. In this form, loading on one bay affects the behaviour of adjacent bays and the beam elements play a role in spanning not only between the pre-stressed ties but also between the masts themselves. There are no special expansion joints as all movement is taken up within the structure itself. Most importantly, the required structural depth is provided outside the building envelope which can thus have a correspondingly lower profile.

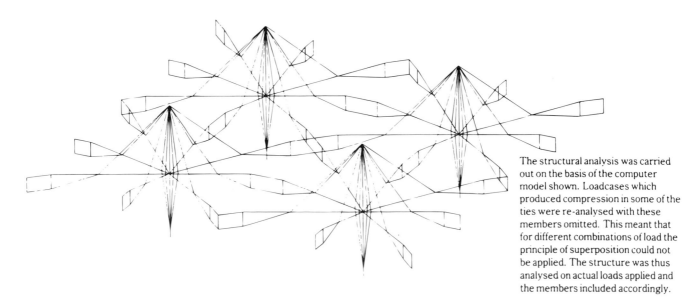

The structural analysis was carried out on the basis of the computer model shown. Loadcases which produced compression in some of the ties were re-analysed with these members omitted. This meant that for different combinations of load the principle of superposition could not be applied. The structure was thus analysed on actual loads applied and the members included accordingly.

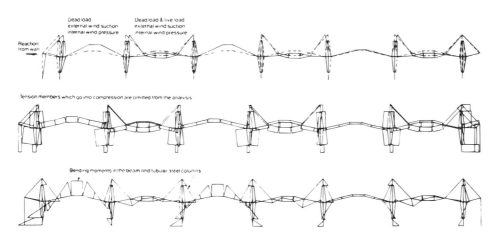

Dead load
external wind suction
internal wind pressure

Dead load & live load
external wind suction
internal wind pressure

Reaction
from wall

Tension members which go into compression are omitted from the analysis

Bending moments in the beam and tubular steel columns

Fig. 12.3
*As above;
computed results
of the stress
analysis of the
extreme load
condition.*

Computer results for one of the grid line frames acted upon by an extreme load case condition. This load case is the "one in 50 year" wind with a dominant opening on the inward face and an adverse distribution of live load.

Top: shows the deflected form of the structure. The dashed line is the original structure position, the continuous line is the deflected shape. Deflections are drawn as 1/10th of the actual value. Where members do not appear on the

drawing, the tension elements have been driven into compression by the deformations of the structure and so omitted from the computer model.

Middle: shows the value of the axial force in the members plotted along

each member. Again tension members pushed into compression are omitted and not drawn.

Bottom: shows the distribution of bending moments in the structure under the particular loadcase.

For reasons mainly of appearance, the structure comprises continuous bending masts pinned to continuous bending beams, linked and stiffened by members capable of taking tension only. This concept means that it is the variations in the conditions of loading which determine the elements which are under stress. The tension members are stressed by the uniform downward loads and destressed, in some cases, by sway and wind uplift forces. In these circumstances, the structure offers only minimal resistance to horizontal disturbances. Consequently, as the engineers describe in their house journal:

"The first aim was to define the members permanently available. We chose to make the structure sufficiently stiff so that modes of failure due to instability would not interfere with yield, and proposed that from Merchant/Rankine ratios of (Pcrit/P) in excess of ten would be sufficient. To achieve this, the ties adjacent to the masts were prestressed to provide not only a moment connection between the beams and columns but also to strengthen and stiffen the columns themselves. The main span tension hangers are principally activated by downward load." (Manning, 1983)

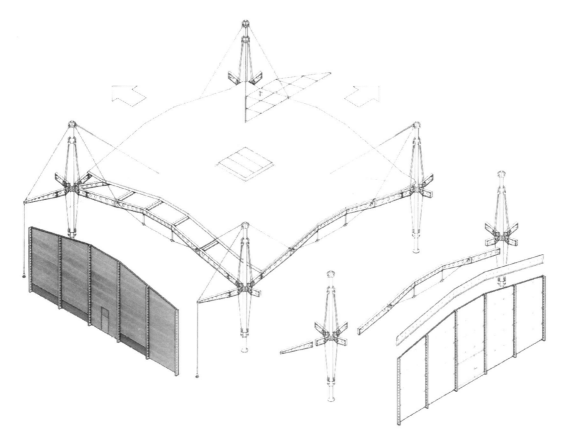

Fig. 12.4
*As above;
exploded view of
the components
of a typical bay
of the building
envelope.*

Analyses were carried out for each of the critical arrangements of loads. The worst loading was associated with a 1:50 year wind, a dominant opening on the windward face and an asymmetric distribution of live load. The factor of safety against destress in the tension members was chosen to be in excess of 1.5 (Figs. 12.2, 12.3). Additional checks were carried out on three of the dynamic features of cable-stayed structures:

i) Eddy shedding in cross-winds producing vibration in the ties.

ii) Down-wind 'galloping' in the ties.

iii) Roof 'snatch' movement under wind uplift producing over-stress in the ties.

12.5
STRUCTURAL FORM

The completed first stage comprises forty-two spatial/structural cells with each cell being 24m square, defined by four 16m high CHS masts. Between the masts, two systems of arched beams, at right angles and diagonally, form the main structure. These beams are trussed at their centres by rods and struts and supported at their quarter points by steel ties connected to the top of the masts. To support the roof decking and the building services, steel purlins are located at 4m centres, spanning between both beam systems and forming a central square rooflight in each module (Fig. 12.4).

The arched steel beams were tapered by cutting the web at an angle, reversing the section, and re-welding. Shear forces are not large in such situations, and the welding was not required to be continuous. The time and money spent in cutting out the 11,000 circular holes in the webs (see Fig. 8.12) was incurred solely for aesthetic effect!

The tie members are Grade 50C steel where they may possibly be destressed, and Macalloy rods form the four pre-stressed ties next to the masts. Stressing this system (which demanded a lot of adjustment) was carried out using the Pilgrim Nut hydraulic jacking system developed originally for stressing nuts in ships' boilers.

12.6
CONNECTIONS

Mechanical connections are used to couple the ties to the masts. To ensure their durability, particularly in the case of those which are exposed on the outside of the building, it was decided that they should be cast, in either iron or steel, to give a smooth, well-sealed profile. The chosen material, spheroidal graphitic cast iron, grade 370/317, acts in a similar way to Grade 43 steel but having been designed to be cast, unlike cast steel, the costs of

casting, heat treating and machining are about half those of the latter.

Quality assurance of the castings was by the testing of manufactured prototypes. By this means it was possible to assess:

i) The likely defect size.

ii) The degree of nodularity and ferriticity.

iii) The crack opening displacement (COD) of the material.

iv) The mechanical properties (yield stress, elongation and charpy values).

v) The ladle analysis.

vi) The velocity of sound which is a measure of nodularity.

The quality control method during production was to compare the ladle analysis and the results of mechanical tests on test bars and to check each piece ultrasonically for defects and sound velocity.

Internal stiffening of the masts at the areas of connection of the ties proved to be impracticable at the time. Consequently, the necessary stiffness was achieved by 'buttering' the surface of the mast with weld metal before the fitting of annular rings to which the vertical connection places were welded. This technique overcame any possible lamella tearing in the mast and the substantial variation of 32mm across the orthogonal diameters of the 457mm masts.

12.7
THE BUILDING ENVELOPE AND ITS SERVICES

The roof decking of 100mm deep corrugated steel units is connected to the purlins so as to restrain their compression flanges against lateral buckling. On top of the decking is laid 75mm of rockwool insulation, held in place by 75mm flat metal disc corner fixings. These are pulled down to the decking by self-tapping screws at centres which vary according to the calculated wind uplift at different points on the roof. This high density mineral wool sheet provides exceptional insulation, and works structurally to provide a dead load against wind uplift.

The waterproof roof surface consists of a single, continuous solvent-welded pvc membrane made of a specially reinforced Trocal 'S' material. It was glued to the fixing discs as it was rolled over them, and formed over pvc coated metal sections at rooflight, eaves and downpipe positions. Waterproofing at the 360 tension rod penetrations is based on a 200 mm pvc patch threaded on during structural assembly. Each rod passes through a hole cut in the decking and the membrane is slit to allow the rod to pass, with a binding of solvent-bonded pvc to ensure a tight fit. The patch was then slid down over the binding and on to the membrane where is was solvent-welded to make a waterproof seal.

Roof drainage is by downpipes within the masts, the flow passing through a fixed moment connection at the base. Outlets enter from the side and rather low down from the top of the deck level outlet. Under extreme rainfall a head of water is deliberately designed to build up on the roof so that the discharge changes from weir to orifice flow, thus increasing the volume which can be drained.

The external wall panels are a low cost system, developed for the project, in which expanded polyurethane foam between two skins of steel provides a high insulation value. The double skin panels span horizontally between vertical mullions at 4m centres, to which they are attached by self-tapping screws, the gap sealed by a neoprene strip. The mullions span between the ground floor slab and the roof, but are restrained at the roof only in the plane normal to that of the wall. In the plane of the wall, the roof is free, vertically and horizontally. The gap at this point, which has to be closed so as to accommodate these movements of +/- 75mm vertically and +/- 30mm horizontally, is sealed by a Neoprene-coated nylon fabric material originally developed for hovercraft skirts, tensioned by the kind of tie-down fixings used in fabric-sided lorries. The poor thermal performance of the Neoprene is balanced by the higher than necessary U-value of the main part of the external wall.

Both the roofing and the decking contracts involved the contractors in design and detail work to meet a performance specification. For the cladding system, Foster Associates' project architect indicated a preferred module within a performance specification, but offered to consider alternatives. In fact, the lowest tenderer was able to offer freedom of choice on both modular length and cladding profile and the chosen section was developed in collaboration with the architects for the project.

The provision of the driverless AGV transport system required the floor level to be within fine limits of +/- 1mm relative to a 1.5m straight edge placed on the surface. The floor construction is of 210mm reinforced concrete with 15mm monolithic granolithic topping on a 300mm blinded slab base and heavy duty polythene membrane. The slab was cast in 4m wide bays across the width of the warehouse.

So far as natural lighting is concerned, this is mainly introduced at the square truncated apex of each module where a combined roof light and automatic smoke ventilation unit is provided in the form of a system of upvc louvres. In addition, twenty-seven north-facing sloping rooflight assemblies are provided in the form of Pilkington's Planar glazing system. These rooflights consist of silicon-bonded 10mm armour plate glass sheets, bolted down to a pvc-coated metal section with a neoprene gasket

between the two. The same system is used for the full height glazing in the showroom area.

The approach to the design of building services is fairly traditional although due emphasis has been placed on energy conservation. Heating is provided by three 700KW gas fired boilers serving the various circuits in the building. For the warehouse, high level down-flow type unit heaters occur at each module. The show room and restaurant are served by low level fan convector heaters specially designed and developed for the project and the workshops, offices and classrooms are heated by warm air systems fed from air handling units.

12.8
THE CONSTRUCTION SEQUENCE

The general sequence of construction was governed by three requirements: first, the need to carry out the foundation construction and steelwork erection during the winter months of 1981-82; secondly, to protect the clay under the warehouse slab from water and damage from construction traffic and, lastly, to lay the high tolerance concrete floor slab under cover so as to be able to control its rate of curing.

For these reasons, the general sequence was as follows:

- Remove all top soil from the site.
- Lay a drainage blanket to limit the water content of the clay fill and ensure its stiffness and stability.
- Excavate and compact the clay to 300mm above the eventual formation level to act as a watertight seal.
- Lay construction roads to protect the clay from traffic.
- Construct foundation pads.
- Erect the steelwork.
- Complete the roof cladding and weather sealing.
- Compact the granular fill forming the final hardcore.
- Cast the monogranolithic slab.

Structural operations began on site with the assembly of the prestressed elements, namely the masts with their four stub beams and eight prestressed ties. These were stressed using Pilgrim nuts, adjusted to achieve the correct loadings and checked for position to a tolerance of +/- 3mm. They were then erected on the bases with eight holding down bolts in a circle. The upper parts of the masts were painted before erection for safety reasons and to achieve shop controlled quality.

The spanning beams along the main and diagonal grids were assembled on the ground with their lower tension members in place. These complete arched units were then adjusted to the exact dimensions required on site by tensioning the tie rods, lifted into place, and pinned in position.

The upper ties, running from the mastheads to the quarter span points, and attached to a stiffening member of the exact straight line length, were then positioned and fixed with finger tight nuts. The stiffening member was then removed. Because of the angle, weight and induced tension in the ties, their profile is sufficiently straight as to make their load extension characteristics virtually elastic. When the steelwork in one bay was complete, the ties around the masts were again checked with the Pilgrim nuts as the masts were plumbed.

12.9
APPRAISAL

This much admired and award winning building has not been without its critics. It has been suggested that the cost of the warehouse area was twice that currently aimed for by commercial pension fund developers, and that the external wall to roof junctions, and several interior junctions, are crude and unresolved (Lyall and Brett, 1983, Pawley, 1983). Moreover, given the architects' professed concern for human values, it is clearly arguable that the money spent on cutting out over 11,000 holes in the roof structure alone, purely for appearance, could have been better spent in providing some eye-level views out for the workers. The architects have shown typical attention to detail and great ingenuity in solving the problems which arose. But it has been argued that these problems have only arisen as a result of early decisions about the general structural concept and its modular expression (Lyall and Brett, 1983).

However, the building undeniably achieves the objectives set by the client: it has proved to be of immense publicity value and its innovative appearance and low physical profile paid off handsomely in increased site coverage and company prestige. For the builders, there was good experience in the precise setting out and the constructional assemblies which will characterise the industry in the future. Lastly, the architects and engineers showed impressive design skills and imagination in further developing the industrial box into a modular organism, in the analysis of masted structures and their behaviour, and in their design and realisation.

Reference sources

- Best, Alistair 'Foster at play' *The Architects' Journal* 1 Dec 1982 pp 40-41.
- Davey, Peter 'Renault Centre, Swindon, Wilts, *The Architects' Journal* July 1983 pp 20-32.
- Lyall, Sutherland and Brett, Peter 'Renault in real life' *Building* 10 June 1983 pp 34-35.
- Manning, Martin 'Renault parts distribution centre, Swindon: The civil and structural engineering' *The Arup Journal* Sept, 1983 pp 2-5.
- Pawley, Martin 'Renault inspection' *The Architects' Journal* 15 June 1983 pp 41-45.
- Renault Centre News Releases, 15 June 1983.
- Waters, Brian 'Framework for Renault' *Building* 22 October 1982 pp 32-40.
- Tietz, Stefan 'Masted Structures' *Building* 20 November 1981 pp. 32-34.
- Thornton, J. A. 'The design and construction of cable-stayed roofs' *The Structural Engineer*, 62A, 9, Sept. 1984 pp. 275-284.

SUMMARIES AND CONCLUSIONS

13

Having completed the explorations and reviews of the various kinds of masted structures that have been proposed or completed, we can now summarise the general characteristics of the genre.

We began by defining the subject matter of the study as being those buildings which embody a tensile structure in which the high level anchorages of the suspension system are provided by tall and relatively slender masts. However, to add point to this basic definition, and to provide some useful comparisons, we have included some buildings which fall outside a strict interpretation of the terms of reference.

This is because the suspension systems vary, and because the masts themselves come in different forms and materials. Consequently, 'borderline cases' are not uncommon. In some instances the suspension system is based on A-frames rather than masts: the Edinburgh Plant House, the Patscenter, and the Sydney Football Stadium, for example. Moreover, some reinforced concrete struts are so substantial as to become heavy pylons rather than slim poles and we have included the Pan Am Terminal, even though its high level masts are not continuous from apex to foundation. These buildings are interesting comparative examples in their own right: they widen the scope of the book and they act as links to other forms of structures.

13.1

THE PATTERN OF DEVELOPMENT

The appraisal of the pattern of development of masted structures over the period of fifty years from 1940 to 1990, involves answers to several questions: how many of such structures have been built, what functional and formal types do they represent, and at what times, and for what reasons have they appeared?

Answers to some of these questions have, in effect, already been provided in the chronological account of 20th century developments in Chapter 5, and the formal and structural characteristics of the genre will be discussed in the next part of this chapter. In terms of numbers of buildings, the earlier analysis showed that mast architecture has increased steadily since its inception, with a surge of examples completed between 1985 and 1990. This rate of increase may decline during the 1990s, due partly to the worldwide recession in industrial and constructional activity. It may also be that as masted forms become more common, their novelty value and visual impact may be lessened, and designers may seek to develop other structural forms. However, even in Europe masted structures are so uncommon that this is unlikely to happen for some time. Elsewhere in the world, they are even more thinly spread, their structural and formal vocabulary is by no means exhausted, and the range of potential applications is so large that we are likely to see many more examples in the future.

In terms of function over the 50 year period, mast architecture has been represented in all those building types which involve large, unobstructed space: that is, in buildings for industry, retailing, warehousing, transport, and sport and recreation. Occasionally, certain clusters of these types of buildings have been related to particular, though still very general patterns of socio-cultural change. For example, the post-war expansion of air travel brought with it the need for wide-span hangars and passenger terminals which provided early opportunities for tensile structures. At the same time, the regular sequence of major international exhibitions, Worlds Fairs and Expos required eye-catching structures for which mast architecture was ideal, and the concern for sport recreation and physical fitness has produced groups of sports halls, stadia and grandstands. For the most part, however, masted structures have occurred at regular intervals across the whole spectrum of functional types, with the exception of residential buildings such as housing, hotels and flats, the multi-cellular nature of which lends itself to more conventional structural systems.

Similarly, in terms of size, there is no particularly uneven pattern of distribution and the occurrence of large-scale, medium or small-scale examples at any one time has been an *ad hoc* one. Masted structures have occurred as solutions to particular problems as and when an appropriate socio-functional programme has seemed to commend itself in that form to a progressive design team and an enlightened or sympathetic client. These circumstances have arisen in relation to projects of all manner of sizes on a variety of occasions with no noticeable patterns in terms of size or date. The most that can be said is that there has been a very general increase in size up to that of the largest example, the Haj Terminal of 1982, but that before and since that structure, the distribution of differing sizes has been a random one.

So far as the general development of mast architecture is concerned, this has been influenced, over the period from 1940 to 1990, by the effects and interactions of three principal processes. The primary process of socio-cultural development has been expressed architecturally in terms of a series of requirements for large unobstructed spaces for the variety of functions mentioned earlier. However, only a proportion of masted structures have taken the form of 'big sheds' of that kind and there has been an equally significant and more varied range of medium and small-scale buildings, often exquisitely designed and detailed, which repay study and appraisal.

The second process has been one of technological development which has been expressed in two distinct fields of construction: first engineering technology and metallurgy, in the form of high strength steels, casting methods and new structural components and connections; and secondly in the form of flexible, single-layer roofing membranes, in weather-proofing, sealing and insulating techniques, and in new decking systems to support them.

The third process has consisted of a developing theoretical and practical understanding of how tensile structures behave under dynamic loading conditions, a process helped considerably by parallel advances in light-weight structures and the availability of computers and computer programs able to make the necessary calculations.

Linking and integrating these diverse processes has been the human factor, that is, those architects and engineers imaginative and creative enough to be aware of the possibilities which were opening up, and who were able to incorporate them into their own design intentions and procedures. The resulting structures have, as we have seen, taken a wide range of forms, the differentiation of which we can now discuss.

13.2
ARCHITECTURAL FORM AND STRUCTURAL EXPRESSION

To explain the formal and structural differentiation amongst masted structures we have based our categorisations on the relationships of the masts to the basic spatio-structural 'cells' which make up the form of the buildings. These basic elements may be enclosed by the building envelope or merely implied by the sheltered space under a roof plane or simple canopy.

There is no doubt that alternative analyses of masted structures can be made, from different stand-points and with different objectives. However, we justify our own approach by the fact that it combines the element of space, which is one of the architect's primary concerns, with the engineer's involvement in its structural articulation; this is intended to satisfy the objective of constructing a taxonomy which combines space and form – the two essential aspects of the architectural subject-matter – and which will be acceptable and relevant to architects and engineers.

The basic, spatio-structural categories of one, two, four and eight mast arrangements, and their one-way and two-way assemblages, have been illustrated earlier largely in terms of the plans of the structures. However, plan pattern alone provides only an initial ordering principle and gives only a limited indication of the structural and formal principles underlying a particular example. In a masted structure, the total spatial and structural logic of the building involves its three-dimensional structural anatomy, the consequent force-paths, the arrangement of major spans, supports and anchorages over the extent of the building, and the particular materials used in the primary structure.

It is these principles of suspension, span and support, and their formal and structural interpretation, which characterise the spectacular variety of masted structures. The basic categories which have emerged, and which order this variety to a large extent, can now be reviewed in more detail.

Single mast structures and assemblages

This category comprises the simplest topological arrangements of a single mast in relation to a basic cell, together with assemblages of single mast cells; however, despite the simplicity of the basic arrangement, the category includes a very diversified group of forms and structures.

The examples cover a wide range of functions, sizes and materials, and the category includes not only conventional enclosed buildings but also open structures in the form of simple or more elaborate canopies; for example, the standard Mobil filling station, the Il de Re toll point, and the stadium canopies at Marl and Marburg.

The comparison of all the structures in this category involves distinctions at three levels: the topological, the geometrical and the constructional. The primary logic concerns the position of the mast in relation to the associated spatial 'cell'. In topological terms, the mast may be located inside the cell, either centrally or off-centre, on its perimeter or outside it. Examples of the former include Fuller's Dymaxion house design, the aluminium pavilion at the Hannover exhibition, and the Knowsley Leisure Centre, whilst the latter sub-group includes the Brentford 'Homebase' Supermarket and the industrial units at Rotterdam.

The two basic topological alternatives can be expressed geometrically in terms of built forms which are square or rectangular, circular or elliptical, or regularly polygonal in plan. This plan geometry, and its proportions, has significant implications for the structural logic. Cells which are square in plan invariably have a central mast with radiating suspension ties, and these cells have ranged from 9.0m to 30.0m square. Groups of such cells can either touch each other, in the form of a simple grid, or be articulated by a minor module to form a 'tartan' grid pattern. In the largest example, the 'Rotaprint' project for Berlin, masts occur in alternate grid modules, forming an 'equal structural tartan' of 20.0m x 20.0m cells. In contrast, rectangular cells, with either internal or external masts, are characterised by two alternative suspension principles: either a system of radiating ties running to the intersection points of an orthogonal roof framework, or a linear system of ties associated with a 'spine' beam of some kind on the long axis of the cell. The stadium canopy at Marl is an example of the former, whilst the Brentford 'Homebase' represents the latter.

The constructional interpretations of these configurations are equally varied: the roof plane may take the form of a simple concrete slab, a grid framework of steel beams, channels or tubes, a timber framework, a pattern of lattice beams arranged diagonally or orthogonally in relation to the planning grid and covered by proprietary decking, or a space deck. At Almere, the suspension ties support truncated pyramids, each with four 'butterfly' roof vents. Small scale structures may have four or eight radiating cables per mast whilst at the other extreme the roof of the Baxter Travenol Laboratory has thirty-two cables from each of its two supports. Expanding the central mast into a four column support, as at Biberach and Bunnik, opens up further spatial and formal possibilities.

So far as assemblages of single mast cells are concerned, one-way repetitions are rare, whereas two way groupings are comparatively common. The latter vary in number of cells from four to one hundred and forty-one, although the great majority fall well below this figure. Architecturally, the most refined detailing is shown in the Rotterdam industrial units by the Cepezed Studio whilst the Brentford 'Homebase' supermarket makes probably the most emphatic visual statement. The most unusual example in this category is the gull-wing canopy of the Swiss Expo Station which was slung, by a series of diverging hangers, from four major suspension cables, each raised up by an inclined mast near to its mid-point.

Two mast structures and assemblages

The structural configurations in this category can also be described with the help of topological and geometrical concepts. In topological terms, the concept of the masts being either inside or outside the originating cellular space is still valid, and examples of both arrangements occur in several buildings. However, the structural logic is more significantly influenced at the geometrical level, in terms of the proportion in plan of the basic cells. In this category, the buildings are all based on rectangular modules and it is this rectangularity which forms the basis of the four topological arrangements of the masts in relation to their associated space. These arrangements consist of masts centrally at the sides, centrally on the ends, or at adjacent or opposite corners (although no instances of the latter arrangement have occurred, nor seem likely to do so).

In these buildings, radiating cables supporting an overall grid framework in the roof do not seem to have occurred. Instead, the primary element of the roof structure is a cable-stayed beam or series of beams forming, with the masts, a linear suspension system which in turn demands a ground anchorage at one or both ends. For this reason, the structures are generally simpler to understand than those in the previous category.

The three topological arrangements of two masts in relation to a rectangular cell, and the one-way and two-way repeats, are easily summarised. The side mast sub-group has text-book examples of a basic cell and an end-to-end repeat in the factory gate lodge at Rotterdam and the Waikita office building respectively. Sideways repeats of a side mast arrangement produce a built form with a series of internal columns and this arrangement can be seen in the SNECMA factory and at the OM exhibition station canopy of 1948. The effect of two-way repetitions of side mast cells is shown in the Transcon lines terminal and the Parker Square development project.

So far as end masts are concerned, the three ice rinks at Arosa, Braunlage and Oxford make an interesting comparison in terms of architectural form, single or dual spine beams and internal or external masts. At a very much larger scale, the Darwin Harbour Complex and the West Japan Exhibition Centre represent comparative approaches to a similar functional problem.

Architecturally, this category includes several buildings of high quality, several of which have been mentioned above. The most complex example is that of Poole Station, a two layer arrangement of different structural systems, aligned in alternate directions. Exoskeletal spine beams characterise the Paco Rabanne Factory and the Hannover Conference Centre.

Lastly, one irregular feature of this category is that occasionally the end masts of the system are omitted so that the basic concept is not physically complete. This occurs, for example, in the SNECMA Factory and in the Berlin Sports Centre. This centre is one of two examples in the last subgroup, i.e. those characterised by masts located at one end of the cell, an arrangement which, when repeated laterally produces a built form with masts along one side. The Woking Pool is the other example of this type.

Four mast structures and assemblages

The key to understanding the structural anatomy of buildings based on four mast cells lies in appreciating that two kinds of structural logic are involved: first, a logic of position, of the masts in relation to the basic spatial compartment, i.e. either at the comers or at the sides and, secondly, a constructional logic of alignments, that is of the suspension systems, which can run either in parallel or at right angles to each other. As in other categories, the proportion in plan of the basic cell, whether square or rectangular, is a significant influencing factor.

The positional logic originates in this category in a single cell with a mast at each of the four corners. The cell can be square or rectangular in plan. We have come across no examples of the former, but the new East Croydon Station is an example of the latter.

The repetition of this arrangement laterally, in the form of a rectangular building with masts down the sides, forms the basis of the Central Washington College gymnasium, the Squaw Valley Stadium, the Napp Laboratories project and the Edinburgh plant house. The first two buildings have outwardly raking masts in a typical 1950s mode: at Edinburgh, the masts are also inclined outwards but in the form of intersecting A-frames, whereas the Napp project is a more straightforward, reticulate structure.

One broader-scale, compositional feature unique to this category is the occurrence of buildings comprising successive parallel blocks of this form, articulated by a minor module. The EBCO Aerospace building and Sainsbury's at Canterbury are based on this strategy which preserves the integrity of each block and provides for the backstay forces to be accommodated, whilst Theme Building envisaged for the future 'Wonderworld' project shows the strategy used on a megastructure scale.

The two-way grid repeats of four mast cells of this basic type include examples with parallel and intersecting structural alignments. The square grids of the Fleetguard and Renault Warehouses, of 18.0m and 24.0m respectively, form the basis of intersecting two-way suspension systems. In contrast, the 28.8m x 14.4m rectangular grid of the shopping centre at Nantes is interpreted structurally as a series of parallel cable-stayed frames.

Changing the positional logic of the four masts from the corners of the cell to intermediate points on the long sides results in a second group of characteristic structures. In the seven buildings of this kind, a 'nave and aisles' pattern of supports results from the repeated bay system, although the 'aisles' between the vertical backstays and the main structural masts are not enclosed in all cases.

In these examples, which have similar plan configurations, the cross section becomes the focus of attention. The proportional aisle/nave/aisle widths vary significantly, in response to the structural philosophy and the activity-space demands. For example, in the ADT canopy, the masts support equal cable-stayed, balanced cantilevers (a 1:2:1 proportion) whilst in the Liquid Ink Factory Project similar balanced cantilevers have an additional roof element spanning between them (a proportion of 1:3:1). All in all, these proportions vary between the 1:1.3:1 of the Craigavon shopping centre to the 1:8.3:1 of the Nice Airport Terminal.

The Airport Terminal at Bundaberg is a single-celled version of this arrangement, although its main beams are concealed within the vault shell thickness. Elsewhere, the number of cells varies between three and fourteen.

As we noted in the main text, the bringing together of two masts to an even closer position on opposite sides of a rectangular cell results in a 'spine' of pairs of supports when the cell is repeated laterally. This configuration forms the basis of a recognisable 'Inmos type', characterised by the masts forming the framework for the linear movement and servicing systems which are flanked by relatively low, but wide-span and column-free spaces. This general form includes the Tosho Printing Works, the Inmos Factory, the Sainsbury Supermarket design by MacCormac, Jamieson and Pritchard, and the Patscenter Research Laboratory – although in that case the dual mast structure is replaced by a series of roof-level A-frames.

The remaining projects in this sub-group consist of narrowly proportioned frameworks designed to structure three entirely different functions: two on a small scale and a third, the UK pavilion at Osaka, larger and virtually on its own typologically.

All these structural configurations result from developmental versions of the basic corner mast strategy. The alternative, generic structural logic is to place the four masts not at the corners nor on two opposite sides but on all four sides of a square, or almost square plan. This implies that the associated cable-stayed beam systems will intersect each other at right angles. This classic 'centralised' logic forms the basis of the Hannover Warehouse and Hall 7 at the NEC in Birmingham, both with two masts per side. The much larger West Swindon Leisure Centre with five masts per side is an extended version of the same principle but the longer span demands a central support in the form of a four mast internal tower.

Centralised 'closed forms' of this kind do not lend themselves to lateral extension whether in one or two directions but the one example which does bear some resemblance in plan to this structural strategy is the Tilburg Station canopy. However, although the pattern of span and supports of the quatrefoil hyperbolic paraboloids forming each structural cell does correspond to the basic arrangement, and although outward-sloping masts do occur along the sides of the canopy, these make only a minor contribution to the overall structural system, which is largely based on the pairs of central, platform supports in conjunction with a fairly cumbersome roof structure.

Membrane roofed structures

In contrast to the previous main categories, masted structures with flexible membrane roofs have few other features in common. In terms of form, they comprise two circular structures, one with a central mast and one with an external raking pylon, four square grid and five rectangular grid structures, and the curious J-shaped barrel vault of the Block A Pavilion at the Tsukuba Expo.

The suspension principles are as follows: first, the two circular structures form a single-masted group with radiating cable stays; secondly, one example, the Yulara Visitor Centre, is roofed with hyperbolic paraboloid awnings spanning directly between the four masts of a series of square cells; thirdly, in all other examples the key issue is whether the tension stays simply raise the tented surface alone or, more rarely, support or are supported by some form of structural framework in addition. Examples of both principles occur with the Haj terminal being an instance of the former, and the Pallet Handling Building at Charles de Gaulle airport in Paris an example of the latter.

Grandstand structures

Taken as a whole, the examples in this functional category do make up a formal taxonomic group if only because they are single-cantilever structures designed to shelter a body of spectators seated on stepped terraces. However, apart from these defining features of the category, each example differs in almost every respect from every other, with the exception of the Mound Stand at Lords cricket ground and the Sussex Stand at Goodwood racecourse. These share a distinct family resemblance, despite having different designers, by each having fabric roof cells drawn up around central masts with horizontal booms and outriggers below. The remaining structures can only be studied, assessed and summarised individually, and on their own terms as each is virtually an individual case, even in morphological terms.

Rotational structures

The principles of support and suspension of the structures of this kind are directly related to the topological disposition of the masts, that is, either on the inside, on the line of, or on the outside of the building envelope. At one extreme one can define a narrow ring of internal masts in conjunction with cable-stayed cantilevers radiating to the perimeter or, at the other, one can have a wider circle of external masts tied back by external outriggers to produce a column-free interior. The Pan Am terminal represents an intermediate position. The choice between these generic topological alternatives will depend on whether the functional requirements are for a core structure with an unobstructed circular perimeter, for a column-free circular enclosure, or for a large space of circular or elliptical form with a minimum number of internal columns.

13.3
STRUCTURAL BEHAVIOUR

We do not propose to deal with the detailed concepts, methods and criteria used in the calculations for masted structures as there is already a substantial literature relating to these matters of which structural engineers will be aware, and with which architects will be only marginally concerned. What seems to us to be important to provide here is a summary of those aspects of structural behaviour which have architectural and engineering implications, jointly, and an indication of some of the resulting formal effects.

The design process

At a certain point in the design process the structural behaviour of cable-stayed buildings becomes a significant architectural determinant. In the initial phases of a project, primary generators of architectural form such as function, movement and site are the basic stimuli and criteria in the production of outline ideas. However, once a masted structure becomes a likely option, other factors come into play and the major architectural statement then takes the form of a structural narrative in terms of a grammar and syntax of prominent engineering components. Levels of function and meaning become identifiable, from the overall configuration of the tensile structure to the physical nature of the principal elements and the design of their junctions and connections. At this point, the designers' responses to the dynamic effects of changing patterns of loading, transverse and longitudinal forces, wind uplift, and in-plane and out-of-plane effects begin to affect the form of the building in earnest.

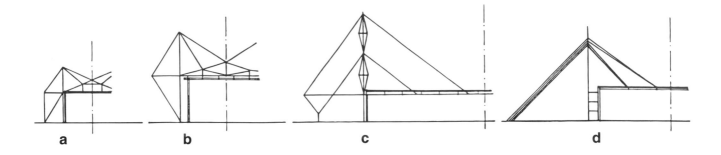

Structural philosophy

The ensuing detailed exploration of structural behaviour can only be meaningfully undertaken in parallel with the development of a more general structural philosophy: for example, is the basic structural concept to be that of a cable-assisted 'umbrella' or series of umbrellas? These might save weight, but do have an unfortunate tendency to fall over! Alternatively, is the structure to be based on cable-stayed beams, used either singly, in the form of the major lattice girder of a framed roof, or as a series of parallel beams or frames, or as an intersecting grid framework? Are there to be one, two or four masts in each spatial/structural cell, and whereabouts are they to be located in relation to it? Which of the alternative tie-down methods is to be used (Fig. 13.1).

It will no doubt become apparent after considering these alternative approaches that each of the generic structural layouts which make up the taxonomy of masted structures described in successive chapters of Part Two is, in effect, a possible structural philosophy. Each is an abstract organising concept of space and structure, capable of being interpreted in a variety of components and materials.

Non-linearity in structural behaviour

Whichever structural philosophy is eventually developed, it is important to remember that masted structures are generally non-linear in their structural behaviour, i.e. that the response of the structure to the applied loadings is not constant. In linear structures, doubling the loads has the effect of doubling the stresses, and reversing the loads of reversing the stresses. In non-linear structures these principles do not apply and the matters involved are extensive and complex.

For example, different patterns of loading may cause individual members to cease to contribute to the structural strength in the way intended: wind uplift can cause the suspension system to go slack so that the structure behaves in an entirely different way, whilst the structural behaviour resulting from the inherent sag in inclined rods and cables also leads to complex situations; out-of-plane displace-

ments in single plane configurations can lead to bending in the masts as well as compression.

These situations will not apply equally to all types of masted structures, nor should the dynamic effects, particularly on roofs, be over-emphasised. Their structural behaviour will depend on mass, stiffness and damping, but mass and damping will not differ significantly from conventional roofs, and stiffness against downward loads will be limited by the code of practice criteria for deflection. Consequently, structural analysis will probably only reveal the need for precautionary measures in extreme cases. However, the detailed design and implementation of designs which embody non-linear characteristics demands a sophisticated understanding and computational resources which not all engineers may be able to bring to bear. This may set limits to the kind of masted structures which can be put forward, although it is true to say that engineering consultancies in the UK are world leaders in these concepts and methodologies.

We will look at some of these aspects of structural behaviour in turn, in relation to their causes and architectural effects.

Vertical loads

Vertical loads on flat or virtually flat roofs are of three kinds:

i) Uniformly distributed gravity loads such as roof decks and level snow loads. These loads are usually applied at roof beam or boom level and their overall support is by the main tension ties from the mastheads.

ii) Patch loading and concentrated gravity loads: these loads, which include drifted snow and rainwater ponding, will not constitute a problem in single-span structures. However, in multiple-span structures, patch loading in one span may lead to an uplift condition in an adjacent span.

iii) Wind uplift: uplift conditions resulting from wind action must be a primary focus of attention. This is because the net uplift can almost equal the self-weight of a light roof. Where the uplift forces are substantially greater than those under dead-load, the need for a different design is perhaps indicated!

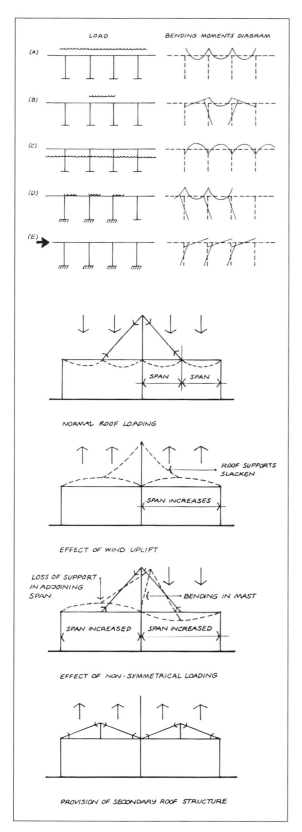

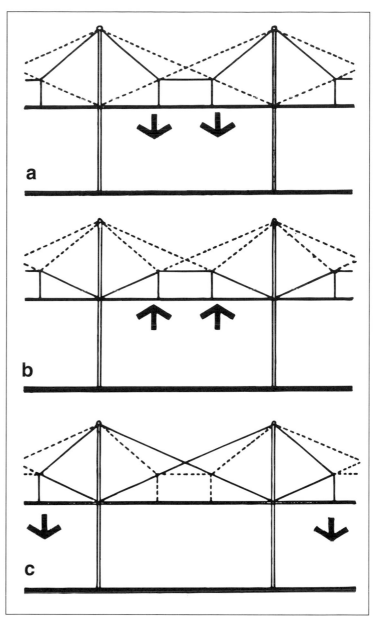

The structural implications of these factors are shown in Fig. 13.2.

Uplift problems and their solution

The loading conditions mentioned under ii) and iii) above represent two characteristic problems in

masted structures, i.e. that the tension system under dead loads becomes inoperative under wind uplift, and that unbalanced live loads in one span can cause uplift in another (Fig. 13.3). They each have the same effect, that is, reversal of loading under uplift causes the tension members to become slack, unless they are prestressed to a level at which they are always in tension. Consequently, the beam, deprived of their assistance and under stress reversal, has to span not between the tension stays but the whole distance between the masts. Their restraint is reduced and, unless they are very stiff, they will become unstable. This in turn allows the suspension points of the loaded span to settle, causing the mast to sway and bend. Several steps can be taken to counteract these uplift conditions, the most obvious being to increase the stiffness of the tension system itself. But this would still not limit the span of the beam to the shorter distance between the sus-

Fig. 13.2
(far left)
Structural
implications of
differing loading
conditions.

Fig. 13.3 *(above)*
Bending moment
diagrams
resulting from
differing loading
conditions.

do much to encourage re-attached air flow and reduce uplift. Hall 7 at the NEC is an instance of this. In grandstands, providing a slot at the rear of the roof and at its leading edge will have a similar effect.

In many cases, however, the preferred solution has been to form a secondary 'inverted tensile system' above the roof – the kind of configuration designed for Fleetguard, for example. This will be more effective in reducing uplift, whilst maintaining the support points of the roof beams under stress reversal, and not causing loss of mast restraint (Figs. 8.10, 13.4). This embodies the principle of designing a structure in such a way that the geometry itself copes with the forces involved rather than the individual members.

This is not to mention the possible alternatives of either choosing a relatively heavy roof construction in the first place, or of deliberately adding extra weight during the detail design of the roof. This principle of adding weight seems inconsistent with the basic aims of structural engineering, but it may be justified architecturally if it also helps in the thermal or acoustic insulation, if heavy materials are more readily available, or if it avoids the need for obstructive tie-downs. The National Athletics Stadium at Canberra is an example of the latter argument.

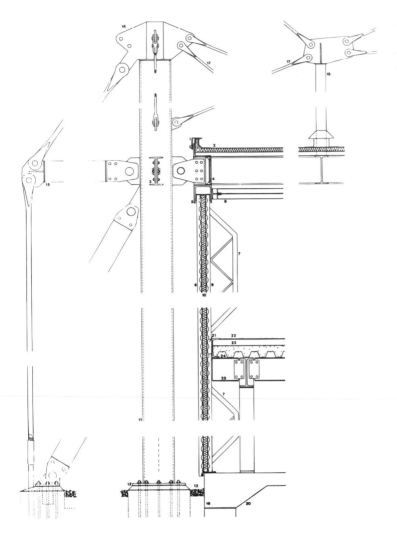

Fig. 13.4
Diagrams showing how the parts of the Fleetguard suspension structure counteract differing patterns of forces:

a. System supporting the roof under downward loading.

b. System to counteract upward loading during wind uplift.

c. System to control the response of the roof to repeated asymmetrical loading, and to limit deflection.

pension points, nor would the bending forces on the mast be eliminated. Consequently, in general terms, attempting to change the stiffness of the system is thought to be structurally inconsistent and inefficient. There is, however, one qualification to this rule in the case of open cable-stayed cantilever canopies. In these instances, the stiffness of the primary supports is usually increased to avoid the need for tie-down cables to restrain the roof under uplift. Cables of this kind would usually be visually unacceptable, but as they do occasionally occur, one should perhaps not rule them out entirely.

As an alternative to increasing stiffness elsewhere, one may deliberately try to limit the bending of the mast so that there is no loss of support to the loaded span. This could be done by increasing the intrinsic stiffness of the mast itself, or by applying external tension stiffeners so as to ensure a fully restrained mast head. But the bending forces involved may be substantial, and resistance to them can absorb a significant amount of additional steelwork, as the Renault building shows.

In the case of enclosed buildings, one alternative is to pay particular attention to the eaves detail which, as wind tunnel tests have shown, can itself

Horizontal stability

The methods of maintaining horizontal stability can be said to be strategic and tactical. The strategic principle is that of providing a spatial/structural zone which is inherently stable in itself and which can thus maintain the stability of the structure as a whole. Spinal and perimeter zones have been used and in spinal masted structures, such as the Inmos factory and the Patscenter, the braced pairs of masts not only frame the circulation and servicing systems, but also provide lateral stability for the whole structure. Stable braced zones have also been defined around the perimeter of some centralised masted structures in the form of a series of in-plane vierendeel frames. In the Hannover warehouse, these frames define a zone 1.4m wide using an outer CHS member and an inner rolled steel section whilst in Hall 7 at the NEC the zone is 3.0m wide, made up of 12m high steel joists. Lastly, in the gigantic Haj terminal, the 12.5m perimeter zone is defined by pairs of standard pattern tapering masts which are quadrupled at the corners in the form of 12.5m square open towers.

At a tactical level, horizontal stability can be achieved either by the frame action of the structure itself or by external bracing. The issue is related to our earlier discussion of the method chosen to reduce the effects of patch loading. Where this is provided by frame action, stability can be achieved by the same method, with simple tie-downs from outriggers to ground anchorages round the perimeter. However, in single bay structures, where frame action is not necessary to resist patch loading, inclined bracing is a more appropriate structural solution.

The alternatives to frame action, namely bracing methods, themselves vary and make an interesting study. At Fleetguard, the tie-downs from the ends of the outriggers run vertically to ground anchorages where they meet the lower ends of inclined, push-pull members running down from eaves level. In more recent designs, at the shopping centres at Nantes and Epone for example, these inclined members run from the ends of the outriggers to the foot of the masts so as to complete an effective portal frame capable of resisting in-plane horizontal loads and maintaining stability. In this kind of configuration, not only is a separate tension anchorage avoided, but also the uplift forces in the inclined member act against the force in the mast thus reducing the total mast base reaction (Fig. 13.1).

Longitudinal forces

Longitudinal stability can, like lateral stability, be achieved in strategic or tactical ways. In strategic terms, the principle of providing inherently stable 'zones' of accommodation or services may be used if the plan of the building is suitable. Alternatively, at a tactical level, inclined tension/compression bracing can be provided at the ends of the building, as at Inmos, or conventional cross-bracing may be introduced into the roof and walls, as at Epone. Where cross-bracing is visually unacceptable, full moment connections have been used in the roof framing. Additional resistance may be provided by the roof beam hangers, and the roof itself may be designed to make a structural contribution as a stressed diaphragm.

Stiffness and deflection

Masted structures are not necessarily more flexible than more conventional structures, nor are deflections necessarily likely to be greater. The stiffness in a masted structure depends primarily on its configuration, which is a matter for good design. Moreover, the large, effective structural depth of a masted system makes a useful contribution to achieving stiffness. However, the factor of span is important because the greater the span the greater the deflection for any particular design-based ratio between them. Consequently, as masted structures are often used over long spans, deflections may be larger than in some conventional structures and the details at the junctions with other building elements will therefore need more attention. But it

must be remembered that deflections have to be kept within the limits set out in the relevant codes of practice in any case.

Wind effects on masts and ties

At certain speeds tension members in structures are liable to vibrate because of an airflow pattern known as vortex shedding. This coincides with the natural frequency of the suspension tie, depending on its length, diameter and tension. When twin ties are run in parallel, this phenomenon can be exaggerated through aerodynamic interaction, particularly at close spacings. Proprietary dampers are used to counteract this.

Similar vibrations can occur in masts, where the mast head is not restrained in both directions. The problem can be avoided by altering the diameter of the mast, by incorporating aerodynamic strakes similar to those used on steel chimneys, or by adding proprietary dampers as mentioned above.

Temperature effects

Because the main components of masted structures are to a large extent outside the building envelope, the effects of temperature can be significant and have to be carefully assessed. Moreover, in a structure of some size, it is not possible to interrupt the continuous tensile system so as to provide an expansion joint of a conventional kind. This too means that temperature stresses can build up and their magnitude and effects have to be taken into account. The temperature differences allowed for will clearly vary with the location of the building.

Two types of situation typically occur: first, where the structure is virtually completely external, the interface between the members and the building envelope will need to allow for movement between them; secondly, where the structure is partly inside and partly outside the building a different kind of differential expansion and contraction will need to be addressed.

So far as the roof covering is concerned, the low thermal mass of lightweight roofing systems can again lead to significant thermal movements. For this reason, the lower strengths of felt roof coverings to BS 747 are inadequate and modern, high performance roofing systems have to be specified. It is essential that all penetrations of the waterproofing membrane are designed, simply and in detail, so that the satisfactory performance of the penetration can be guaranteed in principle rather than entrusted to possibly uncertain standards of workmanship.

Structural behaviour has been a formative factor in most, if not all masted structures and a comparative study of the built examples is an immensely rewarding exercise, especially for students, in showing how movement and its resistance has been reflected in structural provisions and architectural form.

13.4
CONSTRUCTIONAL NOTES

Specific constructional details of recent mast structures are not easy to obtain. The reason is that we are in a period of rapid technological change, not only in the building industry itself but also in technology transfer from the aerospace, boat-building and motor vehicle industries. New materials and components enter production whilst others are discontinued; existing specifications and standards are regularly upgraded and new standards become applicable in new situations. As a result, the leading firms of architects and engineers develop specialised in-house knowledge and experience which, perhaps understandably, is not made generally available.

However, some working details relating to masted structures can be found in another work in this series (Brookes and Grech, 1990), whilst other useful sources are the manufacturers' literature on the materials and components used, and the more technical papers cited in the bibliography (e.g. Thornton, 1984 and Rice, Thornton and Leczner, 1987). But the situation is a fluid one and even 'general principles' can change radically at short notice. Against this background we note in this section some characteristic constructional aspects of masted structures and indicate some possible future developments.

Mast design and construction

Masts have taken many forms and used steel, concrete and timber in the following ways:

- **Steel hollow sections**. Circular tubes have been most widely used because of their efficiency in compression and torsion, minimal surface area to be painted and maintained, minimal wind resistance, easy availability and economy. In larger structures, tubes have been coupled together in pairs, and in the very largest, such as the Peschia Flower Market and the Darling Harbour complex, in clusters of four. This allows heavier loads to be coped with – and four slim tubes are always more elegant than a single bulky cylinder.

  A further variation, seen at the Swiss Expo station, has been the use of four tubes threaded at intervals through circular fish-plate connectors to form a cigar-shaped mast. Seen from a distance this can appear reasonably slender but in close-up the fish-plates are rather clumsy in appearance.

  Rectangular hollow sections, introduced in 1959, and now available up to 500mm x 300mm in size, have also been used as the main members in vierendeel and lattice girders, as noted below.

- **Rolled steel sections**. These off-the-peg components have been used only on rare occasions; they occur as primary members in the Poole Station design, in the Italian Pavilion at the Osaka Expo, and as either one or both members of vierendeel frames elsewhere.

- **Steel lattices**. Towers in the form of steel lattice frameworks replace single member masts in larger projects where the loads are greater and where increased height is required to maintain an effective angle of incidence of the tension ties over a wider span. The Homebase Superstore and the new East Croydon Station are classic examples of parallel-sided towers. In contrast, rather ill-proportioned, stubby cigar-shaped lattice masts occur in the SNECMA Factory and in the Tesco Supermarket in Bristol, whilst a more elegant double-tapered form was used for the inclined masts at the OM Exhibition canopy in Milan.

- **Steel vierendeel frames**. The supermarket at Craigavon, Northern Ireland, is an early example of the use of this design of mast which offers better resistance to bending forces, whilst in the more recent Sheffield Stadium grandstand structure, the vierendeels are used vertically and horizontally to form the most prominent feature of the design.

- **Steel box sections**. Built up rectangular box beams were used in the early days of masted structures, particularly in the USA. They occur vertically and as inclined roof beams, cable assisted, in pitched roofs. The advent of standard rectangular hollow sections in large sizes has rendered obsolete the expensive welding of built-up beams of this kind. Moreover, because tapered box beams have nothing other than visual appearance to set against their additional expense, they too seem to have disappeared from the scene.

- **Tapered steel pylons**. The elegance of circular tapering spires, which can pierce an expressed canopy with some style, often belies their size. In the stadium canopy at Marl, Westphalia, they are 1.6m in diameter at the base and over 31.0m high, whilst in the Haj Terminal they are 2.5m in diameter, tapering to 1.0m over a height of 45.0m. They were designed to provide good lateral stiffness in both cases.

● **Concrete masts**. This second most popular material, in ordinary reinforced or pre-stressed forms, has been used in square or rectangular supports, with broadly rounded corners at the dockside terminal at Piraeus and, unusually, in square form but set on the diagonal at the Central Washington College Gymnasium. At the Max Burren Plant, where concrete was used because its materials were already owned by the civil engineering company client, the masts are octagonally faceted and subtly cigar-shaped over their length.

● **Concrete hollow pylons**. In large-scale projects, concrete is the ideal material to be formed into hollow pylons which replace conventional masts as high-level suspension points. These pylons can act as service distribution ducts, offer a high loading capacity and provide massive lateral stability. In the printing plant at Tapiola, the cylindrical towers are approximately 3.0m in diameter and 21.0m high and in the McCormick Place Development in Chicago, the pylons transfer air from the lower-level mechanical plant mezzanine to the main exhibition hall from where it is extracted via the upper parts of the same supports.

● **Timber framing**. The only example of a masted structure in timber is the small cantilevered canopy for the stage of the Pabst International Music Festival in Milwaukee in which the masts take the form of twin timber members separated by wooden blocks at the bolted through connections.

The choice between cables, rods or tubes, and their connections

The casual observer of tension structures would probably assume that the use of cables in suspension bridges and in the tension ties of fabric and cable-net roofs would transfer easily to the more conventional building technology of enclosed masted structures. This is not so, for two reasons: first, because steel cable has a low modulus of elasticity, the stretch in the ties will be up to four times greater than that of a solid rod, and vertical stiffness is much reduced – in circumstances where stiffness requirements are important. Consequently rods or tubes are more suitable in these structural respects.

Secondly, cables are more difficult to protect from corrosion. Grease introduced during manufacture tends to drift down leaving gaps open to water, whilst galvanising and other proprietary coatings have only a limited life. External protective sheathings may be more reliable over a longer period, but are more expensive and more difficult to repair if things go wrong. In response to these diffi-

Fig. 13.5
The external structure/ building envelope connection detail at the Fleetguard factory, 1981.

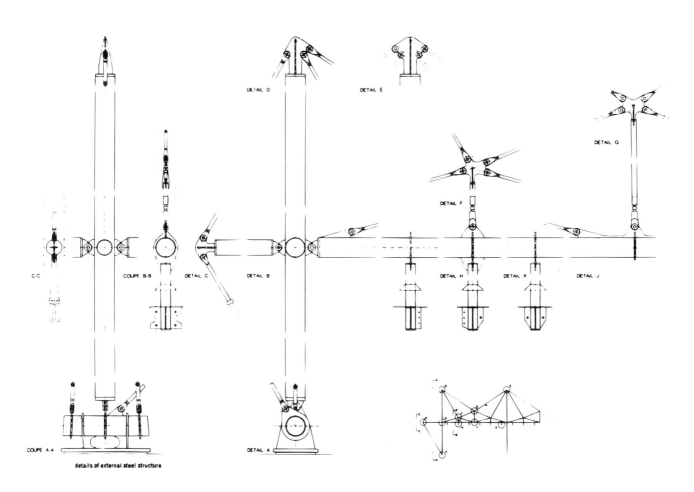

details of external steel structure

culties, stainless steel wire (EN58 to BS 1554) was used in the cables of the Edinburgh Plant House as long ago as 1967.

The main disadvantage of rods, particularly in long lengths, is that they must not be bent, either during transport to the site, or whilst being stored before use. Keeping 50mm rods up to 15m long straight on a building site may be difficult. Moreover, it may also be necessary to provide temporary stiffening members to prevent excessive sag during assembly. However, rods and tubes are cheaper and can be painted and maintained in the normal ways. Stainless steel can also be used in this form, as for example in the Oxford Ice Rink of 1983, and is becoming more frequently chosen.

A third aspect of the comparison between cables and rods is that of the connections between the ties and the rest of the structure (Fig. 13.5). Standard end connectors for flexible cables are readily available from industry, but are relatively clumsy in appearance. So far as rods and tubes are concerned, the magnitudes of the loads means that pinned joints using the fork and eye principle are the general rule. However, useful vocabulary of types of connection can be drawn upon, in terms of pinpointed linkages, profiled mode transfer plates and splice plates of various kinds. Pin joints allow for any slight discrepancies in the angles of the ties as well as rotation with change of sag in the tie, and make assembly relatively simple. The use of pinned connections at all joints in the structure extends these advantages and avoids the generation of moments at the junctions between the roof beams, or booms, and the masts. It also allows a complete family of visually coordinated details to be designed. For all these reasons, rods or tubes will usually be preferred to cables.

The end connections of rods and tubes also need careful consideration, and the study of their design and usage is well worthwhile for designers. Standard cast fork connectors are available from suppliers, but they can be clumsy in appearance and less efficient than a purpose-made component. However, the development and testing of special castings takes time, which may not be available, and the choice of material is important. Such special castings can be machined or flame cut out of plate, or cast in ductile iron or steel.

Cast iron is more consistent in quality and cheaper than cast steel, but cannot be welded. For this reason, some form of mechanical connection to the tie will be needed, and this will probably lead to a bulky appearance, as in the forks of the Renault building. Cast steel is more expensive, less consistent, but can be welded. In both cases the cost of the patterns must be taken into account and variety reduction used to keep costs down, as well as promote visual unity.

However, if members carry different loads, pattern costs may rise unavoidably, and the diverse sizes and shapes may give rise to an incongruous appearance.

Erection and adjustment

The process of erection of a masted structure must be assessed during the design process, and should form part of the tender documents. It is commonplace for erection to be carefully considered by designers and it will be essential in the case of innovative or complex designs. It may also be the case that contractors can suggest equally satisfactory erection procedures which would better suit their own preferences for whatever reason, so the erection process should be suggested rather than mandatory. In any case, a clear indication of what will be involved in the erection of the structure helps to give those tendering some confidence in understanding the project as a whole, and this should encourage a realistic quotation.

The erection and basic assembly of the components should be straightforward enough. Once this has been achieved, there will need to be sufficient adjustment points provided to establish the precise alignments of the basic geometry, and to control the gradual build-up of forces in the system, including the main transfer of the roof loads to the masts in an appropriate sequence. This is often a time-consuming and delicate operation involving strain gauges on most, if not all, of the ties.

Protection against corrosion

The twin features of exposed conditions and structural movement make the protection of steelwork against corrosion a crucial issue. So far as paint coatings are concerned, the main task in designing an appropriate system consists of keeping a balance between the factors involved. These are: the environmental context of the structure, the design life of the system, the cost framework, and whether shop or site application is appropriate. Several coats will build up to the required film thickness but adhesion factors between coats are then multiplied and the paint system may be less flexible in coping with the movement of the structure.

Whichever system is eventually chosen, good preparation is essential: a paint system applied to a properly prepared blast cleaned surface, i.e. to Sa2.5 BS 7079: Part AI: 1989, may be expected to last up to five times longer than the same system applied to steelwork which has been only manually wire brushed.

Paint systems for external use in an industrial or marine environment have until recently been based on chlorinated rubber or epoxy resin. Chlorinated rubber systems are relatively soft and are subject to damage during transport and erection; on the other hand, overcoating the damage re-softens the original coating so that adhesion is good. The main handicap of such products, however, are the environmentally detrimental effects of the chlorine used in their production. For this reason, new acrylated rubber systems are making chlorinated rubber obsolete.

Epoxy resin based paint systems are likely to remain the preferred choice, at least in the short term. Epoxy systems normally consist of three or four coats, totalling approximately 275 microns of dry film thickness, the last coat of which is normally site applied. A typical, three coat system providing a coloured finish will comprise a 75 microns d.f.t. base coat in the form of a good quality zinc phosphate pigmented primer or a zinc rich epoxy containing 90% zinc metal by weight in a dry film. This will have applied to it an epoxy-based, hi-build undercoat to 150 microns and a site-applied epoxy finish to 50 microns. Alternatively, where colour is not important, the weather-coating on the primer can be provided by two coats of an epoxy micaceous iron oxide paint, applied at 100 microns per coat.

A full-coat 'architectural' finish to counter the 'chalking' effect of epoxy coatings will consist of the primer and hi-build epoxy coatings already mentioned, followed by a site coat of a high performance acrylic urethane finish in a chosen colour, this applied in one or two coats depending on the use of brush or spray.

An alternative to multiple thinner coats is to use a 'fast track', one coat primer/finish coating. Two-pack, long term versions will have a life of ten years to first maintenance in an industrial or marine environment. Corrosion protection at the connections involves the connector plate, the joints of the fork, and the pin itself. This latter component can be in stainless steel although even then a small amount of bi-metallic corrosion is to be expected. Elsewhere, the connection can be painted over with the materials specified for the main structure, supplemented by the pointing up with an elastomeric sealant of machined recesses around the pin.

External galvanised surfaces which are to be painted will need to be cleaned with a proprietory industrial detergent to emulsify the grease, washed down with clean water and treated with a Mordant solution to chemically etch the surface. A coat of epoxy-based micaceous iron oxide is then recommended, using the undercoats and finishing coats already described.

Notes on this subject are more than usually provisional: the implementation of environmental protection acts worldwide will involve stringent controls over emissions from solvent-based paints ('Volatile Organic Compounds' or VOCs) by manufacturers and users. Whilst compliant, solvent-based coatings have been developed, new, water based coatings are also available in response to these criteria, and will become increasingly popular. A typical system will include a water based, zinc phosphate primer, a micaceous iron oxide water based intermediate coat and a water based sheen finish.

Lastly, opinions vary about paint specifications for exposed steelwork and there are many possible permutations of different systems and proprietory products for use amongst the range of internal and external environments. The most useful current UK reference is BS 5493: Code of Practice for the protection coating of iron and steel structures against corrosion, which designates the generic types of coatings in relation to differing degrees of exposure and sets standards for each situation. A revised Euro Standard Code of Practice, in the final stages of preparation, will replace BS 5493 in due course.

13.5
ECONOMIC ASPECTS

There is a general belief that mast architecture in some ways 'costs more' than conventional building technology, but this is true only in the most general and therefore fairly meaningless terms. In practice, when outline alternatives for a particular building are being assessed, a masted design should not be dismissed solely for narrow economic reasons without a wider comparative study of all the significant factors and their effects on proposals of equal architectural merit, not simply on other general structural alternatives. Architectural quality must either be built into the comparison in that way or its contribution given a notional value in the assessments.

All this is easier said than done: comparative studies are difficult to cost realistically because the provision of one building element in a particular form will usually have implications for the provision of others. The true net costs are therefore difficult and time-consuming to identify. However, there is good evidence that masted structures have proved to be both appropriate and cost-effective solutions, despite an apparently higher prime cost, but this is not to say that the functional demands, e.g. for unobstructed space, may not be achieved by 'conventional' means in any case.

Three points are particularly important: first, in terms of scale, the larger the unobstructed space needed, the more likely is a masted structure to be an economic and effective solution. For example, Hall 7 at the National Exhibition Centre in England, a major unobstructed space measuring 87m x 104m between supports, was designed, built and occupied in thirteen months and described as 'remarkably economic', whilst the major exhibition spaces measuring 60m x 84m in the Darling Harbour Complex form part of a masted structure considered to be the least expensive solution involving the most efficient use of material.

A second point to be noted is the economic contribution made by a striking visual appearance. Attributes which are difficult to quantify such as appropriateness in function and context, and the publicity value of an eye-catching structure can be crucial in the choice between alternative designs. Where there is a need to attract the general public, and where questions of company prestige are concerned, structural costs can be outweighed by appearance, and at the Renault Centre, the visual attractiveness of the cable-stayed structure more than paid for the higher costs involved by enhancing the development potential of the site.

A third important factor is the expertise and motivation of the design team. A creative and enthusiastic office with a progressive attitude and a reputation to make or to keep up can overturn the conventional economic wisdom and this has been an important factor in the consolidation of masted structures into medium and small-scale buildings. For example, the expertise of the Nicholas Grimshaw Office resulted in the Oxford Ice Rink being by no means an expensive building and its masted structure proved to be substantially cheaper than its nearest equivalent. In another case, the shopping centre at Nantes, the Richard Rogers Partnership produced a first class design within a very low budget (in UK terms, of £300m² in 1986) for a building with high ceilings and full mechanical ventilation. Clearly, in the case of these two design teams, previous experience of cable-stayed structures was an important factor, but other examples are equally encouraging.

In numerical terms, however, the evidence is disappointingly sparse: we know of only two full cost analyses of masted structures (Building Study: Hall 7 Birmingham International Arena, *The Architect's Journal* 11 February 1981 and Building Dossier: Yeovil Football Stadium, *Building* 30 November 1990). Some building descriptions have mentioned savings in material costs of 20% in a competition entry for the Napp Laboratories and, at Fleetguard, of 17% less than conventional structures of 18m bay size. It seems likely that savings of 10-15% can be achieved in an efficient design and this should cover the additional costs incurred. Another indicant of relative economy is that of weight of steel per square metre of floor area (Table 1). But these comparisons can be misleading too; structural costs are not necessarily directly related to the weight of steelwork; complexity of fabrication and erection costs also come into it. A highly-interactive tensile structure, where adjusting one rod involves re-adjusting all the others, and with strain gauges needed to check the loadings, may make erection

the most difficult part of the project. The difference in loadings, too, should be taken into account in assessing the structural economy of different buildings.

Table 1. Weights of Structural Steel

Building	Weight of steel, including cast iron, in Kg/m² of floor space
NEC 1980	105
Fleetguard 1981	46
Inmos 1982	56
Renault 1983	62
Patscenter 1983	45

13.6
VISUAL AESTHETICS

The visual qualities of masted structures are as significant as the structural characteristics because in most cases the prominence of the structure forms the dominant architectural 'order' of the building. Two aspects are important: how the visual implications of the structure are to be resolved architecturally during the design process, and how the building functions visually once it has been completed.

So far as the design process is concerned, the development in detail of an embryonic structural proposal brings with it unavoidable issues of architectural form and expression, the discussion of which raises complex philosophical and perceptual issues. At this time in particular, when De-Constructivism is being promoted as a valid aesthetic principle, and when eccentric and bizarre architectural forms and virtually unbuildable projects are attracting some critical admiration, the propounding of visual principles and precepts is a highly contentious matter. In fact, it is fair to ask if there are any visual principles at all in relation to masted structures. It seems to us that there are certainly some, the reason being that the imperatives of structural engineering, particularly in this field, differ from and take precedence over some of those currently on offer in architecture. In engineering, structural logic, economy of means, and technical rigour are essential design objectives. Their tangible results are always commended and their absence generally deplored and it is neither sensible nor economic to design otherwise. Consequently, in masted structures, capricious formal games are seldom played at the level of the general structural strategy, nor where the pattern of the major structural supports is concerned. This is not to say that, for example, a 'De-Constructivist' approach to a masted structure would not be an exciting aesthetic enterprise, but it is likely to occur in the context of a regular framework of structural order rather than in its absence. A complex structure needs an ordered layout if the complexity is not to slide into confusion – although at this time a minority of designers might consider that to be a valid aesthetic objective!

However, for the most part, ordered relationships and structural truths are still valid precepts, and refinement in detail is still a worthwhile activity. Paradoxically, the architecture and the engineering must work together but still be visually distinct. Moreover, the structure must not be a preconceived visual solution with minimal technical justification: it should emerge naturally as part of the designers' intentions towards a structural anatomy which suits the imperatives of space, site and services, and the visual qualities specified in the architect's brief.

This, too, is easier said than done. Moreover there are three perceptual matters which demand particular attention during the design phase: these are ensuring the 'legibility' of the structural system, clarifying the relationship of the structure to the conventional building elements, and resolving the expression of the external structure on the interior.

So far as legibility is concerned, positioning the structure entirely outside the building envelope obviously offers a virtual guarantee of visual clarity. Not surprisingly, most of the 'classic' masted structures embody an 'exoskeleton' of this kind, positioned over an elegant building volume. In these cases, each of the two elements, the linear structure and the spatial volume, can maintain its own visual integrity and provide a strong image in its own terms, whilst the suspension points impose their own order as integrating elements between the two formal systems. A second visual principle which is useful in clarifying the structural configuration is to reveal it directly on an end elevation.

There remains the difficult problem of how to express inside the building what is a very positive statement externally. Showing the members through openings in the roof or round the walls is certainly possible. Equally surely, false ceilings are deplorable obstacles in this respect.

There are other instances where the complete articulation of the masted structure as a formal element in its own right is not possible. In these cases, the masts form part of the building volume and the successful integration of the two becomes a key architectural issue. Buildings of this kind demand some skill if they are to be visually successful because the legibility of the structure on the exterior is much reduced.

The most awkward instances are those in which the masts simply project out of the roof of the build-ing like an architectural 'compound fracture'. Often, a few tension stays vanish mysteriously into a building mass which is apparently quite capable of supporting itself without their help – a kind of structural ambiguity which runs the risk of appearing banal or confusing. One solution to this problem is to make the building envelope as transparent as possible so that legibility is increased, although light reflections may limit the visibility. This is why the structure of the RAC Control Centre, when internally lit at night, is visually more intelligible than during daylight.

The deliberate pursuit of lightness for aesthetic effect has led to the frequent expression of the roof as an articulated element, either as a floating plane forming a canopy in space, or as a more conventional roof plane articulated by a slip joint at the junction with the walls to cope with the multi-directional stresses at this point. As the Piraeus Dockside Terminal shows, this principle can be visually effective even in reinforced concrete.

As one approaches a masted structure, one perceives a sequence of visual clues to its structural nature. At a distance, the general massing and masted silhouette are identifiable: nearer to, the patterns of masts, backstays and cables become clearer and the suspension points and anchorages become apparent, whilst in close-up, we are presented with an aesthetic of connections – pins, pinjoints and fish-plates, pivots, splices and bolts – a potentially rich and decorative language of essential and significant details for which British architects and engineers have been initially largely responsible and with which the Cepezed Studio, for example, has been successful.

But in visual matters we are not only concerned with perceptual sequences but also with questions of meaning. In this respect, mast architecture functions visually at several levels. In the simplest terms, a masted structure converts a building into a landmark: for example, in the rolling landscape of the Mid-West, the twin masts of the Baxter Travenol Complex identify it visually from the nearby expressway, whilst in England, the Homebase Superstore on the Great West Road out of London was deliberately intended to be a point of reference for passing motorists.

At another level, the general need for a strong visual image – virtually obligatory in exhibition buildings – is a frequent requirement: in Oxford, it was needed to attract visitors to the new Ice Rink; at the West Japan Exhibition Centre the building had to hold its own in the midst of dockside monoliths such as warehouses, factory facilities and fuel tanks and at the Renault Centre, the whole building is an advertisement for company prestige, in yellow, its own 'house colour'.

Lastly in this aesthetic system, architectural metaphors play an important part: at Canterbury, the supermarket masts were said to 'provide a visual echo' of the tower and pinnacles of the cathedral, whilst at the new East Croydon Station, the structure can be interpreted as a wide, shallow entrance portico to the lower-level world of the railway network. Not surprisingly, nautical allusions have been frequent ever since the masted look-out platforms were suspended above the Thames promenade in 1951. At the Darling Harbour and West Japan Exhibition centres, and at Poole Station, the waterside locations evoked metaphors of ships' masts, rigging and dockside cranes in the resulting structures.

There are subtle synectic metaphors, too: an outward-sloping mast, tension stay and back-stay is a visual diagram of the backwards-straining effort of a tug-of-war team member and the Canberra Athletics Stadium is a classic example of this dynamic effect. This direct visual connotation of tension, compression and suspension, and the metaphors which can be invoked, are the sources of the aesthetic potency of the genre.

13.7
BENEFITS AND PENALTIES

To conclude, it is clear that masted structures make up an identifiable and significant class of built forms. In general terms they are important because:

- They represent new ways of achieving column-free space and equally significant architectural form.

- They express the recent progress made in the conceptual analysis and theoretical and practical understanding of how tensile structures behave.

- They demonstrate the successful use of new materials and components, and their fixing and weatherproofing.

- They show how creative architect/engineer collaboration can result in innovative structures which benefit both professions.

- They have introduced a new architectural genre with its own vocabulary and range of structural expression.

At a tactical level there are more specific benefits, to be gained, for example:

- The alternative topological arrangements of masts, tension stays and roof frameworks in relation to spatial/structural cells can meet a wide range of functional demands and be interpreted in a variety of forms and materials.

- The reduction in numbers of internal columns and, in many instances, their complete absence over large areas increases internal flexibility.

- The regularity of the structural systems enables them to be easily extended, often with minimal disturbance to the original fabric.

- The main structural foundations can be concentrated on areas where ground conditions are good, or on a small number of deep foundations where they are not.

- Externalising the structure reduces the visual scale of the building, breaks up the facades, and provides an alternative to anonymous 'big sheds'.

- The consequent reduction in building volume gives a lower profile, useful in environmentally sensitive areas, saves on cladding costs and reduces the internal space to be heated.

- Freeing the roof zone from the main structural elements facilitates the distribution of services internally.

- The structural efficiency of good designs can lead to a reduced weight of steel which can balance the extra costs incurred.

- Reductions in component sizes can reduce transport costs, and lead to rapid and more economic erection.

- The striking appearance of most structures gives them a strong visual identity, a sense of aspiration and excitement with key metaphorical allusions.

Not all these benefits will accrue in every case, nor are they always precisely quantifiable. They depend too on clear thinking and good design, but in total they represent a justifiable set of advantages. On the other hand, there are certain penalties to be expected, for example:

- There are likely to be higher design costs, i.e. in analysis, calculation and checking, and in detailing.

- In all but the smallest examples, there will be increasing thermal movement in the structure which will also need to be taken into account in the design and detailing of both the structure and the building envelope.

- The process of erection and bringing under load of the structure will require more than usual consideration.

- There will be increased costs in corrosion protection of the steelwork.

- High performance roofing systems will usually need to be provided.

Masted structures have a great deal to offer in architectural terms: clear and often breathtaking space; intriguing and often spectacular form, and an authoritative sense of order. In engineering terms they are intellectually demanding and require a clear understanding of the characteristic problems of structural behaviour and the management of the forces involved and the stresses which are generated.

A masted structure must not be arbitrarily chosen for reasons of fashion or bravura, or to attract attention regardless of context. A design should emerge as an appropriate and efficient response to a particular set of functional and contextual problems, in the manner demonstrated by many of the buildings we have described. This response will involve design criteria which are both architectural and technical, and embody the constantly rewarding experience of creative collaboration between mutually supportive disciplines. It is this informed and enthusiastic inter-professional working which will generate the successful masted structures of the future. ■

A SELECTIVE GAZETTEER

YEAR	BUILDING OR PROJECT	DESIGNERS	REFERENCE SOURCE
1825	Theatre Roof Project	Friedrich Schnirch	Rainer Graefe 'Suspended roofs of the 19th century' *Arcus* March/April 1985, pp. 70-81, 94
1834	Aviary, Pfaueninsel, Berlin	Friedrich Rabe	R. Graefe, *op cit*, p. 73
1835	Mast Shop, Naval Arsenal, Lorient, France	M. Laurent	R. Graefe, *op cit*, p. 73 *Engineering News Record* Oct 27 1921, p. 688
1839	Panorama on the Champs Elysee, Paris	Jacques A. Hittorf	R. Graefe, *op cit*, p. 74
1841	Greenhouse Project	Charles Maclintosh	C. Maclintosh, *Book of the Garden*, Edinburgh, 1853, vol. 2 pp. 382- 383
1852	Exhibition Hall Project, New York	James Bogardus	R. Graefe, *op cit*, p. 78
1865	Temporary Hall for the German Song Festival, Dresden	Eduard Muller and Ernst Giese	R. Graefe, *op cit*, p. 76
1890	World's Fair Exposition Building, Chicago	E.S. Jenison	R. Graefe, *op cit*, p. 78
1895	Temporary Exhibition Halls Niznij-Novgorod, USSR	V.G. Suchov	R. Graefe, *op cit*, pp. 78-79
1903	Post Office Savings Bank, Vienna (competition entry version)	Otto Wagner	H. Geretsegger E. M. Peintner *Otto Wagner 1841-1918* Salzburg, Residenzverlag, 1983
1923	Palace of Labour	Alexander and Viktor Vesnin	S.O. Khan-Magomedov, *Pioneers of Soviet Architecture*, New York, Rizzoli, 1983
1924	Aircraft Hangar Proposal	Alexander and Viktor Vesnin	S.O. Khan-Magomedov, *op cit*
1927	Dymaxion House Project	R. Buckminster Fuller	James Meller (ed.) *The Buckminster Fuller Reader*, Harmondsworth, Penguin Books, 1972
1929	Summer Stage Roofing, Central Park for Culture and Leisure, Moscow	Genrikh Lyudvig	S.O. Khan-Magomedov, *op cit*
1933	Travel and Transport Building Chicago Exposition 1933	E. Bennett et al.	*Arch. Forum*, Oct 1931, pp. 451-456 and 501-506
1938	Ice Cream Parlor, River Forest, Illinois	Bertrand Goldberg	*A+U* , 5, 7. 1975, p. 55
1938	Service Station for Standard Oil, Chicago	Bertrand Goldberg	*Architectural Forum*, Mar 1946 pp. 107-115

Service Station for Standard Oil, Chicago.

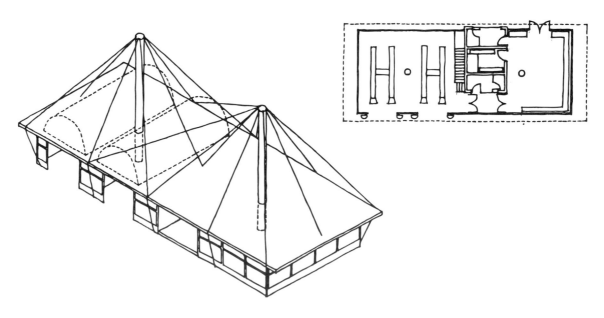

YEAR	BUILDING OR PROJECT	DESIGNERS	REFERENCE SOURCE
1941	Community Centre project	Eero Saarinen	Philip Drew, *Tensile Architecture*, Granada Publishing, 1979, p. 159
1947	Ledbetter Summer Lodge, Norman, Oklahoma	Bruce Goff	J. Cook, *The Architecture of Bruce Goff* Granada, 1978, pp. 46-50
1948	OM Pavillion, Milan Fair, 1948	R. Zavanella	*Ottagono*, 85, Jan 1987, pp. 68-69
1950	OM Pavillion, Milan Fair, 1950	R. Zavanella	*Ottagono*, 85, Jan 1987, pp. 68-69
1950-55	Bavinger House, Nr Norman, Oklahoma	Bruce Goff	J. Cook, *op cit*
1951	The Skylon, Festival of Britain, South Bank, London	P. Powell and H. Moya with Felix J. Samuely	*Architectural Review* June 1951
1951	Viewing platforms, Festival of Britain, South Bank, London	Eric Brown & Eric Chamberlin	*Architectural Review* June 1951
1951	Entrances to upstream and downstream sections, Festival of Britain, South Bank, London	Hugh Casson	*Architectural Review* June 1951
1952	Parker Square Proposal, Wichita Falls, Texas	Ketchum, Gina and Sharp with Severud, Elatad and Kruger	*Architectural Forum*, 98, 3, May 1953, p. 140
1953	Truck Terminal for Transcon Lines	Allison E. Rible with Popp and Ropp	*Architectural Record*, Aug 1953, pp. 178-179
1956	Aircraft Hangar for Temco Aircraft Co. Greenville, Texas	Erwin-Newman Co.	*Acier/Stahl/Steel*, 21, 1956, p. 110 *Progressive Architecture*, 37, 5, May 1956, p. 107
1957	Service Station for Mobil	Whitney Smith and W. Williams	*Architectural Review* Apr 1957, p. 363
1958	USSR Pavilion, Expo 58', Brussels	Boretski, Abramov, Doubov and Polanski	*Acier/Stahl/Steel*, 23, 11, Nov 1958 pp. 459-469
1958	The European Coal and Steel Community Pavilion, Expo 58', Brussels	E. Delatte and R. Maquestieau	*Acier/Stahl/Steel*, 23, 11, Nov 1958
1958	Nicholson Gymnasium, Central Washington College, Ellensburg	R. Buckhard	*The Architect and Building News*, 13 Nov 1963, p. 773 *Progressive Architecture*, 41, 3 March 1960, p. 182
1959	UK Pavilion, Rand Easter Show, Johannesburg	Fleming and Cooke with Ove Arup and Partners	*Design*, 129, Sept 1959 pp. 56-57 *Arup Journal*, Apr 1971 p. 10
1960	Pan American Passenger Terminal JFK Airport, New York	Tippetts, Abbett, McCarthy, Stratton, Ives, Turano and Gardner	*Progressive Architecture*, Dec 1957 pp. 82-85 and Nov 1961 pp. 140-143
1960	Winter Olympic Coliseum, Squaw Valley, California	Corlett and Spackman with H. Brunner and J. Sardis (now Corlett, Skaer and Devoto Architects, Inc.)	*Architectural Forum* February 1960, pp. 104-106 *Progressive Architecture*, Jan 1958 p. 102
1960-61	Tosho Printing Plant, Haramachi, Japan	K. Tange and URTEC with the Yokoyama Engineering Lab	O.W. Grube *Industrial Buildings and Factories* Architectural Press, 1971, p. 82 *Architectural Design*, Nov 1968 p. 536
1962	Aluminium Centre, German Industrial Fair, Hanover	H. Maurer F. Zoschinger	*American Institute of Architects Journal*, 39, 6, June 1963
1962	Works Building, Max Burren AG, Flamatt, Switzerland	Atelier 5	W. Henn, *Buildings for Industry*, vol 2, 1965, pp. 240-241
1962	Pavilion 16A, Hannover Fair Hannover, Germany	not known	Z.S. Makowski, *Steel space structures*, Michael Joseph, 1965, p. 187
1964	Stadium Canopy, Crystal Palace Sports Centre, London	Hubert Bennett and LCC Arch. Dept.	*Arup Journal*, April 1971, p. 17 *Architecture d'Aujourd'hui*, 112, pp. 6-17 *The Structural Engineer* 44, 3 p. 102
1964	New Jersey Pavilion, New York World's Fair	Peter, Quay, Young Associates and Collins, Uhl and Hoisington with N.J. Sonenberger	*Architectural Record*, Feb 1964, p. 141 and July 1964 p. 145
1964	Tilburg Railway Station, Holland	K. van der Gaast	*BOUW*, 18-30 April 1964, p. 648. *Detail*, 1966, 6 Unpaginated
1964	Exhibition Railway Station for Swiss Federal Railways	P. Zoelly with A. Wildberger	*Detail*, 1965, 2, pp. 182-183

YEAR	BUILDING OR PROJECT	DESIGNERS	REFERENCE SOURCE
1965	Printing Works, Tapiola, Finland	A. Ruusuvuori	F. Wilde *Factories* New York Van Nostrand/Reinhold, 1972, pp. 82-83
1965	A Tent for Construction Site, London (unbuilt)	F. Otto with Bernd-Friedrich Romberg	*Architectural Design*, Apr 1968, pp. 173-174
1965	Aviary, London Zoo	Lord Snowdon with Cedric Price and Frank Newby	*Architectural Review*, 140, 823, Sept 1965, pp. 181-186 *Architectural Design* Sept 1965, pp. 452-459
1965	East End Terminal, LaGuardia Airport, New York	William Pereira and Associates with Lev Zetlin and Associates	F. Wilson *Emerging Conversations: Form in Architecture, Conversations with Lev Zetlin*, Cahners Pub. Co. 1975
1966	Tulsa Exposition Centre, Oklahoma	B.R. Griffin with D. Graham and Associates	H. Buchholdt 'Cable structures', Proceedings of the *Conference on Steel in Architecture*, British Constructional Steelwork Association, 1970, p. 131 *Building*, 8 April 1966, pp. 67-68
c.1966	Stadium Grandstand, Laval, France	J. Saint-Arroman with Stephane de Chateau	*Acier/Stahl/Steel*, 35, 11, 1970, pp. 491-494
1967	Plant Houses, Royal Botanic Garden, Edinburgh	G. Pearce with L. Creasy et al. MPBW, Scotland	*Building* 1 Dec 1967, pp. 85-86
1967	Stadium Grandstand, Marl, Germany	A. Riege	*Detail*, pp. 68-72
1968	Ford Pavilion, Hennis Fair San Antonio, Texas	Gunnar Birkerts and Associates	*GA Architect 2* : Gunnar Birkerts and Associates, A.D.A. Edita, Tokyo, pp. 119-121
1968	German Pavilion, Zagreb Fair, Zagreb, Yugoslavia	B. Rasica K. Poltz	*Arhitektura* (Zagreb) 1968, no. 95-96 pp. 33-35
1969-70	Italian Industry Pavilion, Osaka Expo, Japan	Renzo Piano with SERTEC Engineering	*Acier/Stahl/Steel*, 11, 1970, pp. 495-498
1969-70	Kubota Pavilion, Osaka Expo, Japan	Osaka Building Office	*Acier/Stahl/Steel*, 11, 1970, p. 516
1969-70	British Pavilion, Osaka Expo, Japan	Powell and Moya with Charles Weiss and Partners	*Architects' Journal*, 22 Apr 1970, p. 968 *Acier/Stahl/Steel*, 11, 1970, p. 553
1970	Ontario Place, Toronto, Canada	Craig, Zeidler and Strong with W. Hardy Craig and Associates	*L'Architecture d'Aujourd'hui*, 44, 162, 1972, pp. 54-55
1970	Two storey car park, Gessneratte, Zurich	City Parkhaus, AG	*Werk* June 1973, pp 674-675 *Architectural Design* Oct 1973, p. 665
1970	Rest Stand, Cycle Sports Centre, Shuzenji, Japan	Nikken Sekkei	*Japan Architect*, Mar 1972, pp. 63-69
1970-81	Flower Market, Pescia, Italy	L. Savioli et al. Florence	*Domus* Feb 1982, p. 25 *L'Architecture d'Aujourd'hui*, June 1982, pp. 10-13
1971	Service Station, Marburg, Germany	Staatliches Universitats-bauamt Marburg	*Detail*, 1972, 1, pp. 69-70
1972	Motorway Bridge Restaurant, Wrenlos, Switzerland	Dipl. Ing. Dir Stadelmann Meto-Bau AG Zurich	*Acier/Stahl/Steel*, 11, 1974, pp. 453-456

Ontario Place (left), Toronto, Canada, 1970.

Ocean Terminal (right), Piraeus, Greece, c.1972.

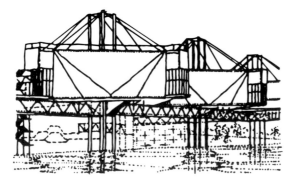
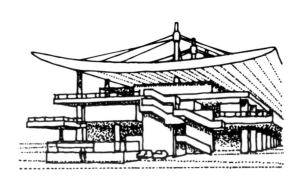

YEAR	BUILDING OR PROJECT	DESIGNERS	REFERENCE SOURCE
1972	Ice Skating Stadium, Braunlage, West Germany	The Westermann Architectural Office with H. von Hirshhaysen	*Acier/Stahl/Steel*, 11, 1974, p. 451
c.1972	Ocean Terminal, Piraeus, Greece	J. Liapis and E. Skroubelous	*Detail*, 1973, 3 May-Jun, pp. 457-459
1973	Covered Cattle Market, Saint Etienne, France	A. Ferra and L. Seignol with S. du Chateau	*Techniques and Architecture*, 294 Oct 1973, p. 58
1974	Quayside Warehouses, Le Havre, France	M. Herbert and Themis Constantinidis	*Techniques and Architecture*, Feb-Mar 1974, p. 80
1974	Mineola Community Centre	Bruce Goff	*Building Design*, Nov 3, 1978, p. 15
1975	Shopping Centre, Craigavon, Northern Ireland	Department of Housing, Local Government with I.G. Doran and Partners	*Tubular Structures*, 25, June 1975, p. 11
1975	Racing Grandstand, East Rutherford, New Jersey	Ewing Cole, Erdman and Ewbank with the Synergo Company	*Architectural Record*, Nov 1975, pp. 135-136
1975-77	Baseball Stadium, Puerto Rico	T. Marvel with Hernandez and Hernandez	*Progressive Architecture*, May 1980, pp. 118-121
c.1976	Stadium at Villeneuve-D'Ascq, France	R. Taillibert	Gaillard, *Architectures des Sports*, Moniteur, Paris 1982, pp. 158-159
1977	The West Japan General Exhibition Centre, Kitakyushu, Japan	Arato Isozaki	*Japan Architect*, 251, Mar 1978, pp. 10-23
1977	Baxter Travenol Laboratories, Deefield, Illinois	Skidmore, Owings and Merrill	SOM, *Architecture and Urbanism*, 1973-83
1977	National Athletics Stadium, Bruce nr Canberra, Australia	Philip Cox and Partners	*Architectural Review*, Oct 1988, p. 67
1977	Aircraft Hangar, Berlin-Tegel Airport	von Gerkan, Marg and Partners	*Architektur*, 1966-78, von Gerkan, Marg and Partners
1978	Ice Skating Stadium, Arosa, Switzerland	A+A Rocco	Karl Kramer Verlag, Stuttgart, 1978, p. 69 *Acier/Stahl/Steel* 4, 1979, p. 153
1978	Pabst Stage, Milwaukee, Wisconsin	Chrysalis East	*A + U*, 91, 5, 1978, p. 69
1978-81	Fleetguard Factory, Quimper, France	Richard Rogers and Partners with Ove Arup and Partners	*Architectural Review*, Feb 1982, pp. 23-30 *Architecture d'Aujourd'hui*, June 1982, pp. 18-25
1979-80	Hall 7, National Exhibition Hall, Birmingham	E. D. Mills and Partners with Ove Arup and Partners	Arup Journal, Jun 1982, pp. 8-10 Architects Journal, 11 Feb 1981, p. 250
1979	NAPP Laboratory, Cambridge (competition entry)	Richard Rogers and Partners with Anthony Hunt Associates	*L'Architecture d'Aujourd'hui*, Jun 1982, p. 28 *Architects Journal* 2 Sept, 1981
1980	Convention Centre, Brazil	A. Peskine, J-P Roulle	*Technique and Architecture*, 334 Mar 1981, pp. 85-86
1980	Exhibition Hall, Pittsburgh	Celli-Flynn and Associates with Bliss and Nyitray	*Engineering News Record*, 200, 19,11 May 1978, p. 23
1980	Municipal Stadium, Bayamon, Puerto Rico	Reed, Torres, Beauchamp et al.	*Progressive Architecture* 5, 1980, p. 118-120
1981	Billingsgate Market, West India Dock, London	N. Levinson and Partners P. Hill and Partners	*Brick Bulletin* Aug 1983, p. 12 *Building* 29 Jan 1982, p. 12
1982	Inmos Microchip Facility, Newport, Gwent, South Wales	Richard Rogers and Partners with Anthony Hunt Associates	*Architectural Review*, Dec 1982, pp. 26-41 *Building Services*, Nov 1982, pp. 24-25
1982	Ice Skating Rink, Kunsteisbahn, Zuchwil, Switzerland	Louis Plüss	*SD* (Space Design), Jan 1989, p. 72
1982	Haj Terminal, Jeddah, Saudi Arabia	Skidmore, Owings and Merrill	*Building Design*, 11 Jun 1982, p. 10
1982	Sainsbury Supermarket (competition entry)	MacCormac Jamieson and Pritchard	*Architectural Review*, May 1983, p. 69 *Architectural Design*, 3/4, 1984, pp. 78-79
1982	Liverpool International Garden Festival (competition entry)	Nicholas Grimshaw and Partners with Ove Arup and Partners	*Architects Journal* 2 June 1982, p. 32 and 21 July 1982, pp. 50-51

(left) Convention
Centre, Brazil,
1980.

(right) Ladkarn
Haulage Limited
building, Isle of
Dogs, London,
1983.

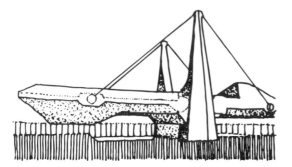

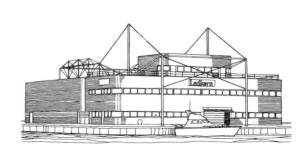

YEAR	BUILDING OR PROJECT	DESIGNERS	REFERENCE SOURCE
1982	Liverpool International Garden Festival (competition entry)	Napper Collerton Partnership with Ove Arup and Partners	*Architects Journal* 2 June 1982, p. 33 and 21 July 1982, pp. 48-50
1982	Reference Collection Complex, Kew Gardens (competition entry)	Ian Ritchie Architects	Architects' own information
1982	The Theme Building, Wonderworld, Corby, Northants, England	Derek Walker and Associates	*Architectural Design*, 52, 9/10, 1982, pp. 6-9
1982	The Stadium, Wonderworld, Corby, Northants, England	Derek Walker and Associates	*Architectural Design*, 52, 9/10, 1982, pp. 42-43
1983	Renault Parts Distribution Centre, Swindon	Foster Associates with Ove Arup and Partners	*Architects Journal*, 15 June 1983, pp. 41-45 *Architectural Review*, July 1983, pp. 20-32 *Arup Journal*, 18, 3, Sept 1983, pp. 2-5
1983	Patscenter, Princeton, USA	Richard Rogers and Partners Ove Arup and Partners	*Arup Journal*, Summer 1986 pp.8-16 *Architectural Review*, Sept, 1986
1983	Liquid Ink Manufacturing and Distribution Centre, Milton Keynes	Nicholas Grimshaw and Partners Ove Arup and Partners	*Architectural Review*, Jan 1984, p. 29
1983	Ladkarn Haulage Limited building, Isle of Dogs, London	Nicholas Grimshaw and Partners Trigram Design Partnership	*Building*, 4 Mar 1988, p. 38 *Nicholas Grimshaw and Partners* 1: 1988 pp. 62-65
1983	Enclosure for Basildon Town Centre, Essex, England	Michael Hopkins and Partners Buro Happold and Partners	*Architectural Design*, 3/4, 1984, pp. 32-34 *Architects Journal* 19 June 1985, pp. 42-53
1983	Ice Rink, Oxford	Nicholas Grimshaw and Partners with Ove Arup and Partners	*Architectural Review*, March 1985, pp. 38-45 *Arup Journal*, Summer 1986, pp. 23-26
1983	House near Crowborough, Sussex	Ian Ritchie Architects with Anthony Hunt Associates	*Architects Journal* 10 Jun 1981, p.1094 and 26 Oct 1983 p. 62
1984	Sainsbury Supermarket, Canterbury, Kent (concept structure by Anthony Hunt Associates	Ahrends, Burton and Koralek with Green and Partners	*Architects Journal*, 5 Dec 1984, pp. 41-48
1984	Swimming and Water-polo Centre, Mladost, Zagreb, Yugoslavia	Vinko Penezic and Kresimir Rogina	*L'Arca*, Nov 1987, pp. 12-19
1984	Montjuic Stadium, Barcelona	Gregotti Associates with CORMA	*L'Arca*, Nov 1987, pp. 72-79
1984	Ret Factory Gate Lodge, Rotterdam	Cepezed Studio	*Ottagono*, 84, March 1987, p. 123
1984	Sports Hall Competition Entry, Frankfurt	P. Cook and Ove Arup and Partners	Peter Cook 1961-1989 A+U extra edition Dec 1989, p. 143
1984-86	Tesco Supermarket, Bristol	D. Daw Architects with Buro Happold and Partners	*The Structural Engineer*, 66, 19, Oct 4 1988, p. A7
1985	Schlumberger Research Laboratory	Michael Hopkins and Partners with Anthony Hunt and Ove Arup and Partners	*Architects Journal*, 1 Feb 1984 pp. 40-47 and 18 Sept 1985, pp. 43-59
1985	Leisure Centre, West Swindon, Wiltshire, England	Thamesdown Borough Architects with Anthony Hunt Associates	*Architects Journal*, 6 Apr 1983, pp. 44-46
1985	Tsukuba Expo, Block A, 1 and 2 Pavilions, Japan	Fumihiko Maki and Associates	*The Japan Architect*, 338, Jun 1985, pp. 176-182

YEAR	BUILDING OR PROJECT	DESIGNERS	REFERENCE SOURCE
1985	Factory at Haarlem	Cepezed Studio	*Ottagono*, 84, Mar 1987, p. 123
1985	Tribunenuberdachung Sport-und Freizeitpark, Vaterstetten, Germany	W. Fauser with H. Tischner	*Detail*, 1984, 2 Mar/Apr
1985	State Sports Centre, Homebush, Sydney, Australia	NW Government Architect with Philip Cox and Partners and Bond, James, Laron and Murtagh	Alan Ogg, *Architecture in Steel: the Australian Context,* Royal Australian Institute of Architecture, 1987, pp. 156-157
1985	Visitor's Centre, Yulara National Park, N.T. Australia	Philip Cox and Partners	*Architectural Review* 177, 1057, March 1985, pp. 46-49
1986	Travel Centre, Newcastle Central Station	N. Derbyshire P. Davis	*Architects Journal*, 12 Feb 1986, pp. 38-49
1986	Paco Rabanne Factory, Chartres, France	Jean-Paul Moneste et al.	*Technique and Architecture*, 367, 1986, pp. 152-153
1986	Temporary Grandstand Canopy, Paris	F. Soler	*Technique and Architecture*, 367, 1986, p. 89
1986	PTT Telecommunication Stand, Amsterdam	F. and P. Wintermans with Ove Arup and Partners	*Arup Journal*, Spring 1987, pp. 8-9
1986	Tourist Centre on A14 Motorway, France	M. Raynaud	*Technique and Architecture*, 366, 1986, p. 120
1986	Factory Units, Nieuwegein, Holland	Cepezed Studio	Architects own information
1986	Retail Food Market and Transport Terminal, Dubhai, UAE	GMW with Cundall, Johnston and Partners	*Architectural Review*, Jan 1986, p. 73
1986	Shopping Centre, Epone, France	Richard Rogers and Partners Ove Arup and Partners	*Richard Rogers 1978-1988 A+U Extra* with *Edition*, Dec 1988, p. 190
1986	Shopping Centre, Nantes, France	Richard Rogers and Partners with Ove Arup and Partners	*Architectural Review* 184 1098 Aug 1988, pp. 34-40
1986	Lightweight Canopy, Victoria Plaza, London	Heery Architects with Anthony Hunt Associates	*Architects Journal*, 29 Oct 1986, pp. 47-50
1986	Showroom for Mercedes-Benz, Vienna	E. Sulke H. Endl	*Bauforum* 20 119 1987, pp. 46-47
1986	Warehouse, Hannover	K. Schuwirth and E. Erman	*Detail* 1986, 4, Jul-Aug pp. 341-344
1986	King Fahd International Stadium, Riyadh, Saudi Arabia	Ian Fraser, John Roberts and Partners	*The Structural Engineer*, 64A, 5, May 1986, p. A4
1987	Snecma Factory, Creusot, France	A. Constantin and P. Rice	*Technique and Architecture*, 378, Jul 1988, p. 86
1987	Massy Autosalon, Massy, France	Richard Rogers and Partners with Ove Arup and Partners	*Richard Rogers 1978-1988 A+U Extra Edition*, Dec 1988, p. 202
1987	EBCO Aerospace, Delta, B.C. Canada	Busby Bridger Architects	*The Canadian Architect*, Mar 1990, p. 44
1987	Natwest Mobile Training Centres, England	Fisher Park with Anthony Hunt Associates	*Building Design* 13 Nov 1987, pp. 17-19
1987	The Mound Stand, Lords Cricket Ground, London	Michael Hopkins and Partners with Ove Arup and Partners	*Architects Journal*, 2 Sept 1987, pp. 37-54 *Architectural Review* Sept 1987, pp. 40-49 *Arup Journal*, Autumn 1987, pp. 2-6

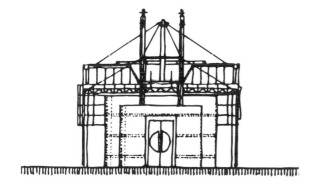

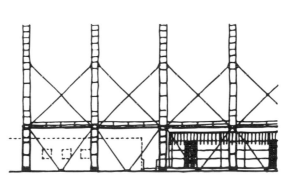

(left) Paco Rabanne Factory, Chartres, France, 1980.

(right) Tourist Centre on A14 Motorway, France, 1986.

(left) Showroom for Mercedes-Benz, Vienna, 1986.

(right) EBCO Aerospace, Delta B.C., Canada, 1987.

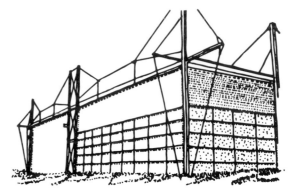

YEAR	BUILDING OR PROJECT	DESIGNERS	REFERENCE SOURCE
1987	Terminal 2, Nice Airport, France	P. Andreu	*Technique and Architecture*, 238 Mar 1988, pp. 56-58
1987-88	Terraced Industrial Units, Rotterdam	Cepezed Studio	Architects own information
1988	Pallet Handling Building, Charles-de-Gaulle Airport, Roissy, France	M.L. Bianchi and M. Malinowski	*Technique et Architecture*, 386, Oct 1989, p. 150 *L'Architecture d'Anjourd'hui* Feb 1990 pp. 84-86
1988	Railway Station, Poole, England	N. Derbyshire and Anthony Hunt Associates	*Architects Journal*, 5 Oct 1988, p. 26
1988	Homebase, Brentford, London	Nicholas Grimshaw and Partners	*Architects Journal*, 20 June 1988, pp. 24-30
1988	Darling Harbour Exhibition Centre, Sydney, Australia	Philip Cox and Partners	*Architectural Review*, Oct 1988, pp. 67-71 *Transactions* RIBA 9, pp. 44-46
1988	Sydney Football Stadium, Sydney, Australia	Philip Cox and Partners	*Architectural Review*, Oct 1988, pp. 67-71
1988	RAC Control Centre, Walsall, England	BDP with Alan Baxter Associates	*Architecture Today*, 3, pp. 34-39
1988	McCormick Place, Chicago	Skidmore, Owings and Merrill	*Progressive Architecture* 2, 1989, p. 76 *Architecture*, Mar 1988, pp. 100-105
1988	Amphitheatre, Ironworld, USA	Damberg, Scott, Peck and Booker	*Architectural Record*, July 1988, p. 53
1988	Frankfurt Airport Expansion Project	Buro AS and P, Albert Speer and Partner, Frankfurt	*Deutsche Bauzeitung* 5, 1988, p. 8
1987-88	La Rampe, Echirolles, Isére, France	F. Confino and Jean-Pierre Duval	*Techniques and Architecture*, Sept 1989, p. 385
1988	Canopy to motorway access point, L'ile-de-Ré, France	J. Sepra, J. Fourquier and J. Filhol	*L'Architecture d'Aujourd'hui* Dec 1988, p. 77 *Architectural Review*, May 1990, p. 100
1989	Rotoprint Factory, Berlin	Richard Rogers and Partners with Ove Arup and Partners	*Building Design*, 13 Jan 1989, p. 10

(left) House on Lake Hossegor, France, 1989-90

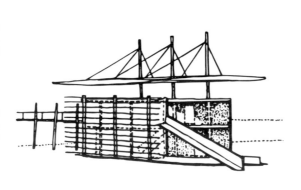

(right) Hanover Convention Center, Germany, 1990.

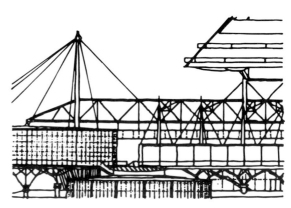

YEAR	BUILDING OR PROJECT	DESIGNERS	REFERENCE SOURCE
1989	Central library of the Pret du Gard, Nimes, France	F. Confino and Jean-Pierre Duval	Information supplied by the architects
1989	House at Kamakura, Kanagawa	Riken Yamamoto and Field Shop	*The Japan Architect*, Feb 1990, pp. 51-57
1989	ADT car auction viewing area, Manchester	Glendinning and Hanson with the Doyle Partnership	*The Structural Engineer*, 21 Nov 1989, p. A5 Architects own information
1989	Airport Building, Bundaberg, Australia	Bligh, Robinson Architects	*Architectural Review*, Dec 1989, pp. 58-61
1989	Swimming Pool, Woking, England	Faulkner Browns	*New Builder*, 21 Sept 1989, p. 4
1989	Events Venue Project, Bents Park, South Shields, South Tyneside	Apicella Architecture and Design with Hunt Projects	*Building Design*, 7 Apr 1989, p. 1
1990	House on Lake Hossegor, France	Jean-Philippe Pargade	*Techniques and Architecture*, July 1990, p. 390
1990	Demountable Exhibition Structure Project	Apicella Architecture and Design	*Building Design*, 28 Apr 1989, p.3
1990	Market Hall, Almere, Holland	W. Stevens and P. Primp, Den Bosch, Architects	*Bouw*, 9, 4 May 1990, pp. 33-35
1990	Office Building Extension Bunnik, Holland	Articon, Amersfoort	*Bouw* 2, 26 Jan 1990, p. 30
1990	Malibu International Kobe Clubhouse Project	Toshibaru Nanba	*SD*, Dec 1990, pp. 36-37
1990	Hannover Convention Centre	Storch, Enlers, Arkitekten	*Building Design*, 16 Mar 1990, pp. 20-21
1990	Escape Stair Canopy, Biberach, Germany	Kaag + Schwarz, Stuttgart	*Werk, Bauen + Wohnen* 4, 1990, pp. 64-65
1990	Sussex Grandstand, Goodwood, Brighton	Arup Associates	*Architecture Today*, 11, Sept 1990, pp. 66-73
1990	Bognor Regis Station Canopy Proposals	Weston, Williamson Architects and Anthony Hunt Associates	*Architectural Review* May 1989, pp. 29-30
1990	Wakita Hi-Tecs, Ohnojo, Fukuoka, Japan	Shoei Yoh + Architects	*Japan Architect*, 9007 pp. 36-39
1991	A1 Galleries Shopping Centre, Hatfield, England	Aukett Associates with Anthony Hunt Associates	*New Builder*, 22 Mar 1990, p. 22

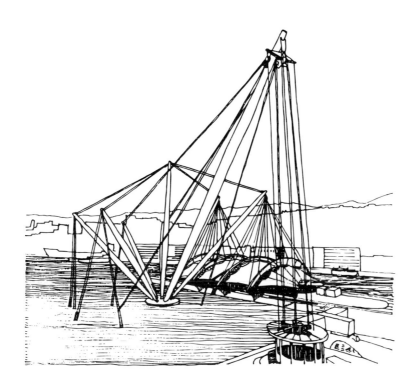

Il Grande Bigo, EXPO 92, Genoa, Italy, 1992.

Proposed Olympic Stadium, Manchester, England, 1993.

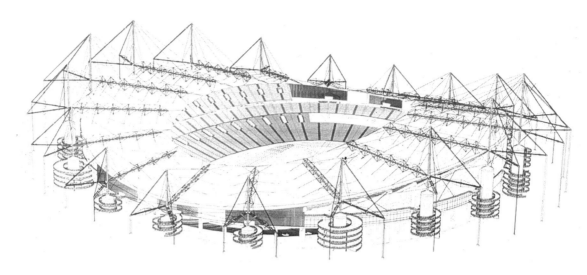

YEAR	BUILDING OR PROJECT	DESIGNERS	REFERENCE SOURCE
1991	Mitsubishi Pencil Gunma Factory, Gunma, Japan	Ken Yokogawa	*SD*, December 1990, pp. 11-12
1991	Don Valley Stadium, Sheffield	Sheffield Council Architects with Anthony Hunt Associates	*Building* , 13 Mar 1990 *Building Design*, 10 Nov 1989, p. 48 *Design Week*, 29 June 1990, p. 13
1991	Sports Centre, Berlin	Christof Langhof	*Architectural Review*, Feb 1991, pp. 50-54
1991	Leisure Centre, Knowsley, Liverpool	Nicholas Grimshaw and Partners with Ove Arup and Partners	*Nicholas Grimshaw and Partners* 1: 1988, pp. 68-69 *AJ Focus*, June 1991, pp. 21-23
1992	East Croydon Station	Hick Derbyshire, Alan Brookes Associates with Anthony Hunt Associates	*Architectural Review*, Dec 1989, pp. 84-87 *Architect's Journal*, 3 Sept 1992, pp. 33-45
1992	Pavilion Gallery, Yorkshire Sculpture Park, Wakefield, England	Fielden, Clegg Design with Anthony Hunt Associates	*Architectural Journal*, 8 April 1992, pp. 22-23
1992	Ingus factory, Cologne, Germany	Nicholas Grimshaw and Partners with Whitney and Bird	*Building Design*, 3 July 1992, p. 15
1992	Il Grande Bigo, EXPO 92, Genoa, Italy	Renzo Piano with Ove Arup and Partners	*Architecture Today* , 29 June 1992, pp. 12-13
1993	Airport Rovaniemi, Rovaniemi, Finland	Heikkinen and Komonen with Erkki Juva of Oy Juva Engineering	*Architectural Review*, September 1993, pp. 67-71
1993	International School, Lyons, France	Jourda and Perraudin	*Architectural Review*, August 1993, pp. 16-21
1993	Proposed Olympic Stadium, Manchester, England	Arup Associates and the HOK Facilities Group with Ove Arup and Partners	*Building*, 27 August 1993, pp. 30-31
1994	TV Studio Cafeteria for Televisa San Angel, Mexico City	TEN Arquitectos with Ove Arup, New York and Salvador Aguilar, Mexico	*Architectural Record*, November 1994, pp. 68-73
1994	Friars Square Shopping Centre, Aylesbury, Buckinghamshire, England	The Stanley Bragg Partnership with Ove Arup and Partners	*Architecture Today*, 46, March 1994, pp. 43-44
1994	Benneton Factory, Treviso, Italy	Afra and Tobia Scarpa with Giandomenico Cocco	*Architectural Review*, January 1994, pp. 30-37 *RIBA Journal*, November 1993, pp. 30-34
1994	Temporary Ticket Office, Green Park, London	Michael Hopkins and Partners	*Architectural Review*, December 1994, pp. 20-21
1995	Dyson Assembly Building, Chippenham, Wiltshire, England	Chris Wilkinson Architects with Anthony Hunt Associates	*Architect's Journal*, 12 Jan 1995, p. 28; information also from the architects
1995	Competition entry for the Imperial War Museum, Hartlepool, England	The Napper Collerton Partnership	Information supplied by the architects

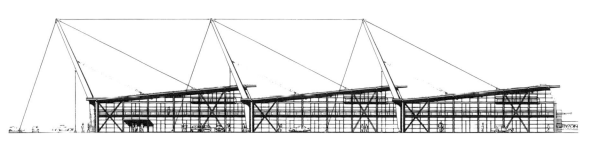

Dyson Assembly building, Chippenham, Wiltshire, England, 1995.

YEAR	BUILDING OR PROJECT	DESIGNERS	REFERENCE SOURCE
1995	Amenity Building, Inland Revenue Headquarters, Nottingham, England	Michael Hopkins and Partners with Ove Arup and Partners	*Architecture Today*, 56, March 1995, pp. 24-33
1995	Competition entry for the Saitama Arena, Tokyo, Japan	The Richard Rogers Partnership	*Building Design*, 7 April 1995, p. 1

BIBLIOGRAPHY

Arup, Ove. 'Structural honesty' .*The Architect and Building News,* 8 April 1954, pp. 410-413.

Arup, Ove. 'Art and Architecture; The architect : engineer relationship'. *RIBA Journal,* August, 1966, pp. 350-359.

Boyd, Robin. 'Under Tension'. *The Architectural Review,* November 1963, pp. 325-334.

Bridges-Adams, W. 'Tension chain-net floors and roofs for spans of 500 feet'. *The Builder,* 6 November 1852, p. 702.

Brookes, A.J. and Grech, C. *The Building Envelope,* Butterworth Architecture, 1990.

Buchanan, Peter, 'High-tech. Another British Thoroughbred'. *The Architectural Review,* July, 1983, pp. 15-19.

Buchholdt, H.A. *Introduction to cable roof structures,* Cambridge University Press, 1984.

Burden, A.R. 'Japanese cable-stayed bridge design'. *Proc. Instn. Civ. Engrs.,* Part I, 1991, 90, October, pp. 1021-51.

Cook, Peter. 'The engineers intervene'. *The Architectural Review,* July, 1983, pp. 48-50.

Crosby, Theo, et.al. 'Frei Otto at work'. *Architectural Design,* March, 1971, pp. 137-167.

Day, Alistair. 'Form finding, control and modification for tension structures'. *The Arup Journal,* **15, 3,** October 1980, pp. 19-20.

Downing, F. and Fleming, U. 'The bungalows of Buffalo'. *Environment and Planning,* **B, 8,** pp. 269-293.

Drew, Philip. *Frei Otto: Forms and Structures.* Crosby Lockwood, 1976.

Drew, Philip. *Tensile Architecture.* Crosby Lockwood Staples, 1979.

Dunnican, Peter. 'The Art of Structural Engineering'. *The Structural Engineer,* **44, 3,** March, 1966, pp. 97-108.

Ferencik, Pavel. 'A suspended roof built in 1826' in *Zbornik Vlaknove Konstrukcie, cable structures, konstruckcii iz gibkich nitej,* Bratislava, 1975, **1,** MIS *(in Russian).*

Forster, Brian. 'The engineered use of coated fabrics in long span roofs'. *The Arup Journal,* **20, 3,** October, 1985, pp. 7-12.

Forster, Brian. 'A brief history of cable and membrane roofs'.*The Arup Journal, 15, 3,* October, 1980, pp. 6-10.

Garbett, E.L. 'A sanitary and floor-ceiling giving the architect no work at all'. *The Builder,* London, December, 1852, pp. 764-766.

Glaeser, Ludwig. *The work of Frei Otto.* New York, Museum of Modern Art, 1972.

Graefe, Rainer. 'Suspended roof constructions of the 19th century' *ARCUS* 1985, 2, pp. 70-81, 94 *(in German).*

Graefe, Rainer. 'Virtuose Sparsamkeit'. *Deutsche Bauzeitung,* July, 1990, pp. 24-31. *(in German).*

Hammer, Karl. *Jakob Ignaz Hittorff.* Stuttgart, 1968.

Hatton, E.M. *The Tent Book.* Boston, 1979.

Howard, Seymour. 'Suspension Structures'. *Architectural Record,* September, 1960, pp. 230-237.

Hruban, Ivo. 'Suspension roofs for Housing and Civic Buildings invented in Czechoslovakia in 1824; in Ferencik, Pavel, *Zbornik Vlaknove Konstrukcie, cable structures, konstruckcii iz gibkich nitej,* Bratislava, 1975, 2, *(in Russian).*

Knight, T. and Weissmann, C. *'The Forty-One Steps'. Environment and Planning,* **B, 8,** pp. 97-114.

Kahn-Magomedov, Selim O. *Pioneers of Soviet Architecture,* New York, Rizzoli, 1983.

Koning, H. and Eizenberg, J. 'The language of the Prairie: Frank Lloyd Wright's prairie house'. *Environment and Planning,* **B, 8,** pp. 295-323.

Lecointe, Alfred. 'A note on some suspended roofs built in France on the model of suspension bridges'. *Allgemeine Bauzeitung,* Vienna, 1843.

Leonhardt, Fritz and Schlaich, J. 'Structural design of roofs over the sports arenas for the 1972 Olympic Games: some problems of prestressed cable net structures'. *The Structural Engineer,* **50, 3,** March, 1972, pp. 113-119.

Leonhardt, Fritz. *Bridges.* Architectural Press, 1982.

MacIntosh, Charles. *Book of the Garden.* **2 Vols.** Edinburgh, 1853.

Manning, Martin. 'Renault parts distribution centre, Swindon: The civil and structural engineering'. *The Arup Journal,* September, 1983, pp. 2-5.

Morgan, M.H. (trans.) Vitruvius; *Ten Books on Architecture.* Translated by M.H. Morgan, New York, Dover Publications, 1960.

Müller, E. and Giese, E. 'The Singing Hall for the first German Song Festival, Dresden'. *Allgemeine Banzeitung,* **32,** Vienna, 1867.

Newby, Frank. 'Hi-tech or Mys-tech'. *RIBA Transactions.* 3, 2, 1984, pp 18-27.

O'Gorman, J.F. 'The Marshall Field Wholesale Store'. *Journal of the Society of Architectural Historians,* XXXVII, 3, October, 1978, p. 186 ff.

Otto, Frei. *Tensile Structures* (2 Vols). Cambridge, Mass. MIT Press, 1967.

Podolny, W.P. and Scalzi, J.B. *Construction and design of cable-stayed bridges.* Wiley, 1986.

Plowden, David. *Bridges: The spans of North America,* New York, W.W. Norton & Co., 1974.

Popper, K.R. *Conjectures and Refutations. The Growth of Scientific Knowledge.* Routledge and Kogan Paul, 1963.

Read, Terry and O'Brien, Turlogh. 'Coated fabrics for lightweight structures'. *The Arup Journal,* **15, 3,** October, 1980, pp. 14-18.

Rice, Peter. 'An Engineer Imagines' *Artemis,* 1994.

Rice, Peter. 'Lightweight structures: introduction'. *The Arup Journal,* **15, 3,** October, 1980, pp. 2-5.

Rice, Peter. 'Patscenter principles'. *The Architectural Review,* July, 1986, p. 47.

Rice, P.R., Thornton, J.A. and Lenczner, E.A.R. 'Cable-stayed roofs for shopping centres at Nantes and Epone', in Topping, B. (ed.) Non-conventional structures. *Proceedings of the International Conference on the Design and Construction of Non-conventional Structures,* Vol. 1, Edinburgh, Civil-Comp Press, 1987.

Roland, Conrad. *Frei Otto: Structures,* Longmans, 1970.

Samuely, Felix, J. 'Space frames and stressed skin construction'. *RIBA Journal,* March, 1952, pp. 166-173.

Scerbo, G.M. 'V.G. Suchov and his network constructions', in *Promyslen noe stroitel'stvo, 5,* Moscow, 1974. (in Russian).

Siliman, B. and Goodrich, C.R. *The World of Science, Art and Industry illustrated from examples in the New York Exhibition, 1853-4,* New York, 1854.

Sommer, Degenhard. *Ove Arup and Partners: Engineering the built environment,* Basle, Boston, Berlin: Stocher and Weisser. Birkhauser Verlag A.G. 1994.

Steiner, F.H. *French Iron Architecture*; Ann Arbor, Michigan, UMI Research Press, 1985.

Stiny, G. and Mitchell, W.J. 'The Palladian Grammar'. *Environment and Planning,* **B, 4,** pp. 115-122.

Stiny, G. 'The Palladian Grammar'. *Environment and Planning,* **B, 5,** pp. 5-18.

Summerson, John. 'The Classical Country House in 18th Century England'. *Journal of the Royal Society of Arts,* **CVII,** pp. 539-587.

Szabo, J. and Kollar, L. *The Design of cable-suspended roofs.* Chichester, Ellis Horwood Limited, 1984.

Thornton, J.A. 'The design and construction of cable-stayed roofs'. *The Structural Engineer,* **62A,** 9 September, 1984, pp. 275-284.

Thornton, J.A. 'Membrane Structures; 1 Developing the form' *The Architects' Journal,* 16 September 1992, pp. 53-61; '2 Getting design on site' *The Architects' Journal,* 23 September 1992, pp. 51-55.

Tietz, Stefan. 'Masted Structures'. *Building,* 20 November 1981, pp. 32-34.

Topping, B. (ed.) Non-conventional structures. *Proceedings of the International Conference on the Design and Construction of Non-conventional Structures,* 2 Vols. Edinburgh, Civil-Comp Press, 1987.

Verantius, Fausti. *Machinae Novae Fausti Fausti Sicari,* 1625.

Vitruvius. *See* Morgan.

Waters, Brian, 'Framework for Renault' *Building,* 22 October 1982, pp. 32-40.

Wilson, Forrest. 'Cable-stayed bridges in crisis'. *Architecture,* **77, 12,** December, 1988, pp. 111-114.

INDEX